BLACK MAGIC

BLACK MAGIC

WHITE HOLLYWOOD AND

AFRICAN AMERICAN

CULTURE

Krin Gabbard

RUTGERS UNIVERSITY PRESS

NEW BRUNSWICK, NEW JERSEY • LONDON

LIBRARY OF CONGRESS CATALOGING-IN-PUBLICATION DATA

Gabbard, Krin

Black magic : White Hollywood and African American culture / Krin Gabbard.

p. cm.

Includes bibliographic references and index.

ISBN 0-8135-3383-X (alk. paper) — ISBN 0-8135-3384-8 (pbk. : alk. paper)

1. African Americans in motion pictures. 2. Jazz in motion pictures. 3. Motion pictures—
United States. 4. Motion pictures and music. 5. Motion picture music—
History and criticism. I. Title.

PN1995.9.N4G33 2004   791.43'652996073—dc22

British Cataloging-in-Publication information for this book
is available from the British Library.

An early draft of chapter two appeared in *Soundtrack Available: Essays on Film and
Popular Music*, ed. Arthur Knight and Pamela Robertson (Duke UP, 2001). Portions of chapter
four appeared in *Masculinity: Bodies, Movies, Culture*, ed. Peter Lehman (Routledge, 2001). An
early draft of chapter six was first published in *Black Music Research Journal* 19.2 (1999). Chapter
seven is an extended version of an essay that appeared in *Ladies and Gentlemen, Boys and Girls:
Gender in Film at the End of the 20th Century*, ed. Murray Pomerance (State U of New York P,
2001). Portions of chapter eight were first published in *Music and Cinema*, ed. James Buhler,
Caryl Flinn, and David Neumeyer (Wesleyan UP, 2000), and in the *American Historical Review*
(October 1997). Chapter nine appeared in slightly different form in *American Music* 18.4
(2000), and in *Postmodernism Music/Postmodern Thought*, ed. Judy Lochhead and
Joseph Auner (Routledge, 2002).

Manufactured in the United States of America

Once again, for Paula

Contents

Acknowledgments

Many colleagues, friends, and loved ones made this book possible. I am especially grateful to the University Seminars Program at Columbia University. Under the administration of the late Aaron Warner and, subsequently, Robert Belknap, the program provided two venues that were essential to the genesis of this book. First, I thank the members of the Jazz Study Group at Columbia, funded primarily by the Ford Foundation and kept healthy and thriving through the efforts of Robert G. O'Meally. At the regular meetings of this group I was able to interact with the best jazz scholars, most of them African American. I would never have written so extensively about black Americans and their achievements had I not come to know so many thoughtful and gracious colleagues. They should certainly not be held responsible for anything weak or foolish in this book, but they may take much of the credit for whatever in it is good. I owe a great debt of gratitude to Bob O'Meally as well as to all members of the Jazz Study Group, especially Mark Burford, Danny Dawson, Gerald Early, Brent Hayes Edwards, Steven Feld, Paula Giddings, Farah Jasmine Griffin, Billy Joe Harris, Vijay Iyer, Travis A. Jackson, Robin D. G. Kelley, George Lewis, Jacqui Malone, Tim Mangin, Ingrid Monson, Fred Moten, Carol J. Oja, Guthrie P. Ramsey Jr., David Lionel Smith, John Szwed, W. S. Tkweme, Chris Washburne, and Salim Washington. The late Mark Tucker, who was a prominent member of the Jazz Study Group, has left behind a profound legacy for jazz studies, and I count myself among the fortunate ones who knew him well. Until the very end, no matter how sick he was, he continued to be an exemplary colleague. The helpful, often brilliant comments he made on early drafts of chapters in this book are especially precious to me.

Another group of colleagues to whom I owe a substantial debt of gratitude are the members of the Columbia University Seminar on Cinema and Interdisciplinary Interpretation. For many hours of stimulating discussions during and after the meetings, I thank the seminar's co-chairs, William Luhr and David Sterritt, as well as Charles Affron, Karen Backstein, Mikita Brottman, Steven B. Elworth, Sid Gottlieb, Pamela Grace, Harvey R. Greenberg, Adam Knee, Jim Latham, Cynthia Lucia, David Lugowski, Paula Massood, Martha Nochimson, Christopher Sharrett, Louise Spence, Elisabeth Weis, and the many film scholars who gave stimulating presentations at the monthly meetings.

Each year since 1987 I have had the pleasure of attending the annual conference on film and literature at Florida State University. I have learned much from the regular members of this group, especially Robert Eberwein, Peter Lehman, Robert T. Self, Fred Sliva, Peter Stowell, and Hans and Bonnie Braendlin.

Bits and pieces of this book were delivered as public lectures at universities and conferences, including Columbia University, the University of Virginia, the University of Kansas, Yale University, the University of Arizona, Colby College, William and Mary, Bowdoin College, the University of Vermont, the University of Leeds, the University of Guelph, and the University of Glasgow. I thank the many colleagues at these institutions who made me feel welcome and who generously shared their thoughts with me.

I sincerely thank all those who read and commented on early drafts of all or part of this book, including Lisa Barg, Emily Bernard, Dennis Bingham, David Brackett, Harriet Castrataro, James Castrataro, Robert P. Crease, Stephanie Stein Crease, Scott DeVeaux, Morris Dickstein, Barbara File, Sandy Flitterman-Lewis, Bernard Gendron, John Gennari, Chris Holmlund, Peter Keepnews, Michael Kimmel, Arthur Knight, Joe Medjuck, Carol J. Oja, Lara Pellegrinelli, Murray Pomerance, Jacqueline Reich, Christopher Sharrett, Sherrie Tucker, Tricia Welsch, Susan White, Pamela Robertson Wojcik, and especially Michael Jarrett, William Luhr, Robert Miklitsch, Louise O. Vasvari, and David Yaffe. Precious bits of information and encouraging words were offered by Michael Cuscuna, Andrea Fabry, Will Friedwald, Jane Gaines, Kyra

Gaunt, Barry Keith Grant, David Hajdu, Christopher Harlos, Michelle Huang, Izabela Kalinowska-Blackwood, Keir Keightley, Brigitte King, Kaye Price Laud, Chi-she Li, Eva Linfield, James McCalla, Susan McClary, Paul S. Machlin, Dan Morgenstern, Mary Morris, Larry O'Connor, Joseph M. Peterson, Lewis Porter, Jeff Smith, John Tofanelli, and Tony Whyton.

Amanda Gabbard and Keith Everett Book were on hand for moral support and good humor on the many occasions when I needed family nearby. As always, my parents, Lucy and Gabby, have been inspirational, to say the least. They have my everlasting love and gratitude for introducing me to the cinema and for tolerating the first stages of my passion for jazz, pop, and the blues. More importantly, they have shown me how life ought to be lived.

My colleagues at Stony Brook have always been valuable resources, especially Joseph Auner, Michele Bogart, Sue Bottigheimer, Román de la Campa, Robert Harvey, E. Ann Kaplan, Shirley Lim, Ira Livingston, John Lutterbie, Peter Manning, Nicholas Mirzoeff, Adrienne Munich, Kelly Oliver, Sandy Petrey, Mary Rawlinson, Jacqueline Reich, James Rubin, Jane Sugarman, and Beni Trigo. Without the daily efforts of Mary Moran-Luba, the extraordinary woman who runs Stony Brook's Department of Comparative Studies, completing this book would have been at best an onerous and overwhelming task.

At Rutgers University Press, I have greatly enjoyed the professional guidance as well as the friendship of Leslie Mitchner. I am especially grateful to you, Leslie, for introducing me to an essential fact-checker, jazz scholar, and native informant, Stuart Mitchner. Thanks also to Marilyn Campbell, Derik Shelor, and Molly Baab for their patience and professionalism.

To those who belong on these lists but cannot find their names, please accept my apologies. This book took shape over several years, and I have not always been as careful as I should have been in keeping track of the many people who have generously assisted me in the research and writing.

And finally, as always, I thank Paula B. Gabbard: companion, lover, wife, editor, friend.

BLACK MAGIC

Sarah in Wonderland

*It is a difficult thing for a white man to learn what a colored man
really thinks; because, generally, with the latter an additional and different
light must be brought to bear on what he thinks; and his thoughts are often
influenced by considerations so delicate and subtle that it would be
impossible for him to confess or explain them to one of the opposite race.*

—JAMES WELDON JOHNSON, *THE AUTOBIOGRAPHY OF AN EX-COLORED MAN* (1912)

Next Stop Wonderland is a sweet little independent film from 1998, written and directed by Brad Anderson. Hope Davis is funny and endearing as Erin, a lonely single woman living in Boston (fig. 1). Because her late father once took her to Brazil, she has developed a passion for the bossa nova. Thanks primarily to recordings that Stan Getz made in the 1960s, this indigenous Brazilian music had a surprise success in the United States just before rock 'n' roll became rock and the Beatles and Bob Dylan became unassailable icons of youthful hipness. The soundtrack for *Next Stop Wonderland* is an almost seamless anthology of the best Brazilian music: Antonio Carlos Jobim, Astrud Gilberto, Jorge Ben, the Tamba Trio, Sergio Brandào, Ary Barosso, Airto Lindsay, and Bebel Gilberto can all be heard, sometimes more than once.

Early on it's clear that the right man for Erin is Alan (Alan Gelfant), but although their paths keep converging, Erin and Alan never actually meet until the film's conclusion. When Erin's mother puts an ad in the personals hoping to locate a husband for her daughter, the young woman reluctantly goes

Fig. 1. Hope Davis as Erin in *Next Stop Wonderland* (1998, Robbins Entertainment). Jerry Ohlinger's Movie Material Store, Inc.

for a drink with each of the unsavory characters who respond. We also see her with friends at a bar and at the hospital where she works as a nurse. Toward the end of the film, when one of Erin's patients softly hums a Brazilian tune, she is intrigued. Andre (José Zúñiga), the one doing the humming, is in fact from Brazil, and he quickly becomes interested in Erin. He eventually invites her to fly home with him, even handing her an airline ticket. Disillusioned by her experiences with American men and intrigued by Andre's Latin charm, Erin accepts the invitation. On the way to the airport, however, she is stuck in traffic and runs to the subway hoping to arrive at the airport in time to meet Andre. En route she finally encounters Alan, whose story has been interwoven with Erin's since the beginning of the film. Exhausted and packed into the cramped subway car, she collapses on Alan's shoulder. Then they look into each other's eyes.

The attractive couple sit on a bench near the ocean and chat about their lives as bossa nova continues to play on the soundtrack. They quickly realize that they are right for each other. Just as Erin is saying that she ought to get back home, Alan asks if she would like to go for a walk. In the film's final line, she immediately replies, "I'd love it." Suddenly the music swells and the majestic voice of the great jazz singer Sarah Vaughan fills the theater. As Erin and Alan walk along the shore, Vaughan sings "Wave," one of several songs in the film by the Brazilian composer Jobim. In fact, the song has already been heard in bossa nova versions earlier in the film. But nothing so far has prepared us for what Sarah Vaughan, nicknamed "Sassy" for her daring, often baroque approach to a song, accomplishes as she transforms the peaceful waterworld of Jobim into a multi-octave tsunami. Fully in control of a vast vocal and emotional range, Vaughan creates a joyous celebration of romance, entirely appropriate to the love affair that is just beginning between Erin and Alan. If anything, the music may be too intense for these two relatively low-keyed people.

The choice of music in *Next Stop Wonderland* is the kind of smart, small gesture that independent films can afford to make and that distinguishes

FIG. 2. Jazz vocalist Sarah Vaughan in the 1940s. Photofest Film Archive.

them from big-budget Hollywood films with their ham-fisted special effects. But it's curious. When Erin is involved with shallow people, the soundtrack features the easy, soothing music of Brazil. When she begins a relationship with someone more substantial, the full-throated voice of the African American Vaughan bursts onto the soundtrack. Why this contrast? In *Next Stop Wonderland,* bossa nova seems to be the music of day to day interactions, sometimes with a little romance, sometimes with less. The film then casts jazz—especially the jazz of Sarah Vaughan—as the music of the real thing, of The Truth. Intentionally or not, *Next Stop Wonderland* supports the notion that the delicate samba rhythms and the teasingly affectless singing of bossa nova musicians were a retreat from the earthy, impassioned expression that has always been at the heart of African American music. Bossa nova was in fact welcomed as such by exponents of more demure music when it made its big splash in the United States between 1962 and 1964. For this same reason it was consistently denounced by jazz purists. In 1977, Sarah Vaughan recorded an entire LP titled *I Love Brazil.* Her affection for the country's music was surely genuine. But when she sings with Brazilian musicians, she digs into their repertoire and lavishly invigorates a music that is not known for extroverted soulfulness.

One of my earlier books dealt with jazz and the American cinema, and there is a good deal about jazz in this one. But I am primarily concerned here with the black people who may or may not make music in films written by, directed by, produced by, and starring white people. I am, for example, struck by the strategic use of one and only one recording by an African American in *Next Stop Wonderland.*[1] Although several African American characters appear in the film, their roles are minor. The two leads interact with many potential lovers, but all are white. None of the black characters on the screen have the potency of Sarah Vaughan, who turns the last minutes of the film into a stirring acknowledgment of real love being born. Despite the transfigurative impact of Vaughan's art, she remains, to use Ralph Ellison's indelible metaphor, invisible.

Farah Jasmine Griffin has written perceptively about the degree to which the black female voice carries emotional authority in American culture. Why else would Whitney Houston be invited to sing the National Anthem at the Super Bowl just as the first Gulf War was getting under way in 1991? And why was an unidentified black woman singing "Amazing Grace" at the funerals after the 1999 shootings at the high school in Columbine? On one news pro-

Fig. 3. Sarah Vaughan
in the 1980s. Photofest
Film Archive.

gram the cameras panned over the crowd of mourners while we heard the
voice, but the editors at the network did not think it necessary to show the
woman as she sang. She became the equivalent of the many black backup
singers who have made crucial but unacknowledged contributions for white
performers such as the Rolling Stones, Carole King, and Talking Heads. The
power and authority of the black female voice is so widely accepted that it
need not be remarked upon, and yet its sound, so essential to the culture's
musical unconscious, is often detached from the human beings who produce it. Although *Next Stop Wonderland* pays tribute to the singing of Sarah
Vaughan, it also continues a long tradition of concealing the achievements
of black people, effectively colonizing them for the benefit of whites. The film
relies upon the magic of Vaughan's voice but discards the rest.

   In twenty-first-century America, the subject of race is as vexed as ever. At
the time of this writing, an American president who came from a highly privileged background and received special preference when he was admitted to an
elite university has unselfconsciously denounced affirmative action because

it gives preference to black people, almost all of whom grew up without his privileges. To cite a more egregious example of white America's racial pathology, Human Rights Watch has reported that, on any given day, one in three young black American males is either in prison, on probation, or awaiting trial. Although blacks constitute thirteen percent of the U.S. population, fully half of the people in prison are black.

And yet it would be impossible to imagine the lives of white Americans without black Americans, if only as images on a television screen and as the source of sounds coming out of radios and stereos. As the theorists of whiteness have pointed out, people often think of themselves as white when there is an Other nearby, usually black. In urban American neighborhoods, children of Irish, Italian, and German heritage (to name just three) have all been taunted by other white children at one time or another as each group assimilated. The arrival of African American families was often instrumental in bringing a sense of solidarity to people who might otherwise think of themselves primarily as Irish, Italian, or German rather than simply as white. If only on this basic level, black Americans perform an important function for whites. Recent American cinema has assigned black people even greater responsibility in their relations with whites. Whether or not they are on the screen—and as in *Next Stop Wonderland,* the important black presences are often offscreen—African Americans radically transform the lives of white characters, usually providing them with romance and gravitas. And although it's seldom acknowledged, representations of black masculinity now provide the model for most of what is considered white masculinity, especially among the working classes. At the same time, however, African Americans often appear in films for no other reason than to help white people reaffirm their own superiority.

Because white culture has assigned black culture a central role in its own self-definition while simultaneously marginalizing or erasing black people, the films that perpetuate this project must often resort to what I have called magic. I use this term literally to describe a group of films in which African American actors play angels who improve the lives of whites; I use this term metaphorically to describe the enchanting effect that black music, black sexuality, and other aspects of African American culture have on movie characters, more often than not when the characters on screen are white.

If I have had my way, the words at the upper left hand corner on the back of this book will *not* say "African American Studies." I'm not really writing about black people, certainly not as individuals or even as movie stars. My real interest is in how white people represent African Americans in movies produced in what I do not think it is reckless to call "White Hollywood." I do not presume any direct correspondence between what is represented on movie screens and how people actually live their lives. In films, a culture holds up to itself what it considers important even if the ostensible occasion is pure entertainment. These representations, however, both affirm and question some basic American values. Because these values are always in flux, and because the films seldom present value systems from a single point of view, audiences are always invited to rethink them at the same time that they are invited to embrace them. My goal is to find the best ways to rethink Hollywood values, especially the inevitable, unquestioned centrality of white people in American stories. Sometimes the rethinking reveals old, malign images so ideologically entrenched that no one seems to notice them anymore. I'm consistently puzzled by how seldom film reviewers and scholars remark upon the bizarre ways in which the races interact in Hollywood films. People must find pleasure in these representations, otherwise we would not be seeing them again and again at the local multiplex. But that pleasure must be thoroughly investigated and demystified.

Since the 1990s, the field of whiteness studies has been a major growth area in universities. Kalpana Seshadri-Crooks has observed that the discipline can no longer be regarded as monolithic, if ever it was. She distinguishes between an ethnographic school and those who write about whiteness "as an ideological construct" (161).[2] I would add that scholars such as Richard Dyer, Eric Lott, and Daniel Bernardi have constructed useful histories of how whiteness has been forged in the crucible of race, especially in European encounters with African and Native American peoples. Throughout this book I am indebted to these writers, but I do not wish to overwhelm my arguments with citations from theorists. Mostly I look closely at how specific films reveal common fantasies about black Americans. Black music and black masculinity, both of which are seldom directly acknowledged in these movies, are crucial obsessions among filmmakers and audiences, driving the plots of films much more than is immediately apparent.

My goals in taking a close look at a group of American films are suggested in Ishmael Reed's *Japanese by Spring,* an entertaining and provocative academic novel (another major growth area in universities). Reed's book begins when a fictional American university is taken over by Japanese businessmen and given a more "rational" curriculum. All of the Humanities are placed into a single unit called Ethnic Studies. "You have African Studies, Chicano Studies, American Studies, Native American Studies and African American Studies. We will have a new department, European Studies, with the same size budget and faculty as the rest" (90). The Japanese curriculum managers feel no particular awe before the authors who dominated reading lists at American universities throughout the twentieth century. To professors of philosophy, the new managers say that they have no use for Plato's "foolishness as to whether the soul has immortality." To English professors they announce that their research has turned up evidence that John Milton was once in prison. He will therefore be left out of the curriculum because "it would not be appropriate to include courses about an ex-convict" (91).

Although Reed is satirizing the desire among university professors to keep disciplinary boundaries firm and reading lists stable, and although he takes great pleasure in cutting the Western canon down to size, I have cited his book because it asks white people to think critically about what it means to have white skin and ancestors from Europe. Instead of organizing our systems of learning around a European heritage, Reed presents American learning as just one possibility among many. As Saul Bellow infamously observed, there is probably no Tolstoy of the Zulus, but then where are the master tribal drummers of nineteenth-century Moscow? My readings of several Hollywood and independent films grow out of the conviction that we must stop thinking about whiteness as "normal" and unproblematic; rather, it is a mostly incoherent set of notions haphazardly drummed into service whenever white dominance must be reinforced. At least since 1904, when the filmed version of *Uncle Tom's Cabin* became a great financial success and the film industry in the United States was taking its first baby steps, the best place to find out how things get constructed in American culture is a movie house. And there is no better way of looking at how whiteness is constructed in movies than by examining how blackness makes these constructions work.

Several first-rate scholars have told the story of blackface impersonation of African Americans by whites and of the borrowing of black cultural capital for the construction of whiteness.[3] For me, racial appropriation in the United States becomes most intriguing when, as with Sarah Vaughan in *Next Stop Wonderland,* it is invisible. The three chapters in Part I examine this phenomenon in depth. Chapter one characterizes the performances of the young Marlon Brando as early examples of the appropriation of black culture without blackface. When Brando first appeared on stage and then in the movies as Stanley Kowalski in *A Streetcar Named Desire,* he found new ways to establish masculinity while building that historic and astonishing performance. Many of his innovations came from a sense of freedom on stage based in the improvisatory aesthetic of African American jazz musicians and dancers. Although he followed the old minstrel performers in playing on the childish license supposedly granted to black men, he also imitated what he perceived as their hypermasculine violence. Brando's haphazard appropriations of what he saw in black culture arrived on the American screen at precisely the moment when a long tradition of blackface performance in the movies was finally coming to an end. His channeling of black culture without burnt cork signified that African Americans had left so profound a mark on performance practice in the United States that blacking up was no longer essential.

The second chapter jumps to films of the 1990s to show how Brando's first steps toward integrating black culture into white performance eventually became the industry standard. Although the opportunities for actual black people in the movies have been narrowly circumscribed, much of African American culture has been thoroughly assimilated by the Hollywood system. While jazz remains a central element in chapter two, the major focus is on the career of Clint Eastwood. Like Brando, we do not usually think of Eastwood as an imitator of black men, but his career is inconceivable without a large investment in black culture, even when (especially when) his Dirty Harry threatens black men with his mammoth pistol. When Eastwood tried to soften his image and project a more romantic form of masculinity in the 1995 film *The Bridges of Madison County,* he turned to the recordings of the African American singer Johnny Hartman. No other singer—not even Nat King Cole—has projected powerful but unthreatening masculinity as convincingly as has Hartman. But like Sarah Vaughan in *Next Stop Wonderland,* Hartman died before *The Bridges of Madison County* went into production. His image never appears on screen, and he is he acknowledged only in the final credits. Nevertheless, Hartman's disembodied voice plays a huge role in transforming Eastwood into the romantic lover he had never been able to embody throughout a long career in films.

Although the two films addressed in chapter three, *Pleasantville* (1998) and *The Talented Mr. Ripley* (1999), engage well-established narrative traditions about black people fighting for their civil rights and passing for white, and although recordings by blacks are essential to the dynamics of both films, black people are virtually absent from both. Stories that would seem to be impossible without black people are entirely dominated by whites. *Pleasantville* relies directly on magic by dropping two teenagers from late twentieth-century America into the black-and-white world of an old television sitcom. As they bring color to the inhabitants of the 1950s town in the television show, the music of Miles Davis, Etta James, and other African American artists plays on the soundtrack. Cranky city fathers—clearly functioning as stand-ins for Southern racists—attempt to stop the colorization of their town, at one point even putting a sign in a store window that reads "No Colored." In *The Talented Mr. Ripley,* the title character "passes" for a white Negro. The film expands the theme of homosexuality that is a small part of the Patricia Highsmith novel on which the film is based, and transforms one of the principal characters from a painter into an aspiring jazz musician. Consequently, the soundtrack of the film is liberally salted with recordings by black jazz artists, many of which ingeniously expand the sexual themes of the film. In addition, the tension between jazz and classical music—and thus between African American and European culture—is constantly played out in the interactions of the two principals. But just as *Pleasantville* never brings black people onto the screen, *The Talented Mr. Ripley* never acknowledges the African American origin of narratives and cultural traditions that drive the film.

The sounds *and* bodies of black men appear in the films addressed in Part II. The dynamic African American actor Delroy Lindo is an important presence in *Ransom* (1996), the first film discussed in chapter four. A black man has an extremely small but significant role in *Fargo*, also from 1996. Except for a brief moment in *Ransom* that features the Crowtations, a group of African American singing puppeteers, neither film has any black music. Or rather, there is only that one moment of music that is clearly the work of African American musicians. Nevertheless, blackness plays crucial roles in both films. In *Ransom*, the overbearing masculinity of an FBI agent played by Lindo provides a strongly marked but unacknowledged racial challenge that the diminutive white hero (Mel Gibson) is constantly prepared to meet. Just below the surface of this film about a kidnapping is the story of an angry white male striving to restore the privileges to which he feels entitled, even in a culture that has empowered black men. The commanding but benign presence of Lindo's character and the constant use of black vernacular by a group of white kidnappers help the film disguise an essentially racist narrative. *Fargo* is also about kidnapping, but it too has much to say about how white masculinity is constructed, appropriately in the snowy white expanses of the upper Midwest. Even the most threatening men in the film are brought to justice by Marge (Frances McDormand), a pregnant policewoman with no claims to potency. In this way the brothers who made *Fargo* consistently reveal the emptiness behind traditional shows of masculinity. While idealizing Marge, however, the film lets minor characters representing a Native American, an Asian American, and an African American exist for no other reason than to set the limits within which the white characters are free to be themselves. Perhaps because of an unconscious agenda of two brothers working together, *Fargo* does not follow through on its critique of American whiteness and masculinity.

Chapter five is most overtly about black magic. In a group of films from the end of the twentieth century, black angels with no real connection to African American culture appear on earth with the sole purpose of making life better for whites. The best examples are *The Green Mile* (1999), *The Legend of Bagger Vance* (2000), and *The Family Man* (2000), though many other films have contributed to the same project. These films may reflect a desire for healing among the races, but this desire coexists with the films' complete unwillingness to relinquish white superiority. So long as the black characters are not of this earth—in one case actually sent down from a heaven visibly administered by white-skinned angels—audiences are not likely to wonder why blacks take unprovoked actions entirely for the benefit of whites. These films seem to be the latest installment in a long history that goes back at least to James Fenimore Cooper and Herman Melville in which white heroes win the complete devotion of a dark-skinned Other.

The several films from documentary traditions addressed in Part III strive to abandon the white mythologies perpetuated by Hollywood, but most still rely on a bit of black magic to tell their stories. If Parts I and II concentrated on films in which the bodies of black people are erased or recruited to serve white interests, what happens when an eminent black man is front and center throughout a film? In chapter six I consider the several attempts to make sense of the brilliant but inscrutable jazz pianist and composer Thelonious Monk. The three jazz documentaries that take more than a brief look at Monk are almost completely incompatible. The 1988 film *Thelonious Monk: Straight No Chaser* emerges from an independent documentary tradition that is as suspicious of conventional notions of insanity as it is fascinated by a black artist's eccentricities. We meet a version of Monk brilliant and dedicated to his music. His bizarre behavior is pictured as the workings of a free spirit, not of an artist suffering from mental illness. The Monk presented in the 1991 made-for-television documentary *Thelonious Monk: American Composer* is certainly not mad. He emerges as a devoted family man and a serious artist contributing to a great tradition of African American composers and pianists. Between 1988 and 1991, jazz discourse was clearly shifting toward a new set of canonizing tendencies that were most apparent when Ken Burns's *Jazz* appeared on Public Television in 2001. In 1995, however, Jean Bach directed *A Great Day in Harlem,* a noncanonizing but thoroughly celebratory view of fifty-seven jazz artists who had their picture taken in Harlem in 1958. The film devotes a great deal of attention to Monk, who emerges as a classic African American trickster. But the film looks at only one day in the life of Monk. Who is he really? How has he magically eluded all attempts to make a coherent narrative of his life? Surrounded by the fantasies of white fans and filmmakers, black jazz artists such as Monk may even be complicit in their own unrepresentability.

Chapter seven deals with a subject I know all too well—collecting recorded jazz and blues. My analysis inevitably turns toward the figure of the nerd, a white man so devoted to collecting the music, to the bohemian rejection of mass culture, and to a hipster aesthetic that he does not attend to his personal appearance or the social graces. Within himself the nerd may have achieved a profound appreciation of the magic in the music, but this does nothing to prevent him from becoming a figure of fun in a variety of films. I look to psychoanalysis and gender theory to explain why a white man's fascination with black music and black masculinity should lead him to obsessive collecting and all that goes with it. The most fascinating film that takes up the subject is the 1994 documentary *Crumb,* an unflinching portrait of the cartoonist R. Crumb. Although he regularly expresses contempt for nearly every aspect of American culture, when Crumb talks about the recordings by pre-modern black bluesmen he has collected, he becomes positively elegiac. R. Crumb's nerdish habits and musical obsessions actually present a radical and legitimate challenge to conventional notions of masculinity, but he may be representable only in a small-budget documentary. When Terry Zwigoff, who directed *Crumb,* made a fiction film for a larger audience, he cast Steve Buscemi as a character with a strong resemblance to Crumb but with few of his redeeming qualities. In *Ghost World* (2001) Buscemi's record-collecting nerd is likely to win the sympathies of a few sensitive souls in the audience, but the film ultimately portrays him as a loser. In this one chapter I let my own experiences as a serious record collector intrude into the discussion.

My working title for the final two chapters was "Syncretic Alternatives," from a term I learned from Ella Shohat and Robert Stam.[4] After cataloguing so many films that press black music and other aspects of African American culture into service for white protagonists, I turn to a pair of films that reverse these trends. Robert Altman's *Kansas City* (1996), the subject of chapter eight, is among the most intelligent fiction films to take up the subject of jazz. Altman hired a full contingent of first-rate jazz artists and then filmed them playing in real time, a practice almost unknown in mainstream cinema. The African American jazz artists, dressed in period costumes and alluding to styles of music from the early 1930s, are integrated into the action in intriguing ways, most notably when a "cutting contest" between two tenor saxophonists is juxtaposed with scenes of black gangsters knifing to death one of their own. Just as he has cut together two quite different cutting scenes, Altman looks at the full range of African American culture in the Kansas City of 1934 without patronizing, pathologizing, or romanticizing his characters.

Spike Lee continues to be among the most consistently thoughtful filmmakers in America. Critics often find flaws in his films, in part because he tackles problems that do not lend themselves to the tidy, satisfying conclusions of the most successful Hollywood films. A chapter on Lee's *He Got Game* (1998) is an especially appropriate way to conclude a book examining so many white stories with invisible black music, because Lee turns the process upside down. Although the film is primarily about the oedipal tension between a black father and his son, Lee regularly inserts the music of Aaron Copland. In an especially provocative use of the music of the composer known as "Mr. Musical Americana," Lee shows a group of young African American men on a Coney Island basketball court fast-breaking, high-fiving, and trash-talking. Copland's "Hoe-Down" from his 1942 ballet *Rodeo* runs throughout the sequence. In *He Got Game,* the director combines music by a gay, leftist, Jewish composer with the magic of black athletic prowess. Lee is often called a black nationalist filmmaker, but his presentation of black men playing basketball to the sounds of Aaron Copland is uniquely American in the fullest sense of the term.

Of course, *He Got Game* has its problems, especially its unembarrassed embrace of discredited forms of masculinity. By no means am I arguing for the flat superiority of a black man's film over a group of films by white men. My point is rather that the various racial agenda driving Lee's films are right out there where we can see and hear them, while mainstream white filmmakers tend to hide or deny much of what is essential about their work. It is always easier to contend with what is there than with what is not there. My primary concern throughout this book is how white filmmakers, acting as what Robert B. Ray has called "great naive anthropologists," have managed America's massively conflicted feelings about race. These feelings may never be resolved. Even though we all know that race is a fiction and that we all share the same DNA, the easy distinction black/white is deeply ingrained in almost every aspect of our thinking.

In criticizing the many absences in white films, I have tried not to be a mere scold.[5] The mostly working-class students at the university where I teach have made me extremely cautious about finger-wagging advocacy. In my large, introductory film classes, I bring up the subject of race frequently, too frequently for many. African American students, who usually make up thirty to forty percent of the enrollment, often look at each other and make gestures that I read as "Does he think *he* can speak for *us*?" Others seem to express puzzlement, wondering why should I care about their lives. Many of the white students *really* want to know why I should care. When these reactions surface, I usually say something about the need to understand how American culture actually works. The marginalized roles that blacks consistently play in Hollywood movies, I tell them, provide some of the best examples of how deeply entrenched myths can be perpetuated. And I often talk about the many smart and witty black people I regularly encounter who are unrepresented in mainstream American entertainment. In movies and on television, when we don't see black men portrayed as criminals and monsters emerging out of the dark, African American characters tend to be loud and obnoxious but full of life and love, usually in contrast to uptight white people. These representations allow us, black and white alike, to laugh at familiar situations. But then I ask, would these situations be as familiar if we did not see them so often in movies and television? Shouldn't we be thinking about why these images and so few others are familiar to us?

In my upper-level courses, I often encounter more sophisticated responses to my lectures about black and white interactions in American culture. After watching *Next Stop Wonderland,* a student told me that he never thought of the voice at the end of the film as coming from a black person. He also insisted that he was not surprised when I showed him the African American face of Sarah Vaughan. For him, race was not a big deal, and it made little difference whether a black woman or a white woman was doing the singing as the film drew to a close. He didn't exactly come out and say it, but his point seemed to be that I was the one who was obsessed with race and that I should get over it. At this point I did not bring up the subject of my large record collection and my life-long romance with jazz and blues. That would have complicated a discussion that was already a bit more personal than I wanted it to be. (Readers interested in my life as a music geek may go directly to chapter seven.) My response at the time was to try to convince the student that race was indeed important, and that it had a lot to do with why he had never heard of Sarah Vaughan but was entirely familiar with innumerable white singers with much less talent who are regularly thrust at us by the media.

This book is in part a more complete response to the student's reaction to *Next Stop Wonderland.* What I should have said then and what I am hoping to communicate here is that ideology works best when it is unnoticed—when it is as invisible as the body of Sarah Vaughan in *Next Stop Wonderland.* Movie music has always relied on a series of codes that send out utterly coherent messages: this is funny, this is scary, this is the moment when you're supposed to cry. After years of watching movies and television, audiences know how to "read" these codes even if the films succeed in preventing us from actually concentrating on the music, a phenomenon that both the theorists and the practitioners of film music know well. The important point is that the codes are as legible as they are invisible. We can read them and understand them without even thinking about them. When a white athlete scores big and does a hip-swiveling victory dance on the playing field, we may not come out and say it, but we know what that means, too. We read the expression of personal celebration as well as the racheting up of intensity through the adoption of black body language. In understanding the motions of the athlete, we are all complicit in a system that abounds with racialized meanings. Hollywood films feed off this complicity and make those meanings seem natural rather than constructed, in the same way that most Hollywood soundtracks rely on deeply established systems of musical signification to produce sounds that supposedly communicate directly and naturally.

I should have told my student that his unwillingness to hear "black" in the voice of Sarah Vaughan was not a mark of distinction. By denying the importance of racial codes in films and in daily life, he was preserving an ideology that nourishes racial hierarchies without calling attention to itself. The student surely "read" the last moments of *Next Stop Wonderland* as a happy ending for two people about to experience "authentic" love. Because Sarah Vaughan knows how to sing from the heart, but also because the blackness in her voice has meanings of its own, the film makes a powerful point completely through aural codes. Many white people use this same set of codes when they wish to express strong feelings of anger or of deep romantic connection. To show that they really, *authentically* mean it, they speak like black people. The codes provided for the film by Sarah Vaughan were entirely legible to my student, and I hope that some day he'll understand why. I also hope that anyone who reads all or part of this book will have a better sense of how the American cinema has made use of black culture.

PART ONE

BLACK MAGIC, DISEMBODIED

Marlon Brando's Jazz Acting and the Obsolescence of Blackface

M arlon Brando may have been the first American actor to practice minstrelsy in whiteface. Before the arrival of Brando, performers such as Al Jolson, Bing Crosby, Fred Astaire, and many others had to put burnt cork on their faces to perform their fantasies of blackness, and their blackface routines were tremendously popular. At the beginning of the twenty-first century, it is more difficult to find white performers who do *not* imitate black people than it is to find those who do. To see and hear a young white pop singer today is to witness a nuanced channeling of blackness, from the husky-voiced melismas of Christina Aguilera to the forcefully articulated rap of Eminem. The swagger of white action heroes—even their stylish approach to handling a gun—is another reminder of familiar representations of black masculinity. Gestures from African American culture are essential elements in mainstream American culture even when actual black people, like Sarah Vaughan in *Next Stop Wonderland,* are not present. White Americans, especially when they are from the working class, base their expressions of joy, anger, and sexual desire almost entirely on what they perceive to be the behavior of black Americans.

After the minstrel show dominated American popular entertainment throughout most of the nineteenth century, blackface performance persisted through the years of vaudeville and then well into the 1950s when white stars blacked up to sing and dance in the movies. Only when blackface was disap-

Fig. 4. Clarinettist and bandleader Benny Goodman in his prime. Photofest Film Archive.

pearing from the screen did Marlon Brando start appearing in movie theaters everywhere. By finding new ways to play out fantasies of African American masculinity, Brando paved the way for what has become essential to Hollywood films, the wide-ranging appropriation of black culture without the actual representation of black people.

Before Brando made his mark in films such as *A Streetcar Named Desire* (1951), *The Wild One* (1953), and *On the Waterfront* (1954), the jazz world was the one place where whites could gain access to black culture without putting dark make-up on their faces. Watch Benny Goodman (fig. 4), for example, in the 1943 film *Stage Door Canteen*. His band plays "Bugle Call Rag" in an arrangement by the great African American bandleader and composer Fletcher Henderson. Goodman solos, as always, in the style of the New Orleans Creole clarinettist Jimmy Noone. In the same film, a smiling young Peggy Lee joins the orchestra to sing "Why Don't You Do Right (Like Some Other Men Do?)," a song written by Joe McCoy of the Harlem Hamfats, one of the first groups to play what we would now call rhythm and blues. In her vocal, Lee adopts the timbre and phrasing of Billie Holiday, the African

American singer who may have been the best of them all. While the blonde, demure Lee sings a black man's song and imitates a black woman's style, Goodman nods and sways insouciantly, very much the white hipster schooled in the vernacular of African American body language. Black music has changed since *Stage Door Canteen,* and so have the gestures with which whites have sought to attach it to their own performance styles. At least in this respect, Christina Aguilera and Eminem are the direct descendants of Benny Goodman and Peggy Lee even if the fans of all four would strenuously deny the lineage.

Less then ten years after *Stage Door Canteen,* Brando had radically updated racial appropriation. Most intriguingly, he did it without playing jazz. This chapter grows out of an attempt to find a place where, like single-cell organisms under a microscope, jazz and acting can be observed exchanging genetic material. This search has been complicated by the shifting meanings of jazz as well as by the vagaries of jazz history, including the highly personal "misreadings" of jazz by painters, poets, filmmakers, choreographers, and photographers.[1] "Jazz" paintings include, for example, the flat geometry of line and color in Mondrian's *Broadway Boogie Woogie* (1943) as well as the playfully perverse representation of Willie "The Lion" Smith at the piano in Bearden's *Lion Takes Off* (1981). In fact, if we consider only the artists' intentions, the two paintings are highly similar, both representing the improvisations of premodern jazz pianists.

In the case of Brando, a jazz influence enters at multiple levels, not all of them readily apparent as jazz or as some aspect of African American culture. A good way to untangle the jazz-like qualities in Brando and his films from everything else that goes on around them is to look closely at the "political unconscious" of filmmakers and their audiences.[2]

I have chosen to concentrate on a film from the early 1950s, when jazz held a powerful appeal for American artists and intellectuals. Although not every aspect of it may appeal to people of different races and ethnicities, the performance of the young Marlon Brando in *A Streetcar Named Desire* embodies, on several levels, a jazz aesthetic.

WHERE JAZZ AND HOLLYWOOD INTERSECT

The story of jazz overlaps at several points with the development of the Hollywood cinema. Both art forms are uniquely American, and both began to develop and mature dramatically after 1900. According to Mary Carbine, black jazz artists were improvising in orchestra pits during the screening of pre-sound films in African American neighborhoods in Chicago in the 1920s (28–29). African American participation at some point in the production and exhibition of the first feature films was, of course, an anomaly. As with most American institutions at the beginning of the twentieth century, blacks were excluded from virtually all aspects of the film industry, with the notable exception of a handful of independent filmmakers, such as Oscar Micheaux, who worked outside the mainstream film industry. The omnipresence of white actors in blackface in D. W. Griffith's *Birth of a Nation* (1914) is the most striking example of Hollywood's long history of relying on myths about African Americans to forge fundamental narratives and ideologies while harshly limiting the actual presence of black actors, directors, writers, and technicians (fig. 5).[3]

The radically different racial orientations of jazz and cinema did not, however, prevent either from being considered low culture during the early decades of the twentieth century. The guardians of America's moral, sexual, and religious health launched similar attacks on both. The two art forms became somewhat more sedate in the 1930s with the rise of superego forces, specifically the Production Code, which made movies safe for children (Doherty, *Pre-Code Hollywood*), and the success of white swing bands, which made jazz safe for Middle Americans (Erenberg). In the 1950s, new scapegoats were found, thus making jazz and film seem less disreputable. Rock 'n' roll replaced jazz just as television replaced movies as new explanations for the corruption of America's youth and the lowering of standards of taste. Coincidentally, claims that jazz and Hollywood films could be "art" first surfaced at about this time in the late 1940s and early 1950s. By the 1980s, after several decades of experimentation, both jazz and cinema fell back into periods of what might be called "recuperation": while some welcomed a return to more classical, more accessible models, others believed that the exhilarating evolution of vital art forms had stopped. At any rate, by the 1990s both jazz and film had begun to acquire the status of elite entertainment. At New York's Lincoln Center, a ticket to a jazz concert cost as much as a ticket to an opera or a ballet.[4] Across the street, at the Lincoln Plaza Cinemas, moviegoers could purchase gourmet food and espresso in the lobby while Baroque music played in the auditoriums before each screening of an "art film."

Fig. 5. The renegade Gus (Walter Long in blackface) is captured by the Ku Klux Klan in *The Birth of a Nation* (1914, David W. Griffith Corp.). Photofest Film Archive.

At least a few critics have speculated about the specific ways in which jazz has actually influenced the movies. Stanley Crouch has made a provocative claim for the importance of Afrocentric practices in American culture, pointing to the call and response dialogue that African American preachers improvised with their congregations and that eventually became the basis for the interaction between blues singers and their audiences and between the brass and reed sections in arrangements played by black jazz orchestras in the 1920s and 1930s. Crouch argues that Hollywood's shot-reverse shot editing is also an appropriation of call and response ("Jazz Criticism" 82).

Crouch has probably exaggerated the actual impact of African American practices on an industry that was much more invested in white mythologies of blackness. Clear evidence of the influence of jazz improvisation in Hollywood is also minimal, especially in the industry's "prestige" products, where a small army of producers and technicians oversees each step in a film's deliberate progress to the big screen. Nevertheless, there may have been a substantial—if highly mediated—exchange between jazz improvisation and film in the 1950s.[5]

Both jazz and the Method acting that made its way into American cinema at this time were part of a modernist mix that also included a romance with psychoanalysis, new forms of racial imitation, the development of postwar masculinities, and a fascination with improvisation. *A Streetcar Named Desire* had a revolutionary jazz-inflected score by Alex North;[6] it was based on the play by Tennessee Williams, who was obsessed with masculine performance; and it was directed by Elia Kazan, who was obsessed with psychoanalysis. The time was right for the youthful Brando's startling innovations.

MYTHOLOGIES OF THE UNCONSCIOUS

Among the many myths and assertions that circulate in jazz writing, three are especially useful for identifying a jazz aesthetic in Brando's performance. Later on I will take up the myths that jazz gives whites safe access to a fascinating but proscribed Otherness and that jazz as an improvised art music can only be performed by disciplined artists. First, however, I would like to explore the myth that improvising jazz artists dig into their unconscious minds and bypass more conventional modes of intellection. Various versions of this myth have circulated since the beginnings of jazz history, when the predominantly African American musicians were considered too primitive to be playing a music mediated by thought. The idea that "primitive" people are instinctual rather than thoughtful goes back at least to fifth century B.C.E. when Herodotus wrote that the Persians, for whom the Greeks coined the term "barbarian," would only make important decisions when they were drunk (I:133).

The trope of the improvising jazz artist as the unthinking explorer of the unconscious is still very much with us. As Will Straw has pointed out, "strength and mastery independent of knowledges" has long been an admired aspect of a musician's stance (8). Certainly, the legend of Louis Armstrong is based more on his propensity, as Robert Goffin once wrote, "to whip himself up into a state of complete frenzy" (Gioia 30) than on his thoughtful and disciplined artistry or on his judicious attention to an extremely diverse body of music. At its most deeply racist, this myth casts black artists as one or two small steps above animals in the jungle. Consider this passage from a 1920 issue of *Revue Musicale,* a French journal aimed at connoisseurs of classical music:

Jazz is cynically the orchestra of brutes with nonopposable thumbs and still prehensile toes, in the forest of Voodoo. It is entirely excess, and for that reason more than monotone: the monkey is left with his own devices, without morals, without discipline, thrown back to all the groves of instinct, showing his meat still more obscene. These slaves must be subjugated, or there will be no more master. Their reign is shameful. The shame is ugliness and its triumph. (Quoted in Attali 104)

There is, however, a spiritual alternative to these grotesque attitudes. Some have suggested that, in the heat of improvisatory creation, the jazz artist achieves a semi-religious state of transcendence. In James Baldwin's 1965 story "Sonny's Blues," the pianist brother of the narrator behaves like a mystic, "wrapped up in some cloud, some fire, some vision all his own" (129). The eponymous hero of Rafi Zabor's novel *The Bear Comes Home* (1997), a saxophone-playing Kodiak with more intelligence and musical talent than most humans, at one point plays with such ecstatic abandon that he is "plucked out of existence like a cheap suit" (454). (In the cinema, the intuitive jazz musician is seldom allowed such transcendence. Consider the Charlie Parker of Clint Eastwood's *Bird* [1988], whose mysterious ways are simply inscrutable or even pathological. Or consider the self-destructive saxophonist played by Dexter Gordon in *Round Midnight* [1986], who needs a sensitive French aficionado to ascertain and then fulfill his needs.)

Between the two extremes of unthinking brutishness and spiritual transcendence is the more modernist notion of the unconscious as the source of creativity. Specific connections between jazz artists and the unconscious mind appeared for the first time in the late 1940s and early 1950s, a heady time for psychoanalysis. John Burnham has shown how a new optimism in the psychiatric and psychoanalytic professions was driven to a large extent by their substantial success in integrating shell-shocked veterans of World War II back into American life. Psychoanalytic concepts of repression and the family romance soon entered popular discourse, and visiting a psychotherapist gained in cachet what it lost in stigma. The fascination with psychoanalysis was especially prominent in the arts, where surrealism and other avant-garde movements had already made the unconscious an essential player in the creative process. The links between jazz and the unconscious were explicit in a number of articles appearing in psychoanalytic journals in the 1950s. Miles D.

Miller, for example, wrote in 1958 that jazz can be "a sublimated means of releasing tension associated with repressed hostile and aggressive impulses" (235). More specifically, Miller associated the sounds of the jazz trombone with "anal expulsive components" that bring delight to audiences who would surely find such sounds objectionable in other situations (237).[7]

The Method acting that Brando helped make famous enjoyed a vogue in the late 1940s and 1950s and was also promoted in terms of what is ordinarily repressed and ignored. Actors sought to build their performances around "affective memory," a term coined to describe pockets of the mind, often unconscious, in which emotional reactions to specific events are stored. Like patients in therapy working through repressed moments from the past, Method actors looked back to incidents in their own lives to find the emotional key to constructing a character. "Draw on them. Turn trauma into drama," Elia Kazan allegedly said (Bosworth 57). Although many of the central ideas in this discipline had already been introduced by Konstantin Stanislavsky at the Moscow Art Theatre in the 1920s, a uniquely American version developed at the same time that intellectuals were especially fascinated by psychoanalysis. In fact, the Actors Studio, the home of the Method in postwar New York, has been conceptualized as a therapeutic institution, with its leader, Lee Strasberg, playing psychoanalyst and his actors playing analysands (Naremore 197). With the help of elaborate exercises, frequently built around improvisation, actors sought to "unblock" themselves and connect with their inner selves in hopes of bringing authenticity and immediacy to their performances.

Some jazz artists engaged in elaborate exercises of their own at the same time that Method acting was gaining in popularity. Although not every jazz artist was seeking to unlock emotional resources through experiments in improvisation, many who fancied the new jazz believed that the musicians were voyaging inward. In his extraordinary autobiography, *Beneath the Underdog*, composer/bassist Charles Mingus seems to understand jazz and improvisation as psychoanalysis "by other means." The pianist Lennie Tristano sought to create an improvised music without key signature that suggested automatic writing, a practice among the surrealists inspired by Freud. The notion that improvising jazz artists rely primarily on emotion and the unconscious is, of course, a gross oversimplification of the process. And as James Naremore has observed, the performances of most actors trained in the Method seldom differ from those with more conventional backgrounds. The specific achievements of the enterprise, he argues, are "difficult to assess" (198). My point is that a new fascination with psychoanalysis popularized discourses of the unconscious and emotional memory that were then recruited to describe both Method acting and jazz improvisation in the years after World War II.

STANLEY KOWALSKI'S COLD PLATE SUPPER

Marlon Brando has been known as an improviser throughout his career. One of his more sensational moments was the tearful speech he seemed to make up on the spot as his character grieved over the corpse of his wife in *Last Tango in Paris* (1973).[8] Brando's most famous piece of apparently improvised business, however, involves Eva Marie Saint's glove in *On the Waterfront* (1954) (fig. 6). The scene is regularly cited as the locus classicus of Brando's improvisatory style in particular and of Method acting in general (Naremore 193–212). Strolling through a playground with Edie Doyle (Eva Marie Saint), Terry Malloy (Brando) picks up the white glove that Edie seems to have dropped by accident. While sitting on a child's swing, Terry absent-mindedly toys with the glove, eventually putting it on his own hand. Brando actually improvised with the glove after Saint accidentally dropped it during a rehearsal while director Kazan was present. At the director's urging, the gesture was preserved when the scene was actually shot (Schickel 91). How much Brando subsequently improvised while the cameras were rolling is open to debate. Indeed, the amount of improvisatory leeway available to an actor—even to one as original as Brando—is extremely limited, especially within the highly conventionalized strategies for achieving "realistic" effects in mainstream cinema. Nevertheless, the variety of gestures that Brando explores with the glove, seemingly without artifice, convinced many that he was letting his unconscious do the work for him and that he was drawing on training based in psychological insights.

For my purposes, however, an even more telling scene takes place in *Streetcar* when Brando ranges through a fascinating variety of stage business. Early in the film, Stanley's wife, Stella (Kim Hunter), serves him a "cold plate" supper so that she and her recently arrived sister Blanche (Vivien Leigh) can go out for dinner and a night's entertainment at Galatoire's. Stanley loudly questions Stella about Blanche, fully aware that she is just around the corner in the bathtub. He is especially concerned about a family inheritance that he suspects Blanche has squandered on clothes instead of splitting with Stella, who must,

Fig. 6. Marlon Brando and Eva Marie Saint in *On the Waterfront*
(1954, Columbia Pictures). Photofest Film Archive.

according to Stanley's highly specific understanding of the Napoleonic Code, share it with her husband. While eating his supper, Stanley explores the clothes and jewelry in Blanche's trunk, recently deposited in the living room.

As with the glove in *On the Waterfront,* Brando is doing much more than reading lines and responding to Kim Hunter in the scene. You can see Brando doing what actors are told to do when they eat—bite small and chew big. You can also see him using the food as a prop and refusing to meet Hunter's gaze (fig. 7). All of these actions present a man for whom appetite is all. Stanley is clearly disappointed by his meager supper, but he is also hungry for information about Blanche, who has profoundly raised his suspicions as well as his sexual curiosity. Like a jazz artist playing changes on a familiar tune, Brando continually finds ways to develop his character as he eats, interacts with Stella, and inspects each of the items in Blanche's trunk. Yet even today, it all seems fresh and "in the moment." The seeming naturalness of his acting in these scenes has made "Marlon Brando synonymous with Stanley Kowalski in world theatre" (Kolin 24). One critic even says he heard a passerby at the filming of a 1983 television version of *A Streetcar Named Desire* ask, "Who's playing Marlon Brando?" (Card 98). Improvisation became the canonical text.

As is often the case with a Hollywood film, we do not know how many takes Brando needed to create effects that seem so appropriate to his character. Nor do we know exactly how much credit must go to director Elia Kazan, to playwright Tennessee Williams, or to Oscar Saul, who is credited with "adapting" Williams's play. I would point out that Kazan came to cinema

Fig. 7. Playing Stanley Kowalski in *A Streetcar Named Desire* (1951, Warner Bros.), Marlon Brando refuses to meet the gaze of his wife, Stella (Kim Hunter). Photofest Film Archive.

from the theatre and was more likely to block and direct his actors in a
"stagey" fashion. And other actors who have played the part of Stanley
Kowalski have scarcely made the part their own as did Brando. The other participants in Kazan's film appear to have stepped back and, like a self-effacing
rhythm section working behind a star improviser, let Brando make the most
of his solo space. More importantly, Brando was *giving the impression* that he
was improvising at the same historical moment that Charlie Parker and a
group of young, mostly black musicians were making improvisation the *sine
qua non* of jazz art.

WHITEFACE, BLACK NOISE

According to the second jazz myth that is relevant to Brando's performance
in *Streetcar,* the white musician can gain privileged access to Otherness
through the music of African Americans. In *Blackface, White Noise,* Michael
Rogin has written that whites have historically benefitted not only from the
surplus value of African American labor; they have also exploited the "surplus symbolic value" of blacks in much of American entertainment (80).
Given this long history of exploitation—from the minstrel show to *American
Idol*—specific cases of white males borrowing from black artists can be described with varying degrees of censure. At one extreme, whites have taken to
black music in ways that are consistent with Fred Pfeil's characterization of
rock music in the 1970s: "rock authenticity means . . . not just freedom from
commerce and opposition to all straight authority . . . but being a free agent
with ready access to the resources of femininity and Blackness yet with no ob-
ligations to either women or Blacks" (79). The same was often true in the
1940s and early 1950s, when jazz was still the music of youthful revolt and
many of the tropes of what was to become rock authenticity, including an
aloof pose on the bandstand and the refusal to play the tepid pop music preferred by the uninitiated, were being developed in the discourses of jazz.

Bebop in particular offered white hipsters a stance of defiance that
linked artistic integrity, a thorough renunciation of bourgeois convention,
and contempt for the institutions of white culture. Rejecting the attempts by
The Wild One's screenwriters to recreate the jive-speak of bop rebellion for a
gang of motorcyclists, Brando drew on his own experiences, including a few
days of hanging out with a real motorcycle gang. At one point Johnny Strabler (Brando) says to his leading lady Kathie (Mary Murphy), "If you're

gonna stay cool, you got to wail. You gotta put something down. You gotta make some jive. Don't you know what I'm talkin' about?" The strained attempt to sound black is unmistakable. Brando could of course pick up a bit of bop talk from motorcyclists or black jazz musicians and then return to his life as a movie star. Unlike Johnny Otis, who lived his entire life as a member of an African American community and never looked back (see chapter 2), any white hipster can abandon the studious appropriation of black bopper discourse and comfortably return to the bosom of Middle America. With very few exceptions, the black artist had no comparable safe haven.

In contrast to this critique of the provisional nature of white investment in black culture, LeRoi Jones (Amiri Baraka) in *Blues People* takes a stance reminiscent of Ralph Ellison when he speaks generously about white artists, such as Bix Beiderbecke, who made a commitment to jazz in the 1920s: "The entrance of the white man into jazz at this level of sincerity and emotional legitimacy did at least bring him, by implication, much closer to the Negro" (Baraka, *Blues People* 151). Beiderbecke approached the music of African Americans at one or two removes, learning his craft almost exclusively from white recording artists such as the Original Dixieland Jazz Band and the New Orleans Rhythm Kings before he had direct experience of black music. But for the many white artists whose performance styles were rooted in black culture, racial appropriation need not be cast as an absolute evil. Other discursive strategies are available. While Baraka has suggested that white jazz artists helped break down the gap between black and white, Eric Lott has employed the phrase "Love and Theft" to describe the ambivalence of whites toward blacks that informed minstrelsy, and David Meltzer has coined the term "permissible racism" to characterize the uncritical adulation of black artists *qua* black artists by white fans (4).

Ellison himself, however, took issue with several of Baraka's assertions in *Blues People,* rejecting his thesis that jazz is the pure expression of a distinctly Negro sensibility. For Ellison, even the most profoundly alienated blacks have always been connected with dominant American culture, during the days of slavery as well as today. While Baraka states that "a slave cannot be a man," Ellison argues that the "enslaved really thought of themselves as *men* who had been unjustly enslaved." If asked what he wanted to be when he grew up, Ellison wrote, the male slave would not have responded, "a slave." More likely he would have said, "a coachman, a teamster, a cook, the best damned steward on the Mississippi, the best jockey in Kentucky, a butler, a farmer, a stud, or, hopefully, a free man!" (Ellison, *Essays* 284).

By including "a stud" among the aspirations of the slave, Ellison hints at why white men seeking to perform their masculinity have so often looked to African Americans. In a culture that consistently denied his manhood, the male slave sought to establish some degree of power within the limitations imposed upon him. He was not likely to be lynched if he became a great musician, a great cook, or, finding whatever privacy was available to him, a great lover. In some cases, he could simply adopt a distinctly manly performance in his way of walking and talking. After Emancipation, the black man succeeded in finding new strategies for projecting manliness without inviting reprisals from whites who were as intimidated by black masculinity as they were fascinated by it. I have argued that, in the early years of the twentieth century, Louis Armstrong was especially adept at coding his masculinity, developing a powerfully "phallic" style with his trumpet while wearing the mask of the harmless jester when the horn was not at his mouth. The garden variety white racist in the audience did not see Armstrong as sexual competition, but clearly many musicians—white as well as black—were able to decode Armstrong's expressions of masculinity and mastery and hoped to recreate them in their own performances (*Jammin'* 138–139). Later on, when men like the boxer Jack Johnson or the singer/actor/athlete/orator Paul Robeson found more conventional means for expressing their masculinity, they suffered from white racism in ways that Armstrong did not, even if they became role models for whites in search of strong masculine personae.

But as Ellison himself has argued, the careful self-masking practiced by men like Armstrong was not simply the result of fear. In "Change the Joke and Slip the Yoke," Ellison says that the black man was just as likely to be motivated by "the sheer joy of the joke" when he hid his identity behind a mask. "We wear the mask for purposes of aggression as well as for defense, when we are projecting the future and preserving the past" (*Essays* 109). For talented artists and entertainers like Armstrong, that "sheer joy" in the performance may have had little to do with a felt need to project masculinity. But this did not stop many whites from seeing masculine performance in the self-presentations of black artists. Nor did it prevent them from seeing "authenticity" in what was essentially another act of masking. And nothing has prevented white performers from engaging in masculinist gestures that bore little resemblance to the black original. John Gennari has suggested that much of the white male appropriation of black masculinity

> operates through gender displacement, i.e., sexual freedom and carefree abandon were expressed through feminized gestures (emotion, flamboyance, etc.) that, paradoxically, end up coded as masculine. I think here of Elvis's hair styling, his obsession with pink, etc.; of Mick Jagger's striptease; the spandex, long-hair, girlish torsos of the cock rockers. To try to get this point across to my students, I show footage of . . . Robert Plant and Jimmy Page talking about how everything they did came out of Willie Dixon and other macho black bluesmen. Then you see them aggressively pelvic thrusting through "Whole Lotta Love," looking like Cher and Twiggy on speed. (Gennari, Conversation with the author)

Even if black men have established the American standard of male performativity, they can hardly be held responsible for the strange attempts by white men to capture some of that magic for themselves.

Like Mick Jagger and many other pop rockers, Brando can be regarded as another member of the white bourgeoisie whose racial and gender borrowings can on some levels be traced to performances by black artists. In spite of the ethnic ring to his last name, as well as the working-class demeanor he convincingly affected in many of his early roles, Brando grew up in comfortable middle-class surroundings, first in Omaha, Nebraska, and later in the Illinois towns of Evanston and Libertyville. As was also true for Bix Beiderbecke, Brando's parents sent him to military school when his behavior disappointed them. But Brando's parents were not the staid burghers who raised Beiderbecke.[9] Both were notorious for their public drunkenness and freely engaged in extramarital affairs. Brando's older sister was already in New York studying dramatic art when Brando arrived there a few years later. Unlike Beiderbecke, Brando did not have to break dramatically with his family when he embraced the bohemian life of the actor. Or when he became interested in jazz.

Peter Manso, perhaps the most diligent of the actor's biographers, reports that Brando grew up listening to jazz—to Louis Armstrong, Jimmy Rushing, and Bessie Smith as well as to Goodman and the Dorseys (43). We also know that Brando had a fascination with dark-skinned women, and that he joined Katherine Dunham's School of Dance in the late 1940s, where 65 percent of

Fig. 8. Jazz drummer Gene
Krupa, typically tousled,
with Benny Goodman.
Photofest Film Archive.

the students were black. There he met Henri "Papa" Augustine, a revered Hait-
ian drum teacher who gave Brando lessons on congas and bongos and introduced him to various aspects of black culture. Among many anecdotes about
Brando's attraction to African Americans, Manso cites Norman Mailer's
party for the Hollywood elite where Brando spent the entire evening speaking
with the bartender, the only black person in the house (285).

Brando once wanted to be a jazz drummer. As late as the Broadway production of *Streetcar* in 1947, he was still keeping a jazz drummer's trap set
backstage along with his bongos and barbells. In high school, Brando briefly
led a few bands of his own at the same time that he tormented his school
band director by playing Gene Krupa riffs in the middle of Sousa marches. The
Krupa connection is revealing. After starring with the Benny Goodman band
in the mid-1930s, the white drummer broke away to form his own band in
1938. Krupa was arrested on a widely reported drug charge in 1943 and forced
out of the music business for several months. For many, the drummer's dangerous romance with proscribed substances only increased his glamour. Even

before Krupa's arrest, however, his band had subversive appeal. In 1941, the new "girl singer" in Krupa's orchestra was Anita O'Day, who projected a more sexually experienced persona than did most of the proper white women, such as Peggy Lee, who sang with the big bands. O'Day raised eyebrows when she refused to wear the prom dresses common among girl singers, choosing instead to wear a blazer like the men in the band. One possible result of this fashion decision was the rumor that O'Day was a lesbian. Also in 1941, Krupa hired the energetic black trumpeter Roy Eldridge and prominently featured his improvised solos and his singing. (After two years of working with the black pianist Teddy Wilson exclusively in recording studios, Benny Goodman first brought him on stage to perform publicly in a trio with himself and Krupa in 1935. Artie Shaw had hired Billie Holiday for a brief period in 1938. Nevertheless, black faces were still extremely rare in the white swing orchestras when Krupa hired Eldridge.) When Krupa's band had a hit with "Let Me Off Uptown," in which Eldridge sang with O'Day, the interracial romance implied in the couple's double entendres was especially daring for 1941. The patter begins with O'Day asking Eldridge if he has been "uptown" and concludes with her urging him, "Well, blow, Roy, blow!" The veiled invitation to interracial oral sex was not lost on the hipper members of the audience. The gender and racial titillation in which Krupa's band specialized may have been as important for the young Brando as Krupa's drumming.

In films such as *Hollywood Hotel* (1938), *Ball of Fire* (1941), *George White's Scandals* (1945), *Beat the Band* (1947), and *The Glenn Miller Story* (1954), Krupa can be observed flamboyantly performing his sexuality and masculinity, often resembling a man approaching orgasm as he flails away with his sticks. Krupa may have been attempting to reproduce what he found most fascinating about black men and their music. Anyone who has watched the great African American drummer Jo Jones in a film such as *Jammin' the Blues* (1944) has witnessed an artist who seems, by contrast, to inhabit his exuberance without affectation. I would speculate that Krupa intentionally went beyond the restrained hipness displayed by his former employer, Benny Goodman. Like the white rockers described by Gennari, Krupa saw and heard sexual power in the work of black artists like Jones and created his own style of bringing it to the surface in hopes of projecting that same power.

At some point in his early life, Brando may have been using Krupa as a transitional figure in his appropriation of black masculinity, just as Beiderbecke first discovered black music through the white artists of the ODJB and NORK. Iden-tifying a parallel phenomenon, Eric Lott has written that imitators of Elvis Pres-ley play out their fascination with black male sexuality safely at one remove by trying to inhabit the body of Presley as he appeared in the 1950s, "as though such performance were a sort of second-order blackface, in which, blackface having for the most part disappeared, the figure of Elvis himself is now the apparently still necessary signifier of white ventures into black culture—a signifier to be adopted bodily if one is to have success in achieving the intimacy with 'black-ness' that is crucial to the adequate reproduction of Presley's show" (Lott, "All the King's Men" 205). By the time he began appearing in movies, Brando had moved beyond Krupa and the channeling of blackness through transitional ob-jects. Indeed, by imitating what he perceived as the *excesses* in black male per-formativity, Brando actually anticipated Presley's breakthrough success with his own uniquely exaggerated imitations of black musical practice.

In 1969, Brando attended a meeting to raise money for the Poor People's March on Washington, sponsored by the Southern Christian Leadership Con-ference in the wake of the assassination of Martin Luther King Jr. The meeting was attended by other Hollywood celebrities, including Barbra Streisand, Harry Belafonte, Natalie Wood, and Jean Seberg, who brought along the man to whom she was married at the time, the French novelist Romain Gary. In his autobiographical novel, *White Dog,* Gary contemptuously describes the behav-ior of Brando at the event. After stressing the need for a steering committee to continue the work of raising money for the poor, Brando asked for volunteers. In a crowd of approximately three hundred, thirty hands went up. "He glares at the audience and at the thirty raised hands. He braces himself, balances his shoulders in that famous half-roll, then the chin goes up. He is acting. Or rather overacting, for the sudden violence in his voice and the tightening of his facial muscles and of the jaws bears no relation whatsoever to the situation." According to Gary, Brando than said, "Those who didn't raise their hands, get the hell out of here!" (172).

Eric Lott is among the few writers who have attempted a history of how white Americans have lived with their conflicted fascination with black Amer-icans. Among many valuable observations in *Love and Theft,* Lott points out that although minstrelsy allowed whites to indulge their contempt and even hatred for blacks, it also invited white people in the early nineteenth century, especially working-class males, to regard black men as sexual role models. Minstrel men constantly played up the supposed hypersexuality, spontaneity, and phallic power of black men. Although his major focus is the nineteenth century, Lott shows continuity between minstrelsy and more contemporary practices. He points out, for example, that adolescent boys today base a great deal of their behavior on their perceptions of African American males. Lott observes that "this dynamic, persisting into adulthood, is so much a part of most American white men's equipment for living that they remain entirely unaware of their participation in it" (*Love and Theft* 53). For the white minstrel man, "to put on the cultural forms of 'blackness' was to engage in a complex affair of manly mimicry. . . . To wear or even enjoy blackface was literally, for a time, to become black, to inherit the cool, virility, humility, abandon, or *gaité de coeur* that were the prime components of white ideologies of black manhood" (52).

The dark side of what Lott describes is especially apparent in *Birth of a Nation,* with its white actors playing former slaves in sexual pursuit of white women. Although the film vividly inscribes the racist myth that black-on-white rape is always imminent if African American males are not carefully policed, the film unintentionally dramatizes the fantasy among white men that inhabiting a black body allows them to unleash their sexual desires. In this sense, the institution of lynching, which almost invariably included the castration of black victims, represents the white man's attempt to repress his own sexual longings by projecting them into the African American male, who is then destroyed for allegedly acting on these desires. As Lott notes, the celebration of the black penis in minstrelsy was "obsessively reversed in white lynching rituals" (*Love and Theft* 9).

Not far from working-class white men, who took their multiple, contradictory pleasures at the minstrel show, stood the abolitionists, church workers, and many other well-intentioned white people of the middle classes with their own sets of complex beliefs about African Americans. Some members of these groups may have regarded African Americans as inferior and thus in need of religious instruction. They may also have regarded African Americans as closer to the spirit and the *gaité de coeur* that Lott mentions. After so many centuries of enforced racial hierarchy in the United States, few whites have been able to look past racist constructions and regard African Americans as individual human beings.

By the first decades of the twentieth century, white connoisseurs of black music were developing their own ambivalent attitudes toward African

Americans. The filmmaker Dudley Murphy cast Duke Ellington in *Black and Tan* (1929), consistently portraying him as a serious composer and a principled bandleader. In the same film, however, Murphy unleashed the black comedians Edgar Connor and Alec Lovejoy as illiterate, shiftless day laborers, very much in the minstrel tradition. Murphy's fascination with black culture led him to prize the dignity of Ellington as much as the tomfoolery of Connor and Lovejoy (Gabbard, *Jammin'* 160–167). Consider also the "Moldy Figs" who waged war with the proponents of modern jazz in the 1940s, insisting that the premodern jazz of New Orleans was the "true" jazz and thus more "artistic" because it was the music of primitive "folk" artists.[10]

More recently, Lee Atwater helped elect George H. W. Bush in 1988 by terrifying white Americans with television commercials about Willie Horton, the sinister-looking African American who assaulted a white couple in their home while he was on "furlough" from a Massachusetts prison. In one commercial, the husband looked directly at the camera and told how Horton left the couple side by side in bed while he raped the wife and held a knife at the throat of the husband. Hardly the first politician to use white America's fear of black male sexuality to win votes, Atwater took the practice to new lengths in a national election, even bragging that he would make Horton the running mate of Democratic presidential nominee Michael Dukakis, then the governor of Massachusetts. In spite of a large early lead in the poles, Dukakis eventually lost the election to Bush, in no small part because of the racist advertisements created by Atwater. But as his biographer John Brady has reported, even while running the Bush campaign, Atwater was an avid fan of Chicago blues and once seized the opportunity to play his Fender Telecaster on stage with B. B. King. A few years later, when he was dying from a brain tumor, Atwater asked African Americans to forgive him for using a presidential campaign to foment racial hatred. Atwater's affection for the sensuality of black blues seems to have coexisted with a loathing that allowed him to make race-baiting a crucial element in the presidential election of 1988. Conversely, some degree of repressed anxiety about black bodies may exist within even the most enthusiastic white believer in the virtue of black Americans. Or as Calvin Hernton has written, "There is a sexual involvement, at once real and vicarious, connecting white and black people in America that spans the history of this country from the era of slavery to the present, an involvement so immaculate and yet so per-

verse, so ethereal and yet so concrete, that all race relations tend to be, however subtle, sex relations" (7).

KIND OF WHITE

Although it would be unfair to diagnose Marlon Brando's advocacy of African
American causes as part of a neurotic fascination with the sexuality of black
men and women, there is no question that his attitudes, like those of most
white Americans, changed dramatically over time. Brando's desire to study
dance with Katherine Dunham in the 1940s is part of the same cultural history as his angry insistence that wealthy celebrities join his steering committee at the meeting in the 1960s that Romain Gary witnessed. In the early 1950s
Brando's negrophilia inflected his stunning performance as Stanley Kowalski.
John Szwed, the author of a superb biography of the jazz trumpeter Miles
Davis, has said that Brando was consciously imitating Davis's voice when he
performed in *A Streetcar Named Desire* (Szwed, Conversation with the author). Coincidentally, Davis seems to have been well aware of Brando at this
time, at one point expressing his great admiration for the jazz-inflected score
that Alex North wrote for *Streetcar*. According to Szwed, after seeing the film
Davis said to his brother, "Fuck jazz! Alex North is the man" (*So What* 151).

In his 1989 autobiography Davis admits to physically abusing virtually
every woman with whom he had a sexual relationship. It is doubtful that
Brando was aware of this aspect of Miles Davis's character, although as Robin
D. G. Kelley has argued, both Davis's seductive music as well as his violent misogyny can be understood as part of a "pimp aesthetic": "listening for the pimp
in Miles ought to make us aware of the pleasures of cool as well as the dark side
of romance. We get nostalgic for the old romantic Miles, for that feeling of
being in love, but who understands this better than the mack, that despicable
character we find so compelling and attractive?" (7). Brando may have sensed
this character in Davis as early as 1950 and brought it into his portrayal of Stanley Kowalski, who abuses and romances his wife with the same intensity.

The Brando/Davis connection can also be traced to Brando's brief encounter in 1965 with Frances Taylor Davis, Miles Davis's second wife. Frances
was in Hollywood, having left her husband a few days earlier because of his
escalating drug abuse. She ended up at a party for Bob Dylan where Brando
was in attendance with Pat Quinn, an actress with whom he was in the middle of an on-again-off-again love affair. According to Manso, when Brando

Fig. 9. Miles Davis, toward the end of his flamboyant career.
Jerry Ohlinger's Movie Material Store, Inc.

became angry that Dylan was paying so much attention to Quinn, he began an intense conversation with Frances Davis. Finding Brando a sympathetic listener, Frances eventually went home with him but was upset when the actor sat her down in front of a pornographic movie in his bedroom. Otherwise he paid her little attention (Manso 619). Brando may also have imitated Davis's notorious practice of leaving the stage while other musicians soloed during his club appearances. Rod Steiger bitterly complained about Brando's behavior during the crucial scene between the two men in the back of a car in *On the Waterfront* ("I coulda been a contenda! I coulda been somebody!"). After the two-shots had been filmed, Steiger says he sat patiently and reacted in character while the camera took close-ups of Brando. But when the camera was turned toward Steiger for his speeches, Brando went home (Manso 365). Steiger's complaint, "He left the set, he left the set," parallels the familiar complaint about Davis, "He left the stage, he left the stage," when the trumpeter made the unusual choice of walking into the wings during the solos of his sidepeople.[11]

In the film of *A Streetcar Named Desire,* Brando's Stanley is prone to preening, sudden violence, and child-like vulnerability, all of them part of white America's construction of black male behavior, especially in the first half of the twentieth century. When he first appeared in *Streetcar* on the New York stage in 1947, costume designer Lucinda Ballard effectively created the vogue for tight jeans by making crucial decisions about how to dress Brando. Ballard kept seven pairs of Levi's in a washing machine for twenty-four hours, then fitted them to Brando's wet body, pinning them tight. Brando's friend Carlo Fiore told a biographer that Brando liked the tight jeans because they made it look as if he had "a perpetual hard-on"; the critic George Jean Nathan went so far as to call *Streetcar* "The Glands Menagerie" (Kolin 28). Ballard also made sure that Brando's u-shirt fit like second skin. Steven Cohan has convincingly described Brando's "gender masquerade" in the section of his *Masked Men* called "Why Boys Are Not Men" (241–252). As the photos in Cohan's book indicate, Brando was more than willing to display much more of a well-muscled physique than audiences were accustomed to seeing. At least some portion of this display surely grew out of Brando's observations of black dancers and athletes.

The menace and sensuality in the persona of someone like Miles Davis appealed to Brando, as did fantasies of how black men treat their women. When Stanley attacks Stella in *Streetcar,* the worst violence is off screen, but he appears to be striking her with his fist. At the beginning of the twenty-first century, when violence against women is increasingly regarded as criminal and immoral, we may lose sight of how differently Americans felt about wife-beating in the years after World War II. Especially because women had so recently been active in the work force and had proved themselves capable of doing "a man's job," some men, white as well as black, felt justified in using violence to restore the pre-war gender hierarchy. Then as now, many white men have regarded black men as more assertive, more capable of controlling their women through violence. Stanley's wild attack on Stella must be understood at least in part in

Fig. 10. Al Jolson as Gus,
an African American trick-
ster/jockey, in *Big Boy*
(1930, Warner Bros.).
Photofest Film Archive.

this context. But Brando's Stanley is also capable of childlike contrition. After his famous tearful cry of "Stella! STEL-LA!," Stanley falls to his knees in front of his wife. The way he buries his head in Stella's stomach has led Ann Douglas to suggest, "It's not just sex he wants, but birth, in reverse" (E24).[12] Some portion of Brando's performance in this scene may be rooted in the hoary fantasy of the child-like black man fixated on a mother that was the creation, most famously, of Al Jolson. With or without the burnt cork, blackface impersonation gave white men license to act out much that was forbidden to them, including hypersexuality, the mistreatment of women without reprisal, and the pathos of the child—all of them extremely prominent in Brando's gender performance.

AFTER BLACKFACE

Blackface disappeared from the American screen in about 1952, at the same time that Brando was appearing on screens throughout the country as Stanley Kowalski. In the film *A Streetcar Named Desire,* Brando played exactly the kind of white working-class male who was both actor and audience at the minstrel shows of the nineteenth century. After a century of prominence on American stages, blackface moved comfortably into American movies, most prominently in the person of Jolson. In addition to his stunning arrival in *The Jazz Singer* (1927) as the first singing movie star, Jolson wore blackface in several subsequent films, including *Big Boy* (1930) (fig. 10), in which he starred as an African American jockey, a part he had created for the stage in 1925 (Goldman 136). In the same year as *Big Boy,* the white actors Charles Correll and Freeman Gosden blacked up to reprise their radio roles as Amos and Andy in *Check and Double Check* (1930). A partial list of white stars who have also appeared under cork would include Bing Crosby in *Holiday Inn* (1942) and *Dixie* (1943), Eddie Cantor in *Whoopee!* (1930) and *Kid Millions* (1934), Martha Raye in *College Holiday* (1936) and *Artists and Models* (1937), Shirley Temple in *The Littlest Rebel* (1935), the Marx Brothers in *A Day at the Races* (1937), Fred Astaire in *Swing Time* (1939), and Mickey Rooney and Judy Garland in *Babes in Arms* (1939). Larry Parks blacked up to play Jolson in two extremely successful biopics, *The Jolson Story* (1946) (fig. 11) and *Jolson Sings Again* (1949). In 1951, Doris Day did a blackface imitation of Jolson in *I'll See You in My Dreams,* a film that also starred Danny Thomas and was directed by

Fig. 11. Larry Parks as Jolson with John Alexander in *The Jolson Story* (1946, Columbia Pictures). Jerry Ohlinger's Movie Material Store, Inc.

Michael Curtiz for Warner Bros. In 1952, however, when Warners celebrated the twenty-fifth anniversary of *The Jazz Singer* by remaking it with Danny Thomas as star and Curtiz as director, there was no blackface performance.

Blackface should have been inevitable in a remake of *The Jazz Singer,* especially because the same studio, star, and director had been involved with a film that *did* include blackface just one year earlier. Although I have found no evidence of a decision-making process at Warner Bros. that resulted in a ban on blackface, it is possible that groups such as the NAACP learned of the film in the early stages and convinced studio executives that the practice was offensive. It is also likely that the men at Warners decided on their own that times had changed and that blackface had become too provocative to be part of mainstream entertainment. After Keefe Brasselle blacked up to play Eddie Cantor in the 1953 biopic, and Joan Crawford appeared under a light coat of dusky body paint in MGM's *Torch Song,* also in 1953, no films with blacked-up actors appeared again until *Black Like Me* (1964), which took the practice in an entirely different direction (but see Lott, "Racial Cross-Dressing"). As Szwed has suggested, the disappearance of blackface "marks the detachment of culture from race and the almost full absorption of a black tradition into white culture" ("Race" 27).

By the late 1940s, when Brando was coming of age as an actor, the African American traditions had become, in Szwed's phrase, so "absorbed" that Brando could partake of a variety of models when he performed his gender. Consider the lyricism and vulnerability that accompanied the assertiveness in the solos of Miles Davis, or the pathos in many of the saxophone solos of Ben Webster and Charlie Parker, of whom Brando was surely aware. Brando was in some ways the nonmusical counterpart of Chet Baker, a white trumpeter who played in the style of the young Miles Davis and flourished in the early 1950s. Baker, the photogenic ephebe turned weathered junkie in Bruce Weber's 1988 documentary *Let's Get Lost,* has been associated with the polymorphous, postwar masculinities represented by film stars such as Brando, James Dean, and Montgomery Clift. In *From Here to Eternity* (1953), Clift projected a gentle/tough masculinity, explicitly connected to a post-phallic trumpet/bugle at the same time that both Brando and Chet Baker were at the peak of their early fame.[13]

In *The Wild One,* also from 1953, Brando took his appropriation of black masculinity a few steps further. Well before Brando developed a jazz aesthetic to play Stanley Kowalski, Tennessee Williams was responsible for naming the heroine of *A Streetcar Named Desire*. Calling a fragile white woman with aristocratic pretensions "Blanche" enhanced the racial subtext of her relationship with Stanley, making him seem more ethnic, more proletarian, and thus quasi-black. But the makers of *The Wild One* seemed even more willing to create a part for Brando that drew upon African American experience. In *Wild One*, Johnny/Brando does after all ride with the "Black Rebels Motorcycle Club." Throughout the film, Brando's graceful menace and what Patricia Bosworth has called his "inarticulate eloquence" (100) strongly suggest black masculinity.

When Johnny and his gang arrive in the village of Carbondale, their contempt for its bourgeois culture is entirely consistent with early 1950s bebop ideology and its opaque white Negro jive talk. A member of the gang even holds out a flat palm to the ancient bartender and asks him to "give me some skin." When Johnny puts a coin in the jukebox, we do not hear rock 'n' roll. (According to Thomas Doherty [*Teenagers and Teenpics* 76], filmmakers did not realize that rock 'n' roll could enhance a film's appeal until after 1955, when "Rock Around the Clock" was ironically inserted over the opening credits of *Blackboard Jungle* and made the film a surprise hit. Elvis Presley, Little Richard, Chuck Berry, and others who ushered in the rock revolution did not begin making rock 'n' roll recordings until 1955 at the earliest. Of course, the term "bebop" was often applied to early rock, just as the jive talk of the jazzers was picked up by rock 'n' rollers.) In *The Wild One*, the jukebox always plays the big band arrangements that Leith Stevens wrote for the film. This music, which is part of the background score even when no juke box is nearby, strongly recalls the recordings of Stan Kenton's big band, at least in part because several members of the Kenton organization play on the soundtrack. At times, however, the music veers toward the large orchestral sounds of Dizzy Gillespie's first big bands, especially when bongos and congas produced that Latin tinge that Gillespie made an essential part of his music as early as 1947 with recordings such as "Cubana Be," "Cubana Bop," and "Manteca." (At this same time, Kenton was adding Latin sounds of his own to big band recordings, such as "The Peanut Vendor" and "Bongo Riff.")

Brando's black-inflected cool in *The Wild One* is set off by the arrival of the "Beetles," a carnivalesque assortment of cast-offs from the Black Rebels Motorcycle Club. Chino (Lee Marvin), the leader of the Beetles, calls Johnny "Sweetheart," repeatedly tells Johnny that he loves him, and takes masochistic

Fig. 12. Though technically innocent, Johnny (Marlon Brando) is seized by a crypto-lynch mob
in *The Wild One* (1953, Columbia Pictures). Photofest Film Archive.

pleasure in provoking him to violence. As Chino, Lee Marvin speaks in sten-
torian, even learned tones. Challenging Johnny to fight for the brass statuette that is a recurring image throughout the film, Chino hands the trophy
to Kathie and loudly declares, "This lovely young lady over here shall hold
this beautiful object signifying absolutely nothing. Now watch closely. See
how the timid maiden of the hill clutches the gold to her breast and see how
she fights back a tear while the hero bleeds to death in the street." He then
delivers a sucker punch to Johnny's jaw. Chino's speech and deportment approach the Falstaffian, but by no means is he cool. Nevertheless, when the
male citizens of the town become dissatisfied with the local policeman's inability to stop the chaos in their town, they rise up as a mob and grab Johnny
rather than the far more violent and unpredictable Chino.

The film had already given Johnny a sympathetic side when he rescued
a terrified Kathie from a roaring circle created by motorcyclists. Now the
prisoner of angry white men, Johnny becomes an innocent victim of what
strongly resembles a lynch mob (fig. 12). After the glorification of Klan violence in *Birth of a Nation,* American films had been highly critical of vigi-

lante violence at least since 1935 when Spencer Tracy is falsely accused of a crime and then nearly burned to death by a mob of rioters in Fritz Lang's *Fury.* Although no black faces appear in *The Wild One,* and although the term lynching is never part of the dialogue, the mob persecution of a man who walks and talks like a black man and who listens to bebop clearly recalls lynching, a well-reported and increasingly reviled phenomenon in Hollywood, even during the paranoid time of the Blacklist. When the state police captain (Jay C. Flippen) arrives late in the film as a *deus ex machina* with the commanding presence and authority to set things right, he lectures the chastened Johnny while a portrait of Abraham Lincoln looms over his left shoulder. Johnny had been falsely accused of murder, but Flippen's Solomonic patriarch learns the truth and clears him of the charges. While Flippen and the Great Emancipator look on, Brando is set free.

FEATHERS IN THE AIR

Brando's performances in films such as *A Streetcar Named Desire, The Wild One,* and *On the Waterfront* were striking primarily because he refused the conventional poses of male stars from the classical cinema, such as Wayne, Gable, and Bogart. His fascination with black male sexuality may be partially responsible for his softer, more sensual masculinity as well as for behavior more typical of children and adolescents than of grown-up men. The incident with Eva Marie Saint's glove was not just a bravura piece of improvisation (if indeed it was by the time the film was shot); putting on the clothing of a woman, Brando's Terry reveals a feminine side as well as an innocent, child-like quality when he sits on the swing. In *The Wild One,* Brando's Johnny is easily intimidated when Kathie accuses him of being afraid of her after he passes up the sexual opportunity she openly offers him. In *Streetcar,* when Stanley inspects the items in Blanche's trunk, he is once again unafraid to handle female garments. He also sulks like a child, paraphrases the Napoleonic Code in the language of a schoolboy, and plays the boy's game of keep-away whenever Stella tries to grab back whatever Stanley has unceremoniously plucked from the trunk. Brando was in touch with a generation of jazz artists, both black and white, who acted out their gender in more subtle ways. The ability of Miles Davis to project vulnerability and even to "cry" with his trumpet became as essential to his gender presentation as his "manly" fascination with boxing and expensive sports cars.

We can also see the influence of jazz improvisers when Stanley manhandles Blanche's possessions. Toward the end of the scene, when white feathers drift away from her stole, Brando tries to pick them out of the air with the purposeful purposelessness of a child. Once again he has ingeniously found a way to react "in character" outside of any scripted directions. In this context, the myth of the jazz improviser as inspired primitive or bold explorer of the unconscious should be placed alongside the equally powerful myth of jazz soloists as disciplined artists in full control of their craft. As Naremore points out, Brando the actor was forging a new level of artifice in order to camouflage artifice. Slipping on Eva Marie Saint's glove or eating a cold plate supper, Brando is so loose and at ease that everyone else around him seems stiff and awkward. This is especially the case with Karl Malden, who plays Mitch in *Streetcar,* and who is *meant* to be stiff and awkward, but Brando makes him seem even more so. We see a virtuoso performance by an actor who knows his craft exceedingly well, and who can convince us that he is making it up as he goes along, not relying on tricks.

IMPROVISATION AS DISCIPLINE

And at least according to some jazz scholars, this is precisely what the jazz musician does. Although jazz musicians, like Method actors, have been constructed as more in touch with their unconscious minds than the rest of us, it is not at all accurate to say that jazz musicians simply dig into their ids during a solo. In fact, Barry Kernfeld has compared the improvising jazz musician to the oral poet, the singer of tales studied by Milman Parry and Albert Lord (Kernfeld, "Two Coltranes"). Parry and Lord carefully analyzed the performances of pre-literate poets in Muslim Serbia in the 1930s in order to explain Homer's method of composition 2600 years earlier. An oral poet like Homer could go on for days seeming to make up new stories in perfect dactyllic hexameter because he had committed to memory a huge reservoir of formulas and epithets and in some cases entire lines of verse that could always be inserted into a new line: "Wine dark sea," "Rosy-fingered dawn," and so on. Similarly, in Kernfeld's argument, accomplished jazz artists have large bodies of music under their fingers and can insert favorite motifs, bits of scales learned in practicing, and fragments of familiar melodies into a performance. They also have different strategies for deploying this material or "running the changes" so that each performance will be different from what they played in the past. This model of improvisation is a long way from the one in which jazz artists simply get in touch with their inner selves.[14]

The improvising jazzman has also internalized a series of musical and physical gestures that connote masculinity. In *Jammin' at the Margins* I argue that jazz artists can learn a set of masculine codes and then signify on them in a variety of ways (138–159). Dizzy Gillespie, for example, could assert himself with fast, loud solos in the upper register whenever he wished. But when young trumpet Turks challenged him in solo duels, he often responded to their lightning-fast assaults on the upper register with short, quiet, often humorous phrases, thus setting himself apart from the pretensions of the challenger and winning a laugh in the process. Affecting a look of well-earned insouciance, Gillespie would signify on the challenger as well as on his own role as the patriarch of the jazz trumpet. Miles Davis surely developed the most flamboyant revision of the trumpet as masculine signifier by seeming to reject conventional virtuosity, preferring instead to strive for raw emotional expression.[15]

The best jazz improvisers do more than simply construct a gendered persona. They also know how to build a solo with structure and logic. Jazz Schenkerians have developed carpal tunnel syndrome transcribing recorded solos in order to demonstrate the structural elegance of a jazz musician's improvisations. In a book about Charlie Parker, for example, Henry Martin takes the different versions of the same song that Parker recorded in a single recording session and then shows how Parker was effectively presenting a more rigorously logical composition in each successive version of the tune. By using the methods of Heinrich Schenker, Martin gives us a Parker more like Johannes Brahms than Cecil Taylor.

And yet, to the uninitiated, black jazz artists seem to be making all of it up as they go along. The accomplished improviser has learned the codes that connote freshness, looseness, and a feeling of spontaneity. Like Miles Davis and the many other jazz musicians who spent many hours in the "wood-shed" with their instruments, Marlon Brando acquired a large reservoir of formulas and gestures after years of training, practicing, and observing other improvisers. This experience bears fruit when he picks those feathers out of the air as Stanley in *Streetcar*. And having learned the secrets of the jazz improviser, Brando makes it seem as if it is all coming to him out of the air, just like the feathers.

CHAPTER TWO

Borrowing Black Masculinity

Dirty Harry Finds His Gentle Side

In choosing to direct and star in *The Bridges of Madison County* (1995), Clint Eastwood once again sought to distance himself from the misogyny and iron masculinity for which most Americans—including at least one former President—have known him. When Ronald Reagan threatened Congress with the line, "Go ahead, make my day," he publicly joined those who associate Eastwood with an unyielding, even sinister assertion of phallic authority.[1] Along with the coolly murderous cowboy introduced by Sergio Leone in the 1960s, the character of Dirty Harry has dominated public perceptions of Clint Eastwood in spite of the actor's repeated attempts to change his image. But Eastwood has also "played" the mayor of Carmel, California, and the esteemed cinematic auteur honored at New York's Museum of Modern Art and at London's National Film Theatre. And in the many films released since 1970 by his production company, Malpaso, Eastwood has often sought to undermine, question, and even ridicule his macho image. As many critics have pointed out, however, many of Eastwood's accommodations of feminism and revised masculinity have been disingenuous or highly provisional within narratives that ultimately restore patriarchal values.[2]

But Eastwood's role in *The Bridges of Madison County* may be something else altogether. Working with screenwriter Richard LaGravenese and playing opposite Meryl Streep, Eastwood has softened the stridently masculine

Robert Kincaid of Robert James Waller's novel. Gone are the Swiss Army knife hanging from Kincaid's belt (117), his self-characterization as "the last cowboy" (141), and the suggestion that he is part gazelle, leopard (82), or some other "graceful, hard, male animal" (105). Furthermore, Streep, as Iowa farm wife Francesca Johnson, does not whisper in Eastwood's ear the words of the novel's Francesca, "Robert, you're so powerful it's frightening" (106). Like the Kincaid of the novel, however, Eastwood does engage in "unmanly" activities such as writing love letters, reciting poetry, peeling carrots, and shedding real tears in conversation with a woman.

Eastwood does *not* pick up a guitar and sing to Francesca as does the Robert Kincaid of the novel (111). Although Eastwood has sung in films before, in *The Bridges of Madison County* he effectively lets the African American vocalist Johnny Hartman (1923–1983) do his singing for him. Hartman's voice, which can be heard during four of the film's most romantic and sexual moments, was an inspired choice, providing the precise musical equivalent of the nonthreatening but undeniable masculinity that Eastwood was trying to project throughout the film. More than any other singer from jazz or popular music, Hartman expressed phallic masculinity at its most unproblematic. Effortlessly displaying a deep, smooth voice, he seems to occupy his manhood with complete confidence and serenity. Just as there is no swagger or menace in his singing, neither is there whining or masochism. Anecdotal evidence suggests that the audience for *Bridges* was predominantly female, but those men who attended the film do not appear to have felt betrayed by Eastwood's lack of weaponry or by his surrender to a woman. Similarly, my survey of the various newspaper and magazine reviews of the film turned up few suggestions that Eastwood fell short of any male ideal.[3] I am convinced that the unambiguously masculine sounds of Hartman's voice were every bit as important to the film's reception as Eastwood's reputation as an exemplar of all things manly. The lack of charges in the popular press that Eastwood was emasculated in *Bridges* suggests that Hartman's voice did in fact work magic.

If the Marlon Brando of the 1940s and 1950s assimilated myths about the hypersexual *and* childish license of African American men in a way that radically updated the old minstrel stereotypes, Eastwood sought out the more romantic, more sensual aspects of African American masculinity that had more recently become part of white America's racial unconscious. Even if critics did not see Eastwood's surrender to a woman in *Bridges* as emasculating, at least since the early 1980s emasculation *has* been an important issue in the literature on Eastwood. More precisely, film scholars have observed how Eastwood's films both "arouse and contain" questions of gender, sexuality, race, and social class, often in ways that can be considered progressive when the films seem to invite different readings from different audiences.[4] Chris Holmlund, for example, has argued that *Tightrope* (1984) repeatedly exposes contradictions within received notions of masculinity and femininity (Holmlund, "Sexuality and Power"). Adam Knee sees the "feminization" of the Eastwood character as early as 1971 in *Play Misty for Me,* with Eastwood playing a radio disc jockey who reads poetry over the air (twenty-four years before he would again recite poetry in *Bridges*). And Robin Wood has written that, as a "buddy film," *Thunderbolt and Lightfoot* (1977) comes close to acknowledging the genre's inevitable homoeroticism, most specifically when the camera cuts to Eastwood preparing to fire a distinctly phallic cannon immediately after Jeff Bridges in drag bends over and lets his dress ride up to reveal a pair of thin bikini panties (Wood 233).

THE LAW OF THE FATHER

Eastwood's creation and maintenance of a powerful, if occasionally complex, masculine persona is best understood with the help of psychoanalytic theory. In an especially useful discussion, Frank Krutnik draws upon Freud's account of the male child's oedipal crises to explain conflicting attitudes about masculinity in the "tough" films of the 1940s. Freud's male child must renounce the mother and accept the authority of the father in order to escape the threat of castration and ultimately to achieve masculine autonomy. To maintain his autonomy the man must avoid a return to the body of the mother—or her surrogates—who hold out the promise of an oceanic feeling, a "desired image of plenitude" (Krutnik 107). For Freud, even "normal" heterosexual desire returns the man to his "infantile fixation on tender feelings for the mother" ("A Special Type" 11:168). These feelings, however, must always coexist with anxieties about castration as punishment for violating the father's law.

Krutnik singles out *The Maltese Falcon* (1941) as the purest representation of "redeemed" masculinity, especially at the climax when Sam (Humphrey Bogart) overcomes his desire for the murderous Brigid (Mary Astor) and hands her over to the agents of patriarchal law on the police force.

A more masochistic scenario was regularly acted out in many of the noir films of the mid- to late 1940s, when the ideals of traditional masculinity were widely questioned in postwar America. In films such as *Out of the Past* (1947) and *The Killers* (1946), soon-to-be macho icons Robert Mitchum and Burt Lancaster betray their father figures and submit to the will of phallic women. Although these films tend to be moral fables about what happens to men who swerve from the true path of masculinity, the films also address male anxieties about living up to impossible standards. For Krutnik, the films allow men to indulge in the satisfying if forbidden fantasy of submitting to a woman who is attractive and powerful and thus a substitute for the maternal body. American films such as *Bonnie and Clyde* (1967), *Body Heat* (1982), and *Basic Instinct* (1992) have continued to offer audiences the complex experience of identifying with men who break the law on multiple levels as they submit to powerful women.[5] At the same time, however, audiences have experienced a steady stream of films about strong heroes who refuse the infantilizing desire for female plenitude while they function as agents of patriarchal law. If a character such as James Bond acts on his desire for a woman, he does so without in any way relinquishing his autonomy or ceding control to the woman, who is almost always objectified to the extreme. And in spite of his sexual dalliances, Bond never betrays the patriarchs and the system they support. Much the same can be said for many films starring action heroes such as Sylvester Stallone, Arnold Schwarzenegger, Bruce Willis, Wesley Snipes, and Jean-Claude van Damme.

With a few notable exceptions, much the same can also be said for the films of Eastwood. If one of his characters becomes sexual, it is because a woman has offered herself and the Eastwood hero can remain in control. Very often an Eastwood character has left romance behind because of a dead but fondly remembered spouse. He has also played a series of characters who have simply been abandoned by their mates. *Tightrope* (1984) includes several reaction shots of the hero's ex-wife, who does little except glare at him. In *The Rookie* (1990), when Charlie Sheen asks the Eastwood character if his wife left him because she hated his passion for auto-racing, Eastwood replies, "No, she loved racing—she just hated me." And in *Bronco Billy* (1980), Eastwood plays a former shoe salesman who shot his wife after he found her sleeping with his best friend. Asked why he shot the wife and not her lover, Billy/Eastwood replies incredulously, "He was my best friend."

While it is true that Eastwood's character rides off with a female love object at the conclusion of *Bronco Billy, Pink Cadillac* (1989), and a few other films, his movies have never shown him in a comfortable, stable relationship with a woman. The single exception came late in Eastwood's career when he directed himself as a happily married engineer in *Space Cowboys* (2000). (But Barbara Babcock, who was cast as Eastwood's wife, was more than twice as old as the woman to whom the real life Eastwood was married at the time. In a way, the female love object in the even more recent *Blood Work* [2002] may be more appropriate; when the film was shot, Wanda De Jesus was probably in her mid-thirties, roughly the same age as Eastwood's own Latina wife.) The trope of placing the Eastwood character's romantic encounters in the past was already present in 1964 in *A Fistful of Dollars*. Eastwood and director Leone departed from their source, Kurosawa's *Yojimbo* (1961), by giving No Name a touch of vulnerability otherwise absent from the seemingly invulnerable protagonist: when a woman asks the gunman why he risked his life to reunite her with her hapless husband, he responds, "Because I knew someone like you once, and there was nobody there to help." (As a perspicacious participant in a seminar on the Western suggested, that woman might have been No Name's mother.) Like many American heroes in both literature and film, the Eastwood character seems to have overcome his oedipal crises and renounced the need for the oceanic feeling offered by union with a woman. In what is surely a consequence of this American myth, romantic relationships tend to resist representation and can only be *referred* to as part of an impossible past. Since this is usually the case in Eastwood's films, *The Bridges of Madison County* becomes all the more remarkable.

The change represented by *Bridges* may result in part from Eastwood's attempts to confront the realities of middle age. Holmlund has argued in "Aging Clint" (1996) that, although the turn-of-the-century Eastwood may simply be too old to continue playing Dirty Harry, his more recent roles do not signal resignation. Like Sean Connery in *The Rock* (1996), *Entrapment* (1999), and *The League of Extraordinary Gentlemen* (2003), the older Eastwood usually plays powerful characters with skills derived from experience, maturity, and painfully acquired wisdom. In *Absolute Power* (1997), Eastwood's master thief Luther Whitney is spry enough to outrun a group of much younger Secret Service agents, but he is even more skillful at outsmarting the president of the United States and his various operatives. In spite of the heart attack that has laid his character low in *Blood Work,* Eastwood has no problem leaping about in abandoned ships to catch the film's villain, nor does he falter when making love to Wanda De Jesus. In *The Bridges of Madison County,* Kincaid is a seasoned traveler who knows how to survive in Africa as well as in Middle America. The film suggests that this kind of knowledge, gained only after many years of experience, lies behind Kincaid's unique and powerful love for Francesca.

When this love is tested and Francesca emotionally accuses Robert of egotism and cowardice, she questions him about his "routine" with the women he romances in his travels. She soon learns, however, that she is not attacking a callow seducer or a passive misogynist. Instead of snarling and tightening his fist in the familiar Clint style, the mature and sensitive Kincaid turns away and sheds tears. In another stark contrast to the usual inarticulateness of his screen persona,[6] Eastwood then eloquently reassures Francesca: "If I have done anything to make you think that what we have between us is nothing new for me, that it's just some routine, then I do apologize." In this scene Eastwood's Kincaid succeeds, at least temporarily, in convincing Francesca that what they are doing is right. Later, however, as they sit at her dinner table for the last time, his words are impotent; he cannot prevent her from staying with her husband. As Francesca explains how she would destroy her husband if she deserted him, Kincaid offers faint assurances that her husband will recover: "People move on." Until his final assertion—"This kind of certainty comes but once in a lifetime"—Eastwood returns to his conventional reticence and frequently befuddled manner with women. Finally, looking old and helpless outside the general store after Francesca's husband has returned, Kincaid stares imploringly at Francesca in a driving rainstorm as the film invokes Ruskin's pathetic fallacy: the sky seeming to weep for him, Kincaid ultimately smiles wanly and slowly turns away. But as I will argue later, Kincaid's smile suggests that Eastwood has not been defeated. In fact, he has preserved his autonomy by moving away from an oedipal triangle.

ONE SINGS, THE OTHER DOESN'T

Before Eastwood gained control over his image by releasing all of his post-1969 films (with the single exception of *In the Line of Fire* [1993]) through his own Malpaso Productions, he was called upon at least once to veer dramatically from masculine autonomy. Playing the benign "Pardner" in *Paint Your Wagon*

Fig. 13. Clint Eastwood as the sexually benign "Pardner" in *Paint Your Wagon*
(1969, Paramount Pictures). Photofest Film Archive.

(1969), Eastwood willingly enters into a *ménage à trois* with Jean Seberg and Lee Marvin. Although he eventually wins complete possession of the Seberg character, he spends a good portion of the film submitting to her desire to live—and presumably have sex—with two husbands. *Paint Your Wagon* is also the first major film in which Eastwood sings. Whenever the film used to show up in the *New York Times*'s television listings, the title was followed by the comment, "Clint sings like a moose." This is an inaccurate characterization of Eastwood's vocal style. His tenor voice is scarcely operatic—in the sense of either Pavarotti or Orbison—but his singing does convey many of the same qualities that Eastwood projects as an actor, including his shyness and his discomfort with romantic expression. When he sings "I Talk to the Trees," his singing style conveys his guilelessness as well as his confusion (fig. 13).

In what may be his most important singing role, when he directed himself in *Honkytonk Man* (1982), Eastwood brings a degree of pathos and even lyricism to a vocal style that is entirely consistent with the role of a struggling alcoholic singer dying of tuberculosis. Unlike films such as *Every Which Way but Loose* and *Escape from Alcatraz* (1979) that fetishize Eastwood's nude or semi-nude body, *Honkytonk Man* almost always shows him fully clothed. Even his walk is hunched over and tentative. As in *Paint Your Wagon,* Eastwood's untrained singing voice expresses his character's suffering and romantic confusion. Earlier, in *The Beguiled* (1971), Eastwood sings behind the opening and closing credits, winsomely intoning an antiwar ballad. As the eponymous hero of *Bronco Billy,* he idly sings along with the voice of Merle Haggard on his car radio. His disembodied voice can also be heard over the opening credits of *Any Which Way You Can,* joining Ray Charles in a rendition of "Beers to You." The mise-en-scène of "Beers to You" is a barroom where men sing of the ephemeral nature of women as opposed to the reliability of male friendships and the taste of cool beer. This is also the only time that Eastwood strives to project a robustly male presence in his singing, and it may therefore be the least successful of his several vocal performances.

It is no longer a secret that masculinity is constantly being constructed and reconstructed in culture, within and across boundaries of race, class, ethnicity, and age, often in contradictory ways. Jonathan Goldberg, for example, points out that when Arnold Schwarzenegger writes about the pleasures of bodybuilding, celebrating the "pump" and its attendant sensation of continuous orgasms all over his body, "this sounds like female orgasms" (175). Not surprisingly, anomalies of masculinity can appear even in a figure like Eastwood, who has consistently succeeded in projecting "the masculine" over the course of several decades. The more threatening aspects of Eastwood's persona are usually subdued when he sings, but "Beers to You"—in which he seems to be trying to remasculinize his voice—exposes an important gap in a supposedly complete inventory of masculinity. As a singer, Eastwood is no Johnny Hartman.

Undoubtedly, Eastwood's vocal performance of "Beers to You" suffers at least in part because of its proximity to the legendary Ray Charles, surely the major influence on a raft of white singers, including Van Morrison, Bruce Springsteen, David Johansson, Billy Joel, Steve Tyrell, and many others who hear "the gravel of authenticity" in Charles's style.[7] In *Any Which Way You Can,* Ray Charles does not appear on camera and is never heard again after the opening moments of the film. Nevertheless, singing with Charles surely represented a profound wish fulfillment for Eastwood, who has been fascinated by black artists and jazz musicians at least since his childhood when his mother first played Fats Waller records for him (Giddins 41). He has told interviewers that he once worked as a jazz pianist, a role he briefly reprises in both *City Heat* (1984) and *In the Line of Fire.* In his debut as a director, Eastwood cast himself as a jazz disc jockey in *Play Misty for Me* and gratuitously included scenes from the Monterey Jazz Festival. He has employed black blues artists in *Honkytonk Man* and *Tightrope,* and the background score for *The Gauntlet* includes several solos by jazz musicians Jon Faddis and Art Pepper.

In this context, the use of Johnny Hartman's voice in *The Bridges of Madison County* may represent the culmination of Eastwood's fascination with blacks and their music as well as his borrowing of their cultural capital.[8] Previously, when acting alongside African Americans as Dirty Harry Callahan or some other tough cop, Eastwood has faced difficult choices about how to treat at least some blacks sympathetically without undermining his status as the guardian of the law-and-order values so dear to American conservatives with their profound suspicion of African Americans. Eastwood and his directors and screenwriters have developed imaginative solutions, such as the one identified by Dennis Bingham in *The Enforcer* (1976). When the head of a black nationalist group tells Harry that he is on the wrong side—"You go out there and put your ass on the line for a bunch of dudes who wouldn't even let you in the front door any more than they would me"—Callahan responds, "I'm not doin' it for them." "Who then?" "You wouldn't believe me if I told you." As Bingham points out, Eastwood is effectively telling the black man, "I'm doing it for you," without abandoning his tough, independent, suspicious stance (189).[9]

In *The Bridges of Madison County* these kinds of elaborate evasions are no longer necessary precisely because the body of the black man is not present, or because blacks are marginalized as an exotic Other during the scene when Kincaid and Francesca dance in an Iowa roadhouse with an otherwise exclusively black clientele. Regardless of whether or not audiences of *Bridges* are aware of Hartman's race, the gentle but unambiguous manliness of his voice seems to emanate from Robert Kincaid himself more than from a singer that few in the audience are likely to know. In *Bridges,* Eastwood has gone further than ever before in expropriating black masculinity and sexuality for one of his own characters.

Fig. 14. Jazz Singer Johnny Hartman, who invisibly transforms *The Bridges of Madison County.* Photo courtesy of Chuck Stewart.

Eastwood had used the disembodied voice of an African American singer at least once before. In *Play Misty for Me,* his first directorial effort, Eastwood and Donna Mills silently enjoy the pastoral countryside and then make love while Roberta Flack sings "The First Time I Ever Saw Your Face." But later in the film, when Eastwood's character wanders through the crowds at the Monterey Jazz Festival, his passion for jazz is more apparent. For *The Bridges of Madison County,* the choice of Johnny Hartman's voice was made well before filming began. According to Bruce Ricker, who served as the film's "music consultant," Eastwood decided to use Hartman's voice one afternoon in his car when the radio began playing selections from Hartman's 1980 LP *Once in Every Life.*[10] In an interview with Bob Blumenthal, Eastwood said that he had been a fan of Hartman ever since he first heard him at a club in the late 1940s (30). He also proclaimed his admiration for Hartman's extraordinary LP with John Coltrane, released on the Impulse! label in 1963. Although the Coltrane/Hartman collaboration would have been an appropriate choice for an action that takes place in 1965, Eastwood chose to make anachronistic use of music recorded in 1980.[11] He bought the rights to *Once in Every Life,* subsequently releasing two CDs on his own Malpaso label combining tracks from the Hartman LP with other soundtrack recordings from *Bridges.*[12]

In Eastwood's film the singing of Johnny Hartman seems exactly appropriate for a director/star hoping to capitalize on the singer's unproblematic masculinity. Nevertheless, Hartman's voice might not have seemed quite so natural if the film had been released several years earlier. Johnny Hartman

Fig. 15. Johnny Hartman at work. Photo courtesy of Chuck Stewart.

was never much of a success prior to his death in 1983, vacillating between the obscurity of jazz singing and the large no-man's-land inhabited by pop singers without a natural audience of youthful or nostalgic fans. Nor did it help that he was short and not especially attractive. In what may be his only appearance on national television, Hartman sang Rodgers and Hart's "It Never Entered My Mind" in an episode of the short-lived *Sammy Davis Junior Show* in 1966.[13] Dressed in a tuxedo, he carried himself very much in the pensive but casual style established by Nat King Cole, the last black entertainer before Davis to have his own network program. People who have listened to Hartman's records in recent years will probably find that the man in the video does not *look* like the man they seem to be hearing on the records. With an unflattering haircut and awkward gestures, Hartman possessed little charisma as a performer. The diminutive "Johnny" seems appropriate for the man in the video just as "Hart-man" seems right for the singer who injects so much feeling into romantic ballads such as "It Never Entered My Mind."

Today Hartman is substantially more popular then he ever was during his lifetime. According to discographer and producer Michael Cuscuna, Hartman's record with Coltrane has become, along with *Giant Steps* and *A Love Supreme,* one of the three best-selling albums of the saxophonist's music. In 1990 media commentator Daniel Okrent celebrated the Coltrane/Hartman LP in *Esquire* magazine as "The Greatest Record Ever Made" in spite of the fact that the record received little attention from critics when it was first released. We can assume that Hartman had a following both inside and outside the jazz world if only because he continued to make records and public appearances for several decades. He usually won sixth or seventh place among male vocalists when *Down Beat* magazine conducted its annual readers' polls in the 1960s, but he was mostly invisible in the magazine's more prestigious critics' polls (although *Down Beat*'s critics voted him the male vocalist most "deserving wider recognition" in 1965). Many jazz critics regarded Hartman as a mere crooner, or worse, a conventional lounge singer. Even Okrent says that Hartman sounded like "a Johnny Mathis for grownups" (46). Although the 1963 LP with Coltrane was not widely admired immediately after its initial release, reviewers in the jazz press regularly greeted subsequent Hartman records with laments about his inability to perform again at the same level he had once achieved.

Born in Chicago in 1923, Johnny Hartman made a handful of records under his own name shortly after he left the army in the late 1940s. He can also

be heard crooning awkwardly with Earl Hines in 1947 and with Dizzy Gillespie's big band in 1948 and 1949. According to an article in *Our World,* a magazine aimed at black Americans, a white booking agent told Hartman in the
1940s that he could not use him because "your voice is too classy for a Negro"
("Struggles" 20). Classy or not, the early Hartman was an insecure imitator of
Billy Eckstine. Especially on "You Go to My Head," recorded with Gillespie in
1949, Hartman sounds like many young singers still searching for a style they
can comfortably inhabit. When he climbs into the upper register, he seems un-
sure of his vibrato and intonation, perhaps trying to shade his timbre and pitch
but falling short of the easy mastery he would later exhibit.

Hartman came of age as a singer when he began making albums under his
own name for the Bethlehem label in 1955. With these recordings he perfected
the art of seeming "natural," performing like the Stanislavskian actor who
seems to "live" his role rather than interpret it. This aspect of Hartman's performance persona may have led Coltrane to take the unique step of recording
with the singer, insisting to producer Bob Thiele that Hartman would be the
best vocalist to complement his ballad style. Most critics and the record-buying
public now agree that Hartman did his best work with Coltrane and the
rhythm section of pianist McCoy Tyner, bassist Jimmy Garrison, and drummer
Elvin Jones. If nothing else, Hartman and the Coltrane quartet made it sound
easy as they recorded a definitive version of "Lush Life," the Billy Strayhorn ballad that poses nearly insuperable challenges to singers as well as to instrumentalists. Even Frank Sinatra was never able to make a satisfactory recording of
the tune (Friedwald 302), although Sinatraphiles would argue that he could
have nailed it if he had really wanted to. According to Strayhorn's biographer
David Hajdu, the Hartman/Coltrane "Lush Life" was Strayhorn's favorite
recording of his composition (Hajdu, Conversation with the author).

Nevertheless, Hartman seldom reached a large audience in the 1960s
and 1970s, undoubtedly two of the worst decades for jazz as a popular art. For
most record buyers during this period, Hartman would have been associated
with bland baritones like Perry Como, whom Hartman has specifically mentioned as an influence (Wilson 36). Nat King Cole, Billy Eckstine, and Frank
Sinatra had all established popularity with large audiences in the 1940s when
the younger Hartman was just emerging. The rage for Swing Era vocalists was
already beginning to play itself out and suffer eclipse behind rock 'n' roll
when Hartman was making his first LPs in the mid-1950s. Jazz critics, mean-

while, were more likely to canonize "hipper" stylists, such as Eddie Jefferson, Mose Allison, or Jon Hendricks, who brought irony or vocal calisthenics to their performances, or gutsier singers, such as Ray Charles, Joe Williams, and Jimmy Rushing, who were more profoundly based in the blues. In 1981 Hartman's *Once in Every Life* was nominated for a Grammy, but the award went to an LP by a more mercurial singer, Al Jarreau.

But Hartman persevered, staying with a style that was romantic and sensual without the menace one hears in the contemporary recordings of Billy Eckstine or the ambiguous sexuality in the records of Johnny Mathis. Even Sinatra, who has sung with a "tear" in his voice as often as he has with a macho swagger, presents a thoroughly problematic male sexuality when compared with Hartman.[14] As a female colleague who recently discovered Hartman's records has told me, "Listening to his voice is like being held by two strong arms." But Hartman did not always project precisely this persona. On a 1966 recording of "Girl Talk," he begins with a spoken introduction before singing Bobby Troupe's lyrics to Neal Hefti's tune. Adopting a jokey, lounge singer's delivery inconsistent with his singing style, Hartman says, "A kiss doesn't mean a thing unless it comes from that special girl. That particular girl. But one thing all girls have in common is that they're all pretty long-winded. Have you ever tried to phone your wife and give her a message—a very important message—and the phone stays busy for hours and hours? And man, don't let it be a long distance call or you'll really blow your top. I know you guys wonder, just what could they be talkin' about that long?"[15] Although the women's movement in America was still in its embryonic stages when Hartman recorded this patter in 1966, not all female listeners may have found Hartman's casual misogyny amusing.

But many women have fallen in love with the Coltrane/Hartman album, recorded even earlier. On the one hand, as a kind of art music, the Coltrane/Hartman album could not have included the narration and direct appeals to audiences associated with less ambitious or more working-class entertainments. On the other hand, when placed in less austere surroundings, Hartman was capable of a practice with which "pure" jazz artists are seldom associated.

As I have argued elsewhere, the claim of jazz to art status has always been subject to the whims of critics, journalists, disc jockeys, audiences, and performers at different moments in the music's history (Gabbard, *Jammin'* 101–137). To be sure, Hartman's thoughtful but unpretentious vocal style has benefited greatly from the recent classicization of jazz that began in the 1980s. Repertory orchestras in Washington and New York—including the Jazz at Lincoln Center Orchestra, for which Wynton Marsalis is artistic director and Albert Murray and Stanley Crouch are his advisors—have both confirmed and promoted the perception that jazz is a legitimate peer of ballet, the opera, the symphony, and the more familiar industries of American high culture. (In 1998, the late, lamented Carnegie Hall Jazz Band, a New York repertory jazz orchestra every bit as worthy as the Lincoln Center band, scheduled an entire evening devoted to the music for Clint Eastwood's films.) Americans have definitely developed a much greater tolerance for jazz, especially the smoother styles of the music that listeners once avoided as scrupulously as they did the more avant-garde or challenging jazz genres.[16] Since Coltrane was regarded as virtually a religious figure by his fans but as a purveyor of cacophony by noninitiates, the Coltrane/Hartman album was not a natural purchase for listeners with little interest in jazz. As jazz began to acquire a new cachet in the 1980s, however, the album became the ideal point of entry into jazz and, in particular, into the music of the profoundly canonical Coltrane, who was at his most restrained and accessible with Hartman. Just as Hartman's "pure" jazz recordings have acquired aesthetic gravity for many audiences, the singer's attempts at reaching a popular audience in performances such as the 1966 "Girl Talk" are likely to strike many in these same audiences as something of an embarrassment. The superb 1980 recordings that so impressed Eastwood and that grace the soundtrack of *The Bridges of Madison County* belong more with Hartman's "pure" jazz recordings. The presence of revered jazz artists such as Billy Taylor and Frank Wess on the 1980 album help place it well inside the domain of jazz art.

BRIDGING THE RACIAL GAP

Regardless of where Johnny Hartman stands in old or new jazz canons, his voice on *The Bridges of Madison County* soundtrack endows Clint Eastwood's actions with real masculine authority at the same time that it heightens the film's romanticism. Hartman's voice is first heard in *Bridges* when Robert Kincaid and Francesca Johnson are chatting innocently at her kitchen table. At the moment when Kincaid initiates more personal conversation by mentioning "his dreams," the radio in the kitchen begins to play Hartman's recording of the slow ballad "Easy Living." Thanks in part to Hartman, a man talking about his inner life—his *feelings*—does not sound emasculated. Just minutes after Hartman's voice first plays on the soundtrack, Francesca takes the crucial step of inviting Robert to dinner. Several musical numbers are heard on radios and on the background soundtrack during the next stages in the romance plot: when Francesca looks out her window and sees Robert washing up in the backyard, a love theme composed by Eastwood and Lennie Niehaus is played by an unaccompanied string section; back in the kitchen a few moments later, Dinah Washington's "I'll Close My Eyes" emanates from the radio; and while Robert reduces Francesca to helpless laughter with his story of the female gorilla, the music is "Poinciana" by the Ahmad Jamal Trio.

When Hartman sings again, the plot has reached the climactic moment on their second evening together when the freshly bathed Francesca walks into the kitchen in the dress she had bought that afternoon, clearly with the expectation of a tryst with Robert. Hartman begins to sing the connoisseur's ballad by Howard Dietz and Arthur Schwartz, "I See Your Face Before Me," at the precise moment that Robert sees her.[v] This is the music to which they will dance and then kiss for the first time. An advertisement for *The Bridges of Madison County*'s soundtrack album that appeared in a June 1995 issue of *The Nation* includes a characterization of the song and its effect:

> *Tell everyone you bought it because of its selection of classic*
> *1964 [sic] gems from the likes of Dinah Washington, Johnny Hartman,*
> *Irene Kral with the Junior Mance Trio, and Barbara Lewis.*
>
> *Play it during your next chess tournament or secret meeting to overthrow*
> *the government and delight your guests with your knowledge that*
> *Clint Eastwood (a true music connoisseur) hand-picked each selection and*
> *even wrote the instrumental (with Lennie Niehaus).*
>
> *We won't tell anyone that you actually listen to it to re-live that scene in*
> *the kitchen where they dance and the whole world changes.*
>
> *Promise.*
>
> (*The Bridges of Madison County* soundtrack CD advertisement)

As the ad suggests, *The Bridges of Madison County* is at its most intensely romantic when Hartman's performance of "I See Your Face Before Me" resonates through the theater. And as the ad implies, however ironically, Hartman's music can do what neither images nor words can do—make us feel what the characters are feeling and somehow connect these feelings to our own experiences. To a large extent all film music functions in this way, but something about that voice must have convinced the advertising executives at Warner Bros. that Hartman's recordings are uniquely capable of achieving this goal, even for the highly suspicious leftists and intellectuals who read *The Nation*.

At another emotional peak in the film, the couple dances among the black patrons at the roadhouse while Hartman sings still another slow love song, "For All We Know." This recording continues as the film cuts to the couple making love back at the farmhouse and then as the narrative flashes forward to the present, where Francesca's daughter is being transformed by reading the account of the affair in her recently deceased mother's diary.[18] Finally, Hartman sings Hal David and Archie Jordan's "It Was Almost Like a Song" at another emotional climax when the lovers eat their final meal together and Robert ineffectually tries to convince Francesca to leave with him. This is also the moment when Kincaid seems to paraphrase the first words of the song, "Once in every life . . . ," when he speaks the line, "This kind of certainty comes but once in a lifetime."[19]

In a trenchant review of *The Bridges of Madison County*, Armond White has raised the issue of the white reception of black music that is crucial to Hollywood and especially to Eastwood's career (White 23). White is highly critical of the film, comparing it unfavorably to the 1948 British melodrama *Brief Encounter*, another story about a woman who reluctantly decides to send away her lover and return to her husband. Whereas the earlier film engaged in an "artfully subtle critique of bourgeois restraint," White charges *Bridges* with squeezing pathos out of the film's validation of conventional marriage and concern with what the neighbors might think. White also suggests that Eastwood and the makers of *Bridges* have condescended to black music by recruiting Hartman and other black artists to dignify a banal story at the same time that *Bridges* and most of Eastwood's films make no attempt to focus on "Black emotional experience" (23).

While I agree with White's assertion that Eastwood has consistently ignored the inner lives of black people, most especially in *Bird*, I must point out that virtually no other element of dominant American culture regularly redresses this omission. I must also resist White's argument that Hartman, Dinah Washington, Ahmad Jamal, and the others on the soundtrack are pulled out of a purely black cultural context. One of the more sensual voices on the soundtrack belongs to the white singer Irene Kral, whose 1963 recording of "This Is Always" can be heard during the erotic moment when Robert and Francesca lie in the bathtub drinking brandy. Eastwood has also placed Kral's version of "It's a Wonderful World" on the radio as an ironic comment on Francesca's pain when she is reunited with her family after Robert's departure. Furthermore, it is not entirely fair to associate the singing of Johnny Hartman, who admitted a debt to Perry Como, exclusively with black culture. After all, white songwriters are responsible for all four of the songs he sings on the soundtrack. In another fortuitous instance of interracial collaboration, Junior Mance, Bob Cranshaw, and Mickey Roker, all of them black, accompany Irene Kral on "This Is Always" and "It's a Wonderful World." Although there is no question that blacks have suffered from the crushing asymmetries of power that have always characterized the meeting of white and black musical traditions, it is also true that the singing style of Johnny Hartman—and for that matter jazz in general—has flourished at precisely these intersections. Since jazz has almost from the beginning relied upon mechanical reproduction for its reception, there have always been patterns of mutual influences among blacks and whites even when they have not played together in the same rooms. As Amiri Baraka has argued, the beginnings of white fascination with jazz marked the crucial moment when an aspect of black culture became an essential part of American culture, when it was "available intellectually, when it could be learned" (Baraka, *Blues People* 155). And of course, black musicians have learned a great deal from white artists, whether it is Louis Armstrong listening to arias from European operas (Berrett), Lester Young listening to Frankie Trumbauer (Porter 33–35), or Johnny Hartman listening to Perry Como.

There are also serendipitous aspects to Eastwood's appropriation of Hartman and other artists. Throughout his career Eastwood has been careful to emphasize interactions among the races as he pays tribute to jazz and American vernacular music. He brought together black blues singers and white country artists in *Honkytonk Man* just as he centered the relationship between Charlie Parker and the Jewish trumpeter Red Rodney in *Bird*. Eastwood told Bob Blumenthal that he shot "virtually the entire festival" at Monterey when he was directing *Play Misty for Me* (Blumenthal 197). That only Cannonball Adderley and Johnny Otis appear in the final film reveals much about Eastwood's understanding of jazz and "black" music. The African American saxophonist Julian "Cannonball" Adderley was leading an integrated group at this

Fig. 16. The incipient love affair in *The Bridges of Madison County* (1995, Malpaso Productions/Amblin Entertainment/Warner Bros.) is temporarily interrupted. Jerry Ohlinger's Movie Material Store, Inc.

time, with the Austrian pianist Joe Zawinul composing and arranging much of the band's music. Johnny Otis, seldom regarded as a jazz artist, is nevertheless one of the most intriguing figures in the history of racial crossover. Although he was born John Veliotes in 1921 to a family of Greek immigrants, Otis regularly refers to himself in his autobiographical writings as black and characterizes African Americans as "my people." In *Play Misty for Me,* Otis is the only white face on stage as his band plays one of its biggest hits, "Willie and the Hand Jive." Like the young Eastwood, Otis felt real affinity for blacks and their music as a young man growing up in California. But Otis did not simply dabble in black culture. Married to the same African American woman for over fifty years, Otis has worked in black Los Angeles not only as a disc jockey, record producer, and performer but also as a politician, community activist, and minister. Otis could reinvent himself at any moment and reassume a "white" identity, but he has never made this choice. Surely these aspects of Otis's life were important to Eastwood when he was deciding which acts to include in *Play Misty for Me.*

As Frank Dobson has pointed out, Eastwood often plays characters who treat their fascination with black culture like a coat that can be taken on and off at whim. Dobson concentrates most closely on *White Hunter, Black Heart* (1990), but he also makes an important observation about an early scene in *In the Line of Fire* (1993). Coming home after a day as a Secret Service agent, Eastwood sheds his professional gear after he picks up a bottle of bourbon and turns on Miles Davis's classic album *Kind of Blue*. Recorded in 1959, *Kind of Blue* featured trumpeter Davis with Bill Evans, one of the few white musicians with whom Davis regularly worked in a small group context. (The group also included John Coltrane as well as Eastwood's old favorite, Cannonball Adderley.) The film portrays Eastwood's transformation from Secret Service agent to jazz enthusiast synecdochically: the camera holds a shot of a table on which Eastwood places a magazine full of bullets and a pair of handcuffs alongside the "jewel box" for the compact disc of the Miles Davis album. When the telephone rings, giving Eastwood his first contact with the film's villain, Eastwood turns off the music and returns to his principal identity as the protector of American presidents. As Dobson points out, Eastwood's jazz-loving character—surely inspired by Eastwood himself—quickly snaps out of his romance with black culture when duty calls.

Wolfgang Petersen, not Eastwood, directed *In the Line of Fire*. Nevertheless, the scene identified by Dobson is emblematic of Eastwood's practice of entering the domain of black Americans only when it suits him. Eastwood may identify with a figure such as Johnny Otis, but he does not seem to understand the patronizing, even colonialist nature of many "hip" appropriations of black culture by affluent whites.[20] Nevertheless, there is no denying the sincerity with which Eastwood has regularly made jazz and black music a crucial part of his projects, bringing music to mainstream audiences that they might not otherwise hear. He must also be given credit for producing (and bankrolling) Charlotte Zwerin's ambitious documentary *Thelonious Monk: Straight No Chaser* (1988) (see chapter six). By the same token, the odd moment in *Bridges* when Francesca and Robert find a black blues club in the middle of the Iowa cornfields can be read less suspiciously as another of Eastwood's attempts to promote interracial cooperation through music. Although the white couple seems to have stepped into an all-black universe, the group on the bandstand is integrated. Led by the black blues saxophonist James Rivers, who also performed over the opening and closing credits of

Tightrope, the band features African American musicians Mark Brooks on bass, Eddie Dejean Sr., on drums, and James Brewer on guitar, as well as the Asian American pianist Peter Cho and Eastwood's son, Kyle, on bass.

I disagree with Armond White's suggestion that the music in *Bridges* has been unceremoniously yanked out of its original context, but he is certainly correct in suggesting that Eastwood has made a film that is in some ways "a yearning dramatization of white incompleteness" (White 23). Like the vast majority of white men growing up in America, Clint Eastwood undoubtedly found some part of his identity in the conduct of African American men. A large portion of that identity was surely related to their displays of masculinity through music, along with sports the most important arena in which whites have partaken of a black male mystique. Throughout his career, Eastwood has carefully maintained the image of an impenetrable, autonomous male at the same time that he has cultivated a passion for jazz and black music. For Eastwood, the two are surely related, as they have been for the last two centuries in the white American imaginary. We can celebrate Eastwood for expanding public awareness of black artists such as Charlie Parker, Thelonious Monk, and Johnny Hartman, but we can only speculate on the extent to which his understandings and misunderstandings of black masculinity are responsible for his cinematic image.

RECLAIMING THE PHALLUS

Even when he reaches out for the masculine authority as well as for the romance in Johnny Hartman's voice, Eastwood may not have drastically departed from his familiar personae by performing as Robert Kincaid in *Bridges*. Like No Name in the Leone films as well as in Eastwood's own imitations of Leone's work, Kincaid rides into town alone, bearing few similarities to and little sympathy for the townsfolk. We might even compare Eastwood's Kincaid with the intruder/redeemer in *Pale Rider* (1985), an inflated remake of *Shane* in which another lone, unnamed cowboy played by Eastwood eventually makes love to a mature woman played by Carrie Snodgress. (Snodgress was thirty-nine when the film was released, roughly the same age as the Francesca Johnson of *Bridges.*) And like all the skillful gunmen that Eastwood has played in his many Westerns and policiers, Kincaid has solid professional competence with his phallic cameras. In one of the more unusual marketing initiatives associated with the film, Warner Books collected the actual photographs that Eastwood took while performing as Robert Kincaid and released them in a book consisting primarily of blank pages that could serve as a diary. For a price of $11.95, fans of the film could assure themselves that Eastwood was not shooting blanks when he aimed his cameras at the bridges of Madison County.

What most separates *Bridges* from the conventional Eastwood film, however, is its emphatic shift away from the masculine quest of the hero and toward the pathos of the heroine. The nonthreatening masculinity of Johnny Hartman's singing may be more consistent with female fantasies than with those of the male. Furthermore, Eastwood exits well before the end of *Bridges* and generously hands over the rest of the film to Meryl Streep, ultimately making a film very much like the classic woman's picture. Like many films in the genre, *Bridges* begins by closely observing the mundane details of the heroine's life and then foregrounds the fetishized souvenirs of her four days with her lover. And like many heroines of women's films from the 1940s, Francesca is not allowed to have it all. The film follows the basic patterns of the "sacrifice" subgenre of the woman's film by asking Francesca to give up her lover for her husband (Haskell 163). But like Jim Mullen, the wag at *Entertainment Weekly* who summed up *The Bridges of Madison County* with the one-liner, "Most men went to this movie only because they thought Clint Eastwood was going to blow up the bridges," I cannot help associating Robert Kincaid with more familiar Eastwood heroes. Kincaid does, after all, regain his masculine independence after he has moved beyond tears and violations of patriarchal law. This would explain the striking lack of conviction with which Kincaid suggests that Francesca leave her husband even while Hartman's records play softly in the background. Thus, when Francesca is reunited with her husband at the conclusion, Eastwood is once again the autonomous male who will not take mother away from father. At one moment in *The Bridges of Madison County,* that father, Francesca's husband, Richard (Jim Haynie), watches *F Troop* on television. In the mid-1960s, with *Rawhide* on television and Leone's spaghetti westerns soon to be playing in theaters everywhere, Richard may have been an Eastwood fan as well.

CHAPTER THREE

Passing Tones

The Talented Mr. Ripley *and* Pleasantville

Both *The Talented Mr. Ripley* (1999) and *Pleasantville* (1998) import significant elements of African American culture into stories about white people
while banishing black bodies almost completely from the screen. They reveal
the extent to which American culture is dependent on the art and history of
African Americans, no matter how indifferent white Americans may seem. In
The Talented Mr. Ripley, Tom Ripley (Matt Damon) is the subject of a "passing"
narrative that recalls novels such as James Weldon Johnson's *Autobiography of
an Ex-Colored Man*, Jessie Fauset's *Plum Bun*, and Nella Larsen's *Passing*, as well
as films such as *Pinky* (1949), *Show Boat* (1936 and 1951), *Imitation of Life* (1934
and 1959), and the novels on which they were based. Also in *The Talented Mr.
Ripley*, Dickie Greenleaf (Jude Law) expresses himself musically on the saxophone by playing "You Don't Know What Love Is," a song historically associated primarily with African American artists.[1] Although the emotional lives of
the film's characters are entirely built around white people, and although *The
Talented Mr. Ripley* was made by white British filmmakers, the cultural dynamics of the film are unthinkable without African American culture.

    Pleasantville goes even further to stage black narratives in whiteface,
completely excluding African Americans from its cast while presenting a
group of white people as the victims of discrimination based on color. Two
teenagers from the 1990s are magically transported into *Pleasantville*, a tele-

vision situation comedy from the 1950s, and gradually bring color to the fictional town's citizens, who are at first shown in the black-and-white tones of
old television programs. The young and adventuresome citizens of Pleasantville change color more quickly than do the more staid members of the
community, who strenuously resist the changes, even placing "No Colored"
signs in shop windows. Later, in a courtroom scene that powerfully recalls *To
Kill a Mockingbird,* a cautiously liberal film from 1962, the townspeople are
strictly segregated, with "colored" people sitting in the courthouse balcony.
In *Pleasantville,* however, to be colored means to be a white person seen in
Technicolor rather than in black and white. The transformative struggles
take place entirely in the realm of empowered and empowering whites. And
in both *Pleasantville* and *The Talented Mr. Ripley,* the music of the great
African American jazz trumpeter Miles Davis invisibly deepens the romance
and sense of wonder in the story.

Innocent explanations of racial appropriation and exclusion in these
late twentieth-century films might reference the free circulation of images
typical of the postmodern moment. With master narratives no longer con-
gealing as they once did, bits and pieces from one story can be moved to another with infinite possibilities for recombination, hybridization, inflation,
and revision.[2] But when patterns begin to emerge in how the elements in a
familiar genre—such as Hollywood's fish-out-of-water stories—are moved
about, ideological projects are quickly laid bare. *The Talented Mr. Ripley* and
Pleasantville reveal the extent to which African Americans both won and lost
the struggles of the 1950s and 1960s. On the one hand, the art of black Americans, especially jazz, has become an official part of American culture; the
civil rights struggles of the 1950s and 1960s are now seen as valid and necessary; and most white Americans are likely to admit that blacks have won the
right to participate fully in American life. On the other hand, these success
stories allow cultural conservatives to claim that wholesale parity now exists
among white and black Americans. Thus, white students can claim to be victims of "racial discrimination" when affirmative action guidelines allow minority students to take a few places in a prestigious university that might
have gone to whites.

As films such as *Pleasantville* make clear, white Americans can even
claim for themselves much of what has been achieved by blacks, even those
achievements for which African Americans have given their lives. In the cin-

ema, the most egregious example of whites taking credit for civil rights victories is Alan Parker's *Mississippi Burning* (1988), which shows white FBI agents fighting for justice after three civil rights workers disappeared in 1964. In fact, J. Edgar Hoover's FBI regarded civil rights workers as communist sympathizers and played virtually no role in apprehending the white racists who were eventually convicted of the murders depicted in *Mississippi Burning*.[3]

RIPLEY UNDER WHITENESS

The Talented Mr. Ripley does not completely expel people of African descent from its mise-en-scène. A scene at an Italian jazz club briefly shows a black woman near the piano, smoking a cigarette and wearing a large flower in her hair à la Billie Holiday, perhaps to add authenticity to a representation of jazz in the 1950s. Later in the film, the camera dwells briefly on a black trumpeter at another Italian jazz venue. But in 1950s New York, where the film's earliest scenes take place, even the help is white, including Tom Ripley. We see Tom as an attendant in a men's room and then as a classical pianist playing alone on the stage of a darkened Carnegie Hall. Although we hear Tom's voice-over narration for only the first minutes of the film, it invites the audience to bond quickly with the character played by the engaging young star, Matt Damon.

By the end, however, we learn that the early voice-over narration immediately follows the events at the film's conclusion, thus turning almost all of *The Talented Mr. Ripley* into one long flashback. Long before we know the murderous path that has brought him to this realization, Tom opens the film by saying how much he wishes he could "rub everything out," starting with his decision to borrow a blazer with a Princeton University crest. His original intention was to look the part as he accompanied a singer before an audience of Manhattan socialites on a terrace overlooking Central Park. Full of class aspiration and seizing an opportunity to pose as an aristocrat, Tom does not disabuse the wealthy Mr. and Mrs. Greenleaf when the jacket leads them to believe that he was once a Princeton classmate of their son, Dickie. Tom soon accepts a thousand dollars from Herbert Greenleaf (James Rebhorn) to bring his son back from Italy, where Dickie lives in the (fictional) seaside village Mongibello. Instead of participating in his father's shipping business, Dickie lives with the aspiring American novelist Marge (Gwyneth Paltrow) while enjoying sailing, swimming, and at least one of the attractive local women.

In order to enter Dickie's affluent world, Tom must, paradoxically, put aside his passion for upscale classical music and learn jazz, the music that Dickie loves but that the elder Greenleaf characterizes as "insolent noise." In early scenes Tom clings to conventional 1950s hierarchies of taste, practically holding his nose as he learns to recognize the playing styles of Charlie Parker, Dizzy Gillespie, Chet Baker, et al. In a comment that resonates with the homoerotic role that Baker's music plays later in the film, Tom says, "I can't tell if it's a man or a woman," as he listens to Baker singing "My Funny Valentine" (Miklitsch 20). When he leaves his apartment for his Atlantic voyage to find Dickie, the soundtrack flatters his aesthetic with an excerpt from J. S. Bach's *Passion According to St. Matthew*. In what is surely an ironic comment on Tom's initial aspirations alongside the murders he eventually commits, Dietrich Fischer-Dieskau sings Bach's text: "Mache dich, mein Herze, rein / Ich will Jesum selbst begraben" (Make thyself pure, my heart, / I will myself entomb Jesus).

Patricia Highsmith introduced Tom Ripley in her 1955 novel, *The Talented Mr. Ripley*. She would bring him back as a protagonist four more times, in *Ripley under Ground* (1970), *Ripley's Game* (1974), *The Boy Who Followed Ripley* (1980), and *Ripley under Water* (1991). At the beginning of Highsmith's first Ripley novel, Tom is a small-time hustler with no interest in classical music and no talent as a pianist. The Dickie of the novel is not a jazz lover and aspiring saxophonist but a painter. Although Dickie's father hires Tom to bring home his son, the Tom of the novel makes no real attempt to educate himself about art. Nor does he bother to comment when he actually sees Dickie's paintings. There is no jazz in the novel or anything that would make Dickie as dramatic as does his passion for jazz in the film. By adding Dickie's love of jazz, screenwriter/director Anthony Minghella was probably attempting to capitalize on the sounds and images that go with the music and lend themselves so thoroughly to cinematic representation. If nothing else, Minghella's revisions of Highsmith's novel gave him the opportunity to create two richly atmospheric moments in a smoky jazz club, both of which became music videos. In one, Americans and Italians create a joyous rendition of "Americano," a song about the European adulation of American culture. In the other, Tom gladly puts aside his aesthetic prejudices and plays the piano while singing "My Funny Valentine" in an excellent imitation of Chet Baker's voice.

By adding the racial politics inescapably associated with jazz and its appropriation by whites, Minghella and his collaborators have complicated much of what is relatively straightforward in the novel. While the novel does include—at least on a subtle, subtextual level—some of the homoeroticism that is central to the film, the jazz elements mark the Tom and Dickie of the film almost as strongly in terms of race as in terms of sexuality. This uniquely cinematic (and uniquely late twentieth-century) play with race and sexuality is immediately apparent when Tom first encounters Dickie on the beach at Mongibello. Looking through his binoculars, the nerdish Tom/Damon sees the golden bodies of Dickie/Law and Marge/Paltrow frolicking gracefully in the Mediterranean. When he approaches them in his bathing suit as they lounge in their beach chairs, the contrast between the perfectly tanned flesh of Dickie and the pale skin of Tom is so obvious that Dickie says, "You're so white!" Then to Marge, "Did you ever see a guy so white?" Tom makes the most of the situation, smilingly insisting that his color is just "primer" and an "undercoat," as if his whiteness were only temporary. The terms also suggest that Tom's pure white color is covering over something else, as is always the case in more conventional passing narratives.

And as in conventional passing narratives, Tom does not change color so easily. Later, he is suspected of being an imposter by Freddie Miles (Philip Seymour Hoffman), who senses immediately that Tom is not a member of the moneyed classes and certainly not someone with the contempt for upper-class decorum that Dickie exhibits in his bohemian passion for jazz. When Tom masquerades as Dickie in an elegant Roman apartment full of the markers of middle-class pretension, he is playing Bach's "Italian Concerto" on his new grand piano when Freddie suddenly arrives at his door. Freddie looks around and remarks, "It doesn't look like Dickie. It's horrible, isn't it? It's so, uh, bourgeois." In most novels and films about passing, the characters who wish to participate in white culture by concealing their African American origins suffer immense anxiety and ultimately regret their renunciation of the people and traditions with which they grew up. James Weldon Johnson's *The Autobiography of an Ex-Colored Man,* for example, ends with the protagonist's confession: "I cannot repress the thought that, after all, I have chosen the lesser part, that I have sold my birthright for a mess of pottage" (154). The 1959 version of *Imitation of Life* ends with the "tragic mulatto" Sarah Jane (Susan Kohner) weeping histrionically over the coffin of the dark-skinned mother she had rejected. Perhaps Tom's regret at abandoning the conventional art music of the aspiring white bourgeois for the more marginal art embraced by

Fig. 17. The young woman who wants to be white (Susan Kohner) with her mother (Juanita Moore) in *Imitation of Life* (1959, Universal International). Photofest Film Archive.

Dickie accounts for his emotional reaction to the high-culture production of Tchaikovsky's *Eugene Onegin* that he watches late in the film.

Dickie is probably a more unpleasant character in the film than in the novel. In fact, the film never really explains Marge's enduring passion for him. Fully aware of his indiscretions and his narcissism, Marge carries a torch for Dickie long after he has been killed by Tom. While everyone else succumbs to Tom's scheme of casting Dickie as a suicide, Marge's inextinguishable love for Dickie seems to give her the unique ability to see Tom as Dickie's murderer. In the novel, by contrast, Dickie never does anything so morally repugnant as carry on with the local woman Silvana (Stefania Rocca) behind Marge's back. In the film, after Silvana becomes pregnant by Dickie and subsequently kills herself, Dickie feels as much self-pity as personal guilt. Playing "You Don't Know What Love Is" on his saxophone is, at best, a stylized means of dealing with a suicide for which he is partially responsible.

But as a work of cinematic art, the film endows Dickie with natural grace and a talent for expressing himself with music, qualities that many Americans associate with black people. Reclining on the beach, coolly greeting Tom, and remarking on his whiteness, Dickie brings to the fore a racial connection that was implicit even before he spoke of Tom's color. As a fancier of European classical music and an awkward presence among people who inhabit their bodies more comfortably, Tom is indeed the whitest person on the beach. Dickie, by contrast, is the hip American whose passion for jazz is consistent with the cool, nonchalant comportment borrowed from African Americans.

"CAN I GET IN?"

As the film progresses, it becomes clear that Tom is not just an aspiring aristocrat posing as a white Negro; he is also a gay man passing as a heterosexual. Unlike jazz, homosexuality *is* addressed in Highsmith's novel. Highsmith herself was a lesbian who lived with several women prior to her death in 1995. Her novel *The Price of Salt,* published in 1952 under a pseudonym and not reissued under Highsmith's name until 1984, may be one of the first lesbian novels in which the main character neither dies nor renounces her homosexuality. Highsmith's final novel, *Small g: A Summer Idyll,* dealt explicitly with gay characters. But even in her earliest work, gay themes and subtexts abound. *The Talented Mr. Ripley* comes much closer to acknowledging the possibility of same-sex love than do any of her four subsequent Ripley novels. At one point in the original novel, Tom overhears Marge speculating to Dickie that Tom might be gay, and Tom kills Dickie at least in part because Dickie has rebuffed him for getting too close.

In the four additional Ripley novels that Highsmith wrote between 1970 and 1991, Tom is decidedly amoral, but he is also a dutiful if not terribly passionate husband to his French wife. Unlike the film, in which Ripley's final murder will likely lead to his capture and imprisonment, in Highsmith's novel Tom kills Dickie and Freddie and then successfully escapes with Dickie's money into the life he had always coveted. In the subsequent novels, he lives a double life as a respectable resident of a small town near Paris as well as a figure with underworld connections possessing few scruples about committing the occasional murder. In its ending, Minghella's film is similar to an earlier film based on *The Talented Mr. Ripley,* René Clement's *Plein soleil* (1960), released in the United States as *Purple Noon.* As Ripley, Alain Delon murders the Dickie Greenleaf character and appears to have successfully evaded arrest until Dickie's body dramatically turns up as irrefutable evidence of Ripley's crime. While *Purple Noon* ended with the crime-doesn't-pay message that French films were required to carry in 1960, Minghella's film departs radically from the novel's conclusion when Tom recklessly kills his new gay lover on a cruise ship and faces certain capture when the boat lands. This ending is vaguely moralistic and consistent with a large body of stories in which gay characters eventually betray their self-loathing, usually with disastrous results.[4]

Minghella has enlarged the novel's gay subtext in subtle as well as obvious ways. Among the less overt references to gayness is the film's fascination with Chet Baker and the Richard Rodgers/Lorenz Hart song "My Funny Valentine," which Baker recorded and performed throughout his career. In the 1950s Baker won the hearts and minds of an audience that was large even by non-jazz standards (fig. 18). Some responded to his youthful beauty (he was regularly compared to James Dean); some heard depths of emotion and sensitivity in his understated singing and playing (his music epitomized the West Coast or *cool* school of postwar jazz); and sadly, some cast him as jazz's Great White Hope, the anointed heir of Bix Beiderbecke and a paragon of the more sedate, less threatening strains of jazz that have always coexisted alongside the more intense music associated with African Americans. Given the elaborately conflicted attitudes toward blacks in the conscious and uncon-

Fig. 18. Jazz trumpeter/vocalist Chet Baker in the full flower of his youthful beauty. Photofest Film Archive.

scious minds of most white Americans, it is not surprising that Baker's image struck a chord with many whites who loved black music more than they loved black people. Baker became a "transitional figure," not unlike the white impersonators of Elvis Presley identified by Eric Lott who channel their fascination with black music through a white artist (see chapter one).

Baker's story is especially intriguing because he often seemed to value his music less than the massive doses of illegal drugs he ingested almost continually from his early twenties until he died at the age of fifty-nine in 1988. Pursued by a long line of beautiful women as well as a group of hopelessly devoted male admirers, Baker was pathologically incapable of sustaining a relationship with any of them. He paid attention to people only when they could competently assist him in obtaining controlled substances. Diane Vavra, the most loyal of his female lovers, who stayed with him almost until the end, ruefully remarked that the key to maintaining a relationship with the trumpeter was knowing that "You really can't rely on Chet" (Gavin 339). One of those charming sociopaths who are accustomed to having everything their way, Baker could affectlessly narrate stories full of self-aggrandizing details that often turned out to be fabrications. Most famously, Baker regularly told interviewers an elaborate story about his first meeting with Charlie Parker in the late 1940s. At the conclusion of his tale, Baker has Parker calling up Miles Davis, Dizzy Gillespie, and Lee Morgan—the premier jazz trumpeters of the day—and warning them that "there's a little white cat on the coast who's gonna eat you up" (Gavin 53). The words have been reported uncritically by many jazz writers. Other than Baker's statements, however, there is no evidence that Parker said any such thing.[5]

Baker's lack of regard for others and his sense that he *deserved* love and adulation suggests a comparison with Jude Law's Dickie Greenleaf in the film version of *The Talented Mr. Ripley.* Like Baker, Dickie possesses youthful beauty and natural grace and unself-consciously carries great appeal for men as well as for women. Also like Baker, Dickie is accustomed to being adored and does little to repay the love he receives from Marge, Silvana, and of course Tom Ripley. In order to make an early, positive impression on Dickie, Tom pretends that several jazz LPs, including a copy of *Chet Baker Sings,* have accidentally dropped out of his briefcase. When Dickie picks up the Chet Baker LP, he says "This is the best." Minghella may or may not have known Baker's biography well enough to see how much he shares with the Dickie of his film. Regardless,

"My Funny Valentine" is an especially appropriate choice for Minghella's version of *The Talented Mr. Ripley*. When Tom/Damon uses his prodigious abilities as a mimic and sings in a Bakeresque voice ("You can't tell if it's a man or a woman") while Dickie and a group of male musicians accompany him, he enjoys the homoerotic thrill of sharing an intense moment with Dickie.

"My Funny Valentine" carries a gay sensibility if only because the author of its lyrics, Lorenz "Larry" Hart, was a closeted gay man. In fact, according to one man who says that he slept with him, Hart would retreat to a closet after a sexual encounter: "He'd get up and go into the closet. You'd wake up and you'd find him in the closet. . . . Sex frightened him. He didn't know what to do or how to do it. But he wanted to, desperately" (Nolan 238). Hart wrote several songs that invite queer readings, including "Tell Me I Know How to Love," in which the singer asks a lover of unestablished gender to dance as well as to lead. In "This Funny World," Hart may be telling gay lovers to follow his example and leave their emotions in the closet:

> *If you're beaten, conceal it. There's no pity for you.*
> *The world cannot feel it. Just keep to yourself. Weep to yourself.*

Robert Miklitsch perceptively reads the lyrics to "My Funny Valentine" in the same spirit, even suggesting that Hart found heterosexual romance to be comic. The lyrics and the *music* to "My Funny Valentine," as well as to other Rodgers and Hart songs, also suggest that love is a subject best treated with pathos. Minghella has unleashed the sadness and homoerotic elements in both the career of Chet Baker and the song by Rodgers and Hart and let it all play across the themes of his film. But many of the most compelling versions of Rodgers and Hart songs have been performed by black artists, including Miles Davis, who made two extraordinary recordings of the team's "It Never Entered My Mind." And Baker's treatments of "My Funny Valentine" were heavily influenced by African American jazz artists. Appropriating the music of Baker and Rodgers and Hart is consistent with the film's immersion in that part of white American culture that is inconceivable without African American culture.[6]

Just as many gay people choose to remain closeted in hopes of succeeding in mainstream society, gay characters in fiction either confront this dilemma or, like Proust's Albert/Albertine, play their roles in drag. In Highsmith's subsequent Ripley novels, Tom's wife, Heloise, is vaguely complicit in her husband's schemes while remaining discretely in the background. There never appears to be much romance in their marriage. In fact, Heloise functions more like the loyal male companions of unmarried heroes in detective fiction. But in the first Ripley novel, as in Minghella's film, Tom himself is a gay man passing for heterosexual. More commonly in the American cinema, however, passing stories are about racial identity, often with white actors playing characters with black African ancestors. This was especially the case in the 1940s and 1950s, when the figure of the tragic mulatto provided great opportunities for white actresses in search of juicy roles. In spite of Lena Horne's strenuous efforts to land the part, Ava Gardner played Julie in the 1951 *Show Boat.* In 1949 Jeanne Crain played the title role in *Pinky,* and Susan Kohner played an African American woman in the 1959 remake of *Imitation of Life.*[7] With a character passing as a white Negro, *The Talented Mr. Ripley* is another film that appropriates an African American tradition for whites *without* making black characters part of the story.

But *The Talented Mr. Ripley* borrows more than the narrative of passing from black cultural texts. When Tom first impresses Dickie with his collection of jazz recordings, Dickie exclaims that Charlie Parker, nicknamed "Bird," is not a man but a god. He has even named his sailboat *Bird* in honor of Parker. And yet we never see Parker's photograph, and no one mentions that he is African American. His music becomes the possession of whites, especially later in the various performance scenes in which virtually all of the musicians on camera are white, even as they play in the modernist style that Parker was prominent in creating. This is not to say that white artists have no business playing jazz or that white audiences should not be attracted to the music. Jazz itself would never have developed in the United States without the constant dialogue between African and Euro-American traditions. Furthermore, the international success and diffusion of jazz was vastly facilitated by white musicians, promoters, and true believers. Nevertheless, there is no denying that African American musicians have been exploited—sometimes viciously—by white artists and entrepreneurs. The fact that Tom is only *pretending* to admire a black musician like Charlie Parker makes the film's unintentional subtext more apparent.

Although Tom reaches a pinnacle of sorts when Dickie's saxophone embroiders his appropriately androgynous performance of "My Funny Valen-

tine," there is an even more significant jazz moment in the sexual tension between the two men. In a deeply homoerotic scene, full of tight close-ups and
pregnant pauses, Tom and Dickie play chess while Dickie sits nude in the
bathtub. The music is "Nature Boy," recorded by Charles Mingus in 1955 for
his own Debut label and featuring the trumpet of Miles Davis. Still in his shirt
and trousers, Tom runs his fingers through the warm bath water and says,
"I'm cold, can I get in?" Slightly uncertain but not afraid to let a note of teas-
ing into his response, Dickie says no. He then leaves the tub, exposing his
nude body to Tom as he walks away to pick up a towel. He looks over his shoulder to see that Tom is watching him in the mirror. Tom quickly turns away.

This is the turning point in Tom's erotic fortunes. For Dickie, Tom has
become a burden, as much because of his emotional vulnerability as because
of his need to keep Dickie on his own timetable. Moments after the scene
with the bathtub and "Nature Boy," Tom is literally shut out of Dickie's life
when Freddie Miles (Philip Seymour Hoffman) arrives and almost completely steals Dickie's attentions (fig. 19). When Freddie pulls up at the outdoor café in Rome where Dickie sits chatting with Tom, the music of a jazz
saxophone seems to be coming out of his car radio. The music, however, continues uninterrupted into the next scene at a record store where Freddie literally seals himself into a listening booth with Dickie so that they can share
a set of headphones. Tom is on the outside looking in, devastated that Dickie
is much more in his element with Freddie. The music is "Tenor Madness,"
featuring the tenor saxophones of Sonny Rollins and John Coltrane, both of
them African American. Freddie adopts an almost ghoulish posture as he
slowly gyrates to the music and fixes his gaze on Tom, clearly aware that he is
looking at a parvenu upstart. At this point, Dickie only wants to lose himself
in the music and cares little about his schedule for the rest of the day. Nevertheless, Tom taps on the listening booth's glass door to announce the departure time of the train they had planned to take back to Mongibello, clearly
hoping that Dickie will join him. Freddie shakes his head and snorts with de-
risive laughter at Tom's joyless, compulsive behavior.

The switch from Davis's "Nature Boy" to "Tenor Madness" is as striking
as the arrival of Freddie, played with immense confidence by Hoffman. In
both cases, the music occupies an ambiguous register in the world of the
film. We do not see a record player or radio while Dickie is in the bathtub,
and the music briefly continues into the next scene with Tom and Dickie

Fig. 19. Freddie Miles (Philip Seymour Hoffman, *right*) disrupts Tom Ripley's (Matt Damon, *left*)
idyl with Dickie Greenleaf (Jude Law) in *The Talented Mr. Ripley* (1999, Mirage
Enterprises/Miramax Films/Paramount Pictures). Jerry Ohlinger's Movie Material Store, Inc.

fully clothed at a bank. At the record store, although Dickie and Freddie appear to be listening closely to music in the booth, the audience hears the
seamless continuation of music that played when Freddie drove up in his
sports car in the earlier scene.

Regardless, Minghella has exploited all of the eroticism, yearning, and
tension in the slow version of "Nature Boy" as well as the more boisterous, ag-
onistic spirit of "Tenor Madness." In Mingus's "Nature Boy," Davis's trumpet,
elegantly softened by the stemless harmon mute that was so often in its bell,
plays over the delicate chimes of Teddy Charles's vibraphone, the subtle
brush work of drummer Elvin Jones, and the steady heartbeat of Charles
Mingus's bass. At this stage in his career, Davis was developing an intimate,
even introverted approach to improvisation that was completely unlike the
style of the phallic extroverts who preceded him in the roster of great jazz
trumpeters.[8] And like Chet Baker at this same time, Davis was learning not
to leave a song's melody behind for the sake of elaborate improvisation. Both
trumpeters took the melodies seriously, as if they were singing rather than
playing the songs. The album on which Mingus and Davis perform "Nature
Boy" was released as *Blue Moods*. Listening to their collaboration today, it is
difficult to hear the tension between the bassist/leader and the trumpeter.

According to John Szwed, Davis would not walk the two blocks to the *Blue Moods* recording session because he had been promised a ride. "And once he got the ride, he told the driver, 'I hope I won't have to hit Mingus in the mouth'" (Szwed, *So What* 117). The choice of the recording of "Nature Boy" from the *Blue Moods* session, with its looming tension between two men sharing a moment charged with musical eroticism, was especially appropriate for the scene in which Tom approaches Dickie in the bathtub. It even anticipates the additional tension of Freddie's arrival.

In spite of what we know about Miles Davis's tempestuous past, his music from the 1950s has since provided many young men with the perfect music for sexual seduction. Davis himself was uncomfortable with the idea that he was providing little more than sex music for the many white people in his audience. Partially as a result, he made the still controversial move toward jazz-rock fusion in the late 1960s. We also know from Davis's autobiography that he was hardly the vulnerable, romantic figure he presents in his music, especially after he began taking large quantities of drugs and alcohol throughout substantial portions of his career. Under the influence of various substances, he frequently abused women, even those who were closest to him. The black feminist writer Pearl Cleage was among many women appalled by passages in *Miles: The Autobiography,* such as Davis's description of how he shared laughs with policemen while his wife, Cicely Tyson, hid downstairs after she had called the police to report an incident of abuse. In her essay, "Mad at Miles," Cleage wonders how she could have fallen in love with the music of a man capable of such brutality toward a woman. Nevertheless, Davis's "classic" recordings of the 1950s and 1960s still play behind a great deal of lovemaking, and not just in the cinema. In the words of Art Farmer, a jazz trumpeter who listened carefully to Davis in developing his own approach, Miles Davis "played the way he wanted to be" rather than the way he was (Farmer, Conversation with the author).

The choice of "Nature Boy" for Tom's first, uncertain sexual overture to Dickie is also significant because of the mysterious aura with which the song first became known. "Nature Boy" was a hit in 1948 for Nat King Cole, who brought an especially reverential delivery to the song. Eden Ahbez, who claimed that he wrote the song, wore his hair long, recalling popular images of Christ, and affected a hippy demeanor well before it became the fashion. He was anything but a conventional avatar of American masculinity. According to legend, Ahbez appeared at the stage door where Cole was performing and handed him the lead sheet for the song. Cole's people had to track down Ahbez to tell him that Cole wanted to record it. Although Ahbez probably stole the song and eventually settled a copyright infringement lawsuit out of court, his image as a simple man living close to nature, eating only fruits, vegetables, and nuts, increased the song's association with profound truths and the mysteries associated with love (Gourse, *Unforgettable* 110–112). When Mingus recorded the song with Miles Davis, the Cole version was still in the ears of most listeners.

The unheard lyrics to "Nature Boy" contain the phrase, "The greatest thing you'll ever know, is just to love and be loved." Although Davis and Mingus were at odds when they recorded "Nature Boy," the song and its words have little in common with "Tenor Madness," taped one year later. "Tenor Madness" is the happy result of John Coltrane's decision to tag along with the rhythm section that Sonny Rollins took into the studio for a record date on May 24, 1956 (figs. 20 and 21). That rhythm section was the core of Miles Davis's working group in 1956. Because Davis also employed Coltrane as the band's tenor saxophonist at the time, Coltrane was right at home with the rhythm section. "Tenor Madness" consists of muscular, up-tempo blowing by Rollins and Coltrane, two larger-than-life tenor saxophonists who only recorded together on this one occasion and only on this one cut on the LP. If "Nature Boy" features a hornman speaking clearly about love while Tom tries to move closer to Dickie, "Tenor Madness" is the hot-blooded confrontation between two masters of the horn while Freddie barges in and snatches Dickie away from Tom.

In each case, African American musicians are as essential to the film's meanings as the passions for jazz exhibited by Dickie and Freddie. In spite of his low tolerance of jazz, and in spite of the later scene in which Tom sheds tears at *Eugene Onegin* after he has killed Dickie, the recording of "Nature Boy" seems to be entirely consistent with his emotional yearnings. Unlike the performance of *Eugene Onegin,* however, the music of Davis, Mingus, Coltrane, and Rollins is not part of an elaborate performance in front of a large audience.[9] Like Johnny Hartman in *The Bridges of Madison County* and Sarah Vaughan in *Next Stop Wonderland,* their music is as invisible as it is essential.

Shortly before Tom kills Dickie in a small rowboat outside of San Remo on what Dickie purposefully identifies as their last trip together, the two men sit at an outdoor café listening to the muscular bebop of the great British alto

Fig. 20. Sonny Rollins works his saxophone magic in "Tenor Madness" while Freddie steals Dickie from Tom in *The Talented Mr. Ripley.* Photofest Film Archive.

saxophonist Peter King. As soon as we hear the last of this music, *The Talented Mr. Ripley* departs from the borrowing of black culture and drifts into a murder and suspense narrative. Tom kills Dickie and then Freddie. He is subsequently exonerated and named the heir to Dickie's fortune. Although Tom appears to have achieved the aristocratic life to which he had always aspired, as the film comes to an end he kills his first real male lover, Peter Smith-Kingsley (Jack Davenport). On the boat taking them to Athens, Peter sees Tom kissing Meredith Logue (Cate Blanchett), a wealthy, single woman traveling in Italy, apparently with hopes of finding a husband very much like Dickie. Because Tom first posed as Dickie Greenleaf in early scenes with Meredith, and because she still believes Tom to be Dickie, she could easily link him with the two murders. The film ends ambiguously as Tom kills Peter because of fear of exposure, continuing gender confusion, or some combination of both.

Black music is not, however, completely absent from the last half of the film after the death of Dickie. There are two significant moments. First, when Dickie's father comes to Italy to investigate the disappearance of his son, he sits in an outdoor café as a street musician with a tenor saxophone plays a jazz version of "You Don't Know What Love Is," the same song that Dickie had played on his saxophone after the death of Silvana. No fan of jazz or the saxophone, Greenleaf Senior suffers from the sounds, even muttering that he would gladly pay the man a hundred dollars to "shut up." Significantly, the busker is white. Although Mr. Greenleaf is surely unaware of Dickie's connection to the musician's song, he must know that Dickie was an aspiring saxophonist. The elder Greenleaf seems to care deeply about his son, but his passionate reaction to the performance of "You Don't Know What Love Is"—inevitably tinged with racial prejudice—demonstrates how strongly he resents the way his son has rejected his values. It also signifies the continuing presence of white Negro aesthetics in the film even after Tom's musical life has returned to the European classics. Perhaps unintentionally, the film has let race play a prominent part in the aesthetic conflicts that drive the characters.

The unwillingness of *The Talented Mr. Ripley* to acknowledge its racial thematics is especially clear as the end credits begin to roll. Once again we

Fig. 21. John Coltrane joins Sonny Rollins in a stirring performance of "Tenor Madness" on the soundtrack for *The Talented Mr. Ripley.* Photofest Film Archive.

hear "You Don't Know What Love Is." For the first time, however, the song is sung rather than played. Although the gruff, possibly damaged voice of the singer clearly recalls Louis Armstrong, Ray Charles, and an unquestionably African American tradition of jazz singing, the vocalist is white. He is John Martyn, not well known to American audiences but popular in England as a folksinger. In fact, the jazz musicians throughout the film have been white Englishman, virtually all of them playing in styles closely associated with African Americans. Peter King and the other first-rate British jazz musicians led by trumpeter Guy Barker in the film's several performance scenes deserve credit for creating music that meshes elegantly with the events of the film. So does Anthony Minghella, who appears to be a man of musical sophistication working closely with the musicians. Martyn, Minghella, Barker, and the other British jazz artists have all made the most of African American culture to create some of the best moments in a mostly thoughtful film. But the film contains no discussion of race and elides any real dialogue between black American culture and the white musical cultures of America, England, and Italy as surely as it elides any representation of African Americans as speaking, acting subjects. The film also neglects to interrogate the white Negro aesthetics of Dickie and Freddie, who purposefully embrace a jazz aesthetic even as they would certainly exclude black people from their lives.

STUCK IN NERDVILLE

Pleasantville begins by gently parodying the nostalgia for a false past that drives the revival of old television programs on cable channels such as Nick at Night and TV Land. Moments later, the film is more heavy-handed as it catalogues the social and environmental crises of the late twentieth century, not to mention the bizarre courting rituals of postmodern teenagers. The nerdish David (Tobey Maguire) seems thoroughly demoralized as his high school teachers talk about AIDS, ozone depletion, and world famine. He is equally discomfitted by the attractive girls at his school whom he is too timid even to approach. Unlike his sister, Jennifer (Reese Witherspoon), who is brazenly successful in winning the attention of high school hunks, David finds solace in returning repeatedly to old episodes of the television sitcom *Pleasantville*. The program is clearly inspired by *Father Knows Best*, an extremely popular series with runs on three television networks between 1954 and 1963. Although he seems to pay little attention during his classes, when a friend quizzes David on the trivial details of *Pleasantville* episodes, he displays an extensive knowledge of the program.

Don Knotts, who became a permanent part of television memory after five seasons as the bug-eyed, self-important sheriff's deputy Barney Fife on *The Andy Griffith Show* (1960–1965), makes a cameo as an omniscient, magically empowered television repairman who transports both teenagers into the black-and-white world of *Pleasantville*. Although they might simply be on a television shooting set, the two soon discover that they are, in fact, in 1958 and that all the characters are earnestly playing out the lives they lead on the old program. Jennifer/Witherspoon, now known as Mary Sue or "Muffin," is appalled by the cheerful, banal exteriors of her sitcom parents (William H. Macy and Joan Allen), who do not seem to notice that she bears little resemblance to the actress who had previously played Mary Sue. David/Maguire, who is now called "Bud" (the same name as the son in *Father Knows Best*), adapts more quickly, even taking pleasure in knowing to say "a new Buick" when a neighbor asks him what kind of a car his father recently purchased.

Both teenagers are amazed by the grotesque bounty of pancakes, waffles, bacon, sausage, and hamsteak stacked high at their breakfast table (fig. 22). Just as the film had exaggerated the hopelessness of life in the late 1990s, it goes even further with images of simple-minded abundance in the Middle America of the 1950s. While David is at first content to live in the sitcom utopia, hamsteak and all, Jennifer is horrified to be "stuck in Nerdville." Only when she meets the blandly handsome Skip (Paul Walker) does she reconsider.

Pleasantville was the first major film directed by Gary Ross, who had previously written two successful comedies built on similar fish-out-of-water plots. In both *Big* (1988) and *Dave* (1993), a self-effacing everyman is thrust into a new life for which he is completely unprepared. The eleven year-old protagonist of *Big* suddenly acquires the body of a thirty-year-old, and in *Dave*, an imitator of the president of the United States steps in when the real president goes into a coma. Although the heroes in both films know that they are imposters, virtually everyone accepts them as authentic. *Pleasantville* was not as successful as the two films Ross had previously written, but it represents a more complex treatment of his usual theme, bringing both a woman *and* a man into a new environment that is, at least at first, completely alien to one and strangely familiar to the other.

Fig. 22. Reese Witherspoon is dismayed by the fulsome breakfast served by Joan
Allen in *Pleasantville* (1998, New Line Cinema). Photofest Film Archive.

In his commentary on the DVD of *Pleasantville*, writer/director/producer
Ross speaks of the challenges of placing contemporary teens in the world of
1950s television. He points out how the black-and-white scenes were shot in the
style of late twentieth-century Hollywood rather than with the shot selection
and camera movement typical of 1950s television. This is not the only way that
the film does not conform to the conventions of early sitcoms in general and of
Father Knows Best in particular. Many of the episodes of *Father Knows Best* dealt
with the real anxieties of career, family, and social status that were not at all re-

pressed in many of the television programs of the 1950s. By contrast, the characters in *Pleasantville* simply seem oblivious to any complexity in their lives. Furthermore, affluence and excess were never as conspicuously displayed in *Father Knows Best* as when the mother in *Pleasantville* dishes out those gargantuan portions of breakfast in the first black-and-white moments of the program.

To use his own word, Ross has "rationalized" his parodic view of *Father Knows Best* and its genre by giving us a Pleasantville in which the citizens only know as much about life as was shown on television in the 1950s. Since the characters never have sex, they have never seen a double bed. Since we never see anyone going to the bathroom, there are no toilets. Since the inhabitants of *Pleasantville* never travel beyond Main Street, no one knows of any world outside. And since no one reads books in the television show, every book in the library consists of blank pages.

As Ross explains repeatedly on the commentary track, the people in Pleasantville turn from black and white to colorful when they change in some important way. Since young people are most open to change, and since sexuality makes for fast and fundamental transformations, the town's teenagers are the first to earn their colors. Later on, characters change color because they have become angry or highly emotional. After Jennifer hustles Skip off to Lover's Lane for his first sexual encounter, he sees a vivid red rose on a bush as he drives home. As Jennifer the sexual adventuress begins to influence behavior throughout the high school, color suddenly appears as a pink bubble of gum emerging from a girl's mouth and as a red taillight on a car from which hang the suggestively swaying limbs of young lovers. Everything else in these early scenes remains in black and white.

The sexual awakenings brought to Pleasantville by Jennifer include a scene in which Betty (Joan Allen), the mother of Mary Sue and Bud, appears to be masturbating in the bathtub. Mary Sue/Jennifer has just told her about sex, more importantly that "there are other ways to enjoy yourself . . . *(pause)* . . . without dad." As Betty approaches orgasm, the items in her bathroom take on color. When she climaxes, a tree in the family's front yard magically explodes into blazing orange and red flames. Since Pleasantville has never had a fire, the firemen only know how to bring kittens down from trees. David, however, understands the hydraulics of a fire truck, calls the firemen, and instructs them on the use of a water hose to extinguish the blazing tree.

The sexual changes also involve Mr. Johnson (Jeff Daniels), who runs the soda shop where Bud/David works after school. Although David has initially been reluctant to change the lives of the citizens in his antique television idyll, he takes pity on Mr. Johnson, who would like to do something more meaningful than tend to the daily routine in his shop. He says he most enjoys painting a Christmas scene each year on his shop's large picture window. When David brings him a book of European paintings by the most color-conscious of the old masters, Mr. Johnson begins by painting a colorful, cubist Santa on his window. After he begins an affair with Betty (her new sexualization has led her to act on a series of glances they exchanged earlier in the film), Mr. Johnson replaces his Santa with a nude portrait of Betty.

THE INVISIBLE CODES OF COLOR

Like so many other American films, *Pleasantville* abundantly recruits the music of African American artists to define and refine the transformations of its characters. When Jennifer first begins seducing Skip exclusively in black and white, the audience hears the wholesome voice of the white Pat Boone singing the pop ballad "Mr. Blue." Later, when the camera picks up the bright red taillight and slowly pans across the cars full of young people exploring their new sexuality on Lover's Lane, the music on the soundtrack is "Be-Bop-a-Lula," performed by Gene Vincent. To use a phrase coined by Michael Jarrett, Vincent was a "white black singer" (Jarrett, Conversation with the author). Vincent's 1956 recording of "Be-Bop-a-Lula" was clearly inspired by the success of Elvis Presley's early forays into black rhythm and blues; Vincent sings in the hiccuppy vocal style that Presley and the first white imitators of black rhythm and blues borrowed from Otis Blackwell and other African American singers of the 1940s and 1950s. Although there was little of what jazz canonizers would now refer to as bebop in the music of Vincent, he was almost as prominent as Presley in scandalizing Middle America with his appropriation of sexually suggestive gestures from black musical traditions. In Vincent's mouth a simple word such as "bebop" somehow took on sexual connotations:

> *Be-Bop-a-Lula, she's my baby.*
> *Be-Bop-a-Lula, I don't mean maybe.*

Just seconds after "Be-Bop-a-Lula" comes to an end with a montage of changes in Pleasantville, David arrives for work at the soda shop, where several teenagers have already turned completely colorful. In one of the film's few sight gags, the cherry on Jennifer's otherwise black-and-white soda is a lusty red. When a teenager inserts a coin into a fully colorized jukebox, we hear the sounds of Lloyd Price's rambunctious "Lawdy Miss Clawdy." Larry Williams, who sings on the version heard in the film, and Lloyd Price, who wrote and first recorded "Lawdy Miss Clawdy," are both African American. The choice is significant and probably not the result of a random selection made by the film's music supervisor.[10]

The move from bland white pop ("Mr. Blue") to black-inflected white pop ("Be-Bop-a-Lula") to "authentic" black rhythm and blues ("Lawdy Miss Clawdy") sets the stage for a similar move from white jazz to black jazz a few scenes later. Although the townspeople do not know that Betty's sexual awakening caused the fire outside her house, David is hailed as a hero for rallying the firemen to put out the flames. The day after a public ceremony in his honor, David once again arrives for work at the soda shop. In his commentary, Ross says that he wanted to transform the shop—previously represented as a place where teenagers gossiped and flirted over cheeseburgers and milk shakes—into something more like a coffee house where beats and bohemians would have congregated in the 1950s. Ross and his crew create the effect partially by turning down the lights and foregrounding the noir effect of the shop's venetian blinds. More importantly, the music of the Dave Brubeck Quartet plays through the first part of the scene.

Although most jazz purists today have little respect for Brubeck, it is impossible to overstate his importance to jazz's reception after World War II. By the late 1940s, the popularity of the swing bands had largely vanished along with the popularity of what we now think of as jazz. The mostly austere and inscrutable black musicians who played bebop were extremely successful among jazz writers but not at all with audiences (Gendron 143–147). Jazz was increasingly a music for connoisseurs and insiders. Thanks to Brubeck and very few others in the 1950s, jazz developed into an upscale music with an important following among college students.[11] Although large portions of this audience would soon drift away to Joan Baez, Bob Dylan, and the Beatles, Brubeck convinced many that jazz could stand up to classical music as a legitimate art form. Having studied with the eminent French composer Darius

Milhaud and experimented radically with time signatures in composition and improvisation, Brubeck prominently presented jazz as worthy of sophisticated listening. It did not hurt that he wore thick horn-rimmed glasses and resembled a professor more than a hipster. And of course he was white, still another artist who may have served as a transitional object for those fans who preferred their jazz cooked rather than raw.

When David approaches the soda shop after his triumph with the fire department, we hear the Brubeck Quartet playing "Take Five," a composition by the band's alto saxophonist Paul Desmond, first recorded in 1959. Unlike virtually every other jazz tune, "Take Five" was written in 5/4 time, giving it an unusual pattern of emphases by adding an additional beat to the conventional four-beat measure. But the band, which also included Joe Morello on drums and its one black member, Gene Wright, on bass, is comfortable with the meter, allowing the song to swing gently if idiosyncratically. The music adds equal portions of sophistication and hipness to a scene in which young people are exposed to what are, at least for them, radical new ideas and sensibilities.

MILES FROM HOME

Up until this point, the changes that came with rock 'n' roll and rhythm and blues on the *Pleasantville* soundtrack had been primarily sexual. But as "Take Five" plays in the background, the young people in the shop ask David how he is able to know about fire. The film associates jazz with thinking rather than with feeling. Not yet willing to explain his impossible presence in Pleasantville, David coyly suggests that there may be more to life than his peers suspect. He soon discovers that the teens in the soda shop have multiple questions for him. One of them has been reading *Huckleberry Finn,* thanks to a halting attempt by Jennifer to tell the boy what ought to be inside a book with blank pages. Since she only read up until "the part about the raft," only the first pages of the book have, according to the logic of the film, filled themselves in. David, however, has been more conscientious about his homework. The wide-eyed congregation of teenagers is suddenly obsessed with what happens to Huck and Jim.

The camera closes in on the face of the perky blonde cheerleader Margaret (Marley Shelton) as she asks David to tell them what happens in the novel. As David begins to talk about Huck Finn and watches while *all* the pages in the book are dutifully filled in, Brubeck's music gives way to a new recording. We then hear what is surely the most elegant music in the film and unquestionably one of the most important recordings in the history of American music, the Miles Davis Sextet's 1959 recording of "So What," the first track on the great *Kind of Blue* LP. *Pleasantville* disposes of the introductory duet between bassist Paul Chambers and pianist Bill Evans, the only white member of Davis's group at the time. The music starts abruptly with the second statement of the tune's sketchy "melody" as the three black hornmen (Davis, trumpet; John Coltrane, tenor saxophone; and Cannonball Adderley, alto sax) answer the assertions of the bassist with the two-note phrase suggesting the title, "So What" (phrased as a judgment, not as a question). Ultimately, the audience only hears the solo of trumpeter Davis, and even that has been edited down to roughly half its length on the original recording. But Davis's solo occupies almost a full minute of *Pleasantville*'s soundtrack while a great deal happens on the screen. The elegant but vernacular sounds of Davis's trumpet accompany the discovery among the town's young people of a literature that is about as radical as the timid liberalism of the film is prepared to endorse. Even though David's interpretation of *Huckleberry Finn* is basically a conservative one, the film uses Davis's music to impart a sense of wonder and experimentation as David tells the town's teenagers about Huck and then about *Catcher in the Rye*. The music continues as young people line up at the doors of the library and proudly display their new colors.

The placement of "Take Five" and "So What" in a crucial scene in *Pleasantville* is not accidental. Ross says that he wanted the increase in "complexity" as the soundtrack music moves from Brubeck to Davis. (He does not say that the two selections parallel the earlier transition from "Be-Bop-a-Lula" to "Lawdy Miss Clawdy," but two prominent pairs in which black music follows white music suggest that the filmmakers are multiply color conscious.) Recorded just a few months apart and initially received warmly by very similar audiences, "Take Five" and "So What" have taken two completely different directions as markers in jazz history. Brubeck and Desmond were tampering with jazz meter on "Take Five" as well as on the album, appropriately titled *Time Out,* on which the tune first appeared. Miles Davis and his five sidepersons were playing largely without chord progressions, relying instead on what has been called "modal" jazz.

Time Out and *Kind of Blue* were not the only important jazz records released in 1959. This was also the extraordinary year in which Charles Mingus came of age as a composer, combining elements from Duke Ellington, Jelly

Roll Morton, Charlie Parker, the new avant-garde movements in jazz, the sanctified church, and the Western canon with his recording *Mingus Dynasty*. In the same year John Coltrane brought a new level of intensity and complexity to jazz improvisation with his "sheets of sound" on the album *Giant Steps*. Also in 1959, Ornette Coleman recorded *The Shape of Jazz to Come*, which took the music about as far afield from conventional chord changes and key signatures as was possible without losing a connection to jazz. Coleman's music still stands as a monument in what John Szwed has called "The Permanent Avant-Garde."

Although Mingus, Coltrane, and Coleman may have been more radical than Davis in moving jazz into new territory, the interventions of Miles Davis are probably more significant for jazz history. If nothing else, *Kind of Blue* has become the best-selling jazz record ever. Brubeck's *Time Out* has also been a money-maker for Columbia Records, but it has hardly had the same impact on subsequent jazz artists as has *Kind of Blue*. The coffeehouse hipness that Gary Ross heard in "Time Out" still clings to the song and marks it as an artifact of the 1950s. "So What" has acquired more of what we might call "timelessness" and plays a much more convincing role as *Pleasantville*'s signifier of profound transformation. More importantly, as black music, the Miles Davis recording carries with it an aura of the forbidden and the transgressive that *Pleasantville* needs as it moves the narratives of the civil rights movement to a small town devoid of African American faces.

EXPLICATING HUCK

"So What" plays these important roles in the film just as David begins to explain what happens in *Huckleberry Finn*. For obvious reasons, David refers to Nigger Jim as "the slave." In his attempt to convey the meaning of the novel to the innocents sitting in the soda shop, David explains that "in trying to get free, they see that they're free already." After he utters this one sentence, every one of the pages in the book fills with print and the story of Huck and Jim becomes available to all the town's young people. In his commentary, Ross says that *Huckleberry Finn* is a "picaresque adventure" about getting knowledge, an important theme he claims for his film. He also mentions the many times that the book has been banned, but he neglects to mention that the book is banned not because of politics or scatology but because of its repeated use of the word "nigger." In the 1950s there were no national movements to ban the book. Only after black students began making demands in the 1960s did the book begin to disappear from libraries and reading lists. The other book that David introduces to the curious young people, *Catcher in the Rye,* first published in 1951, has been banned for different reasons, specifically for the explicit language used by its teenage narrator. For Ross, however, the two controversial books are an appropriate pair to drive home his theme that knowledge—especially knowledge that is controversial or threatening—has the power to change people.

Although there is virtually nothing in his commentary about the film's appropriation of civil rights imagery, Ross does take a few moments to talk about his father, Arthur Ross, who was active in political causes in the 1950s. In addition to founding the Hollywood Committee for a Sane Nuclear Policy, the father organized rallies to oppose anti-ballistic missile development and took an activist role in other organizations devoted to nuclear disarmament. Gary Ross mentions that his father was actually blacklisted for his efforts in the 1950s. The son then goes on to speak about how he grew up in a household where liberal causes were always being promoted, and although he backs away from embracing his father's politics, he presents himself as someone with strong beliefs about political as well as personal freedom. But like his father, whose most memorable project as a screenwriter was *The Creature from the Black Lagoon* (1954), Gary Ross is content to make small liberal gestures within a typically conservative Hollywood product. Although the younger Ross directly endorses nothing so radical as social justice for black Americans, he does come out against burning books.

The racial displacements in *Pleasantville* resonate in David's reading of *Huckleberry Finn.* David does not mention that the book upset African Americans for its use of "nigger," nor does he point out how Huck sees through the racism of his culture and discovers humanity in Jim, even putting his own future at risk in order to help Jim escape to the North and to freedom. Instead, David conveniently defines freedom as something that is internal rather than as a right than can be granted or taken away by the state. By having David ignore the realities of slavery in the United States—and by extension the legacy of slavery in the political and social life of Americans in the 1950s—the film draws attention away from the fact that the only people in the film who are discovering their internal sense of freedom are white. Thus they can identify with African Americans like "the slave," who suffer discrimination and small-town small-mindedness but who can supposedly find true freedom simply by looking inward.

Just as *The Talented Mr. Ripley* made social class a substitute for race, the quotation of the courtroom scene from *To Kill a Mockingbird* at the climax of *Pleasantville* powerfully suggests that David, Mr. Johnson, and the rest of the liberated citizens of the town are at the mercy of bigots from a lower social order. In *To Kill a Mockingbird,* the usual Hollywood bias against southern accents and dialects pervades the courtroom scene. With perfect general American speech and great dignity of bearing, Gregory Peck courageously defends an innocent black man against charges made by the local proletariat and enforced by a slouching, drawling prosecutor (fig. 23). *Pleasantville* recruits this spirit of class prejudice by showing the most aggressively conservative city fathers at a bowling alley and by giving an especially bad haircut to their leader (J. T. Walsh). And of course, the music of Miles Davis and Dave Brubeck is emblematic of the higher status of the colorful in *Pleasantville,* in spite of the fact that the music was scarcely associated with the higher classes when it first appeared in the 1950s.[12]

Fig. 23. Gregory Peck knows that a white woman of the lower classes was not raped by a black man in *To Kill a Mockingbird* (1962, Universal International). Photofest Film Archive.

Fig. 24. Vocalist Etta
James brings spring
colors to Pleasantville.
Jerry Ohlinger's Movie
Material Store, Inc.

The invisible color-coding of the film's music is also apparent when David asks Margaret for a date. After she accepts, we briefly hear Elvis Presley singing "Teddy Bear" as David leaps over the fence on the way home. Moments later, as David drives Margaret to Lover's Lane and all of nature bursts into the vibrant colors of early spring, the radio plays Etta James's "At Last." This well-known recording carries a depth of romantic feeling that has little in common with the playful come-on in Presley's tune.[13] Once again the film has signaled a switch in intensity—in this case in David's relationship with Margaret—with a change from white to black music.

The racial dynamics of *Pleasantville* almost become explicit after the scene at the lake when Margaret falls for David and turns colorful. Had it not been for the arrival of David into the world of the sitcom, she would still be dating a boy named, provocatively, "Whitey." The black-and-white members of the community have turned on the newly colorful by this time, placing "No Colored" signs in store windows and even burning books. In this spirit, the still colorless Whitey utters threatening words to David and to Margaret, referring to her as David's "colored girlfriend." A bit later, Mr. Johnson's nude painting of Betty on the soda shop window is smashed by angry citizens who hurl a park bench through the glass. The sequence features camera views from both inside and outside the shop. Immediately after the park bench goes through the window, angry citizens throw a garbage can through the door of the shop, thus recalling a film that directly addresses racial conflict, Spike Lee's *Do the Right Thing* (1989). At the climax of that film, as Lee's character Mookie hurls a garbage can through the large window of Sal's Pizzeria, the film gives us both inside and outside views of the shop window breaking. Referring to a memorable moment from Spike Lee's film is one of the more artful ways in which the film suggests racial conflict while eliding race itself.

Pleasantville also links right-wing politics, sexual anxiety, and suggestions of racial prejudice with the "Code of Conduct" laid down by the colorless city fathers. Lover's Lane and the library are ordered closed until further notice; the "non-changes view of history" must be taught exclusively in schools; and all music is banned with the exception of "Johnny Mathis, Perry Como, Jack Jones, the marches of John Philip Sousa, and the Star Spangled Banner." In a second commentary on the *Pleasantville* DVD, Randy Newman talks about the music he wrote for the film's soundtrack, but also makes a few stray comments of his own. Concerning the list of acceptable vocalists, Newman wonders why Johnny Mathis was included, suggesting that he was pretty "hip" for his age. Newman may have been referring to the alternative sexuality that Mathis projected in his singing or simply to the fact that Mathis represents the only black music in the city fathers' list. It is also possible that Newman, like all of us, has specific memories of hearing a particular artist at particular moments in his life and has read those experiences back into the music.

Nevertheless, as the odd list of permitted music makes clear, the film casts civil rights as popular entertainment rather than as the fundamental restructuring of American society. And as far as the film's white appropriation of blackness is concerned, that's as far as it has to go. When David outsmarts the city fathers and provokes them into turning colorful, he says, "It's in you and you can't stop something that's inside you." Just as David suggested that the freedom sought by Nigger Jim was always already there inside him, he now reveals that everyone in Pleasantville was already colored. All strife ends when everyone discovers this truth. But *Pleasantville* disingenuously sidesteps any substantive issues by presenting everyone as *also* the same on the outside. Thanks to the magic of the movies, we're all colored. The allusions to civil rights, an unstated part of the film's dynamic from the outset, no longer matter.

Jennifer, meanwhile, turns colorful only after reading *Lady Chatterley's Lover*. Even though she brought about the initial colorization of the town by introducing sex into the lives of the young people, she herself has remained black and white, presumably because for her sex long ago ceased to be transformative. Only when she expands her mind can she earn her colors. As the film reaches its conclusion with the entire town thoroughly colored, Jennifer decides to remain in Pleasantville, where she will attend college and become something more than a "slut," her own term for her past self.

David, however, has learned that his retreat into the *Pleasantville* television series has denied him a life of real discovery and romance. He returns to the present with an entirely new level of wisdom. Of course, the present to which he returns is not the one at the beginning of the film in which AIDS and ozone depletion were held out as inevitable. David returns to a much more manageable situation. He immediately encounters his divorced mother (Jane Kaczmarek) crying over something much less apocalyptic. She has broken up with her boyfriend, her junior by nine years. David consoles her with the knowledge he has gained through his egalitarian adventures in Pleasantville. When his mother tearfully recalls, "When your father was here, I used to think—this is it. This is the way it was always going to be. I'd have the right house, I'd have the right car, I'd have the right life." David assures her that "there is no right life, there is no right car." A lesson that was initially linked to the evils of racism and the glorious possibilities in diversity transmogrifies into the conventional postmodern lesson that consumerism is all.

EXIT MUSIC

As in *The Talented Mr. Ripley, Pleasantville* moves away from black music well before its conclusion. After Etta James's "At Last" disappears from the soundtrack at the film's midpoint, the closest thing to black music the audience hears is Buddy Holly's version of "Rave On." Like Gene Vincent, Holly borrowed a few elements from rhythm and blues, and his music too was often called "bebop." This usage was even present in the 1978 biopic *The Buddy Holly Story* when teenage girls ask Buddy to play them some "bebop." As Ross points out in his commentary, the tom-tom sounds on the record also inspired more conservative listeners to call it "jungle music." "Rave On" is played on the jukebox by David's allies after the city fathers have begun burning books and persecuting "colored people." Presumably, it symbolizes the rebellious spirit still alive in the young people. But it is a spirit of rebellion that lost its edge for Americans a long time ago. What was "edgy" for 1950s listeners has since become comfortable "golden oldies." The rest of the film's music is by Randy Newman. Although Randy Newman has recorded numerous songs that take a jaundiced view of America—including "Rednecks," with its critique of racial hatred in the South—everything he has written for *Pleasantville* fits the conventional, late romantic paradigm for movie soundtracks. When the credits roll, the music is Fiona Apple's ethereal, arty version of John Lennon's "Across the Universe." Black music, like the discourses of the civil rights era, has served its purpose, and the film has moved on to safer territory.

The lyrics to "Across the Universe" include the refrain, "Nothing's going to change my world." The irony is surprising if unintended. *Pleasantville* has shown how at least one world can be changed while thoroughly supporting the status quo in contemporary America. The final shots of the newly colored Pleasantville are entirely reassuring. It is still a nostalgic misrepresentation of small-town Americana, abundantly referencing the magazine covers of Norman Rockwell. But it would be unfair to blame Rockwell for the imagery at the end of *Pleasantville*. Rockwell prominently and provocatively included the bodies and faces of black Americans in his paintings. Like *The Talented Mr. Ripley, Pleasantville* detaches narratives essential to the African American experience and recycles them to give substance to white characters. And both films sexualize and even dignify their white characters with the invisible sounds of black Americans on the soundtrack. The recordings of Miles Davis in particular are wrenched out of the context in which they might have the most consequence, either as revolutionary music or as the expressions of a man with a deeply troubled and troubling past. Instead, the music simply serves white characters in a movie. As is so often the case in American films, even postmodern ones, black men and women are not allowed to participate in stories that would seem to be inconceivable without them.

SERVING THE WHITE AUDIENCE

CHAPTER FOUR

The Racial Displacements

of *Ransom* and *Fargo*

T he American film industry's project of keeping white characters on top
is not as easy as it used to be. Trying not to offend the large black audience and seeking to avoid charges of racism, Hollywood has been especially
inventive in placing potent African American characters in stories that ultimately do little to disturb the fundamental American hierarchies of race.
And as Clint Eastwood has figured out, a film can acknowledge the masculine and romantic power of a black singer while concealing his African American body and placing the sound of his voice entirely at the service of the
white hero. *Ransom,* directed by Ron Howard in 1996, and Joel and Ethan
Coen's *Fargo,* also released in 1996, come from two different strains of the
American cinema, but they have much more in common than a kidnapping
narrative to focus audience interest. *Ransom* is a high-profile Hollywood film
with a bankable star and director as well as some engrossing action sequences. *Fargo* comes from two brothers who usually work at the margins of
Hollywood, making "independent" films that combine large portions of
irony with more familiar genre material. And yet both films powerfully affirm the centrality of white people in America's racial universe. *Ransom* is
more concerned with the white hero's attempts to assert his masculinity and
to control events when a hypermasculine African American man stands in
his way. *Fargo* seems to critique bourgeois culture and white masculinity, but

Fig. 25. Tom Mullen
(Mel Gibson) with
his son (Brawley Nolte)
in *Ransom* (1996, Imagine
Entertainment/Touchstone
Pictures). Photofest
Film Archive.

it also places "non-white" characters well outside the domain of whiteness and casts their behavior as pathological. In both films the whites retain their centrality, whether on the mean streets of New York City or on the snow-packed plains of the upper Midwest.

"SOMEONE IS GOING TO PAY"

An early scene in *Ransom* presents an image that symbolizes the gender anxieties of both the hero and the film. We see Tom Mullen (Mel Gibson), the wealthy owner of an airline company, his wife, Kate (Rene Russo), and their son, Sean (Brawley Nolte), at a science fair in New York's Central Park. The boy has built an airborne device that consists of a video camera attached to two orange, helium-filled balloons. Using a remote unit, Sean, who looks about nine years old, controls the flight of the balloons as well as the direction of the video camera. Suddenly, kidnappers seize the boy while both parents are momentarily distracted. We then see the balloons drifting slowly out of the park. The possibility that his son has been kidnapped begins to dawn on Tom just as the balloons collide with the cornice of an apartment building. One of the balloons bursts, sending the video camera plummeting to the sidewalk. The falling camera functions as a synecdoche for the son, who has been seized while deploying that camera over the rooftops of New York City. With its two large spherical balloons, the contraption is also a metaphor for Tom's prominent but threatened masculinity: his "balls."

Those who threaten Tom and his status as a powerful member of a white ruling class include not only the working-class kidnappers but also an African American FBI agent (Delroy Lindo) who seeks to control Tom's negotiations with them. The racial thematics of the film function entirely apart from the narrative, but they create similarities between *Ransom* and the growing number of films in the "angry white male" genre. The familiar white male heroics of Mel Gibson are deployed primarily against the persona of Lindo, who plays Special Agent Lonnie Hawkins. Lindo's character speaks with a slight accent associated with working-class black people, but otherwise he comports himself very much as an assimilated member of the American middle class. The white kidnappers, however, are much more likely to engage in signifying practices associated with African Americans. Nevertheless, it is Lindo's black FBI agent who embodies white anxieties about black masculinity and its imagined threat to the dominance of white men, particularly for a character played by Mel Gibson, whose lack of physical stature may be partially responsible for his desire to project a hypermasculine image in most of his films.[1] In the case of *Ransom*, Gibson's character encounters a man whose size (and color) threaten his quest for masculine dominance.

Sean's attempts at urban surveillance foreshadow a series of gazes directed at Tom Mullen as he endures the pain and humiliation caused by the kidnapping and attempts to regain control of his life. As psychoanalytic film theory has taught us, looking in movies usually involves empowerment while being looked at can mean the opposite. From his penthouse apartment near Central Park, Mullen can look out over the city from a privileged location consistent with his financial and social position.[2] Once his son has been kidnapped, however, that lofty position becomes systematically less available. Tom learns that his movements are being carefully monitored not only by the kidnappers but also by the FBI, the media, and random on-lookers, almost all of them from the working class. Although the plot of *Ransom* is driven by Tom's attempts to retrieve his son, the film is in many ways more involved with Tom's needs to retrieve his manhood, in particular that version of manhood that has little to do with the daily demands of fatherhood. The film repeatedly dramatizes Tom's paranoia as he confronts emasculating forces linked to family, class, and—most disturbingly in a film that presents the familiar face of "liberal" Hollywood multiculturalism—race.

MY FATHER THE HERO

The prominent image of large but fragile balls floating inexorably toward destruction can also be read as a symbol for Tom's vulnerability as a father. Although the film repeatedly pays lip service to the importance of families, *Ransom* reveals the tension between life in the nuclear family and the aspirations of the American hero, especially the familiar type that Robert B. Ray calls "the outlaw hero," the ubiquitous figure in American narratives who runs away from home and rejects values associated with domesticity and conventional social organization. American heroes of this breed make their own laws, answering to an internal but infallible sense of right and wrong. The hero often risks his life to save the people he cares about, but he usually moves on as the narrative ends, still resisting the compromises and entanglements that come with family and stability.[3] Clark Gable, Humphrey Bogart, and John Wayne made careers playing this character. More recently, Mel Gibson has joined Clint Eastwood, Tom Cruise, Bruce Willis, and various others who continue the tradition. It is difficult to imagine any of these actors playing a domesticated man in a stable relationship with a wife and child. As I argued in chapter two, a psychoanalytic reading of these films suggests that an idealized masculinity is dependent on the rejection of unity with a woman, if only because it returns the man to a state of child-like dependence on the mother with the corresponding, overriding fear of the father's wrath. The cinema's presentation of the most "masculine" characters is incompatible with the daily frustrations and accommodations of conventional family life even if their "back stories" often include a wife who is deceased or estranged. For these characters, a stable loving relationship cannot be represented, only referred to in the past. Although Gibson plays a family man in *Ransom,* he spends most of the film asserting his manhood, in effect violating the family conventions that are missing from the films of most male action stars. The fundamental and incoherent project of *Ransom* is to represent Tom Mullen as, simultaneously, a family man and a "real" man of the action cinema.

Ransom is especially unusual for creating a character like Tom Mullen who reclaims his masculinity by resisting union with a woman but who does

Fig. 26. Glenn Ford and Donna Reed in *Ransom!* (1956, MGM). Photofest Film Archive.

so from *within* an idealized family structure. While the fathering of children gives men a certain degree of phallic authority, it also erodes their autonomy and draws them back into the world of the child, the mother, and the oceanic feeling from which the adult male in dominant American narrative must escape. *Ransom* dramatizes what happens when myths of the American hero are superimposed on myths of the bourgeois family. Something's got to give.[4]

In the script by Richard Price, Jonathan Gold, and Alexander Ignon, the hero defies his wife and Agent Hawkins by refusing to pay a $2 million ransom. Convinced that the kidnappers will kill his son as soon as they receive the ransom money, Mullen appears on television and promises the ransom money to anyone who provides information leading to the capture of the kidnappers, dead or alive. If the kidnappers return his son, Mullen will withdraw the reward.

In the 1956 film *Ransom!*, when the son of Glenn Ford and Donna Reed is kidnapped, the father decides to change the ransom money into reward money.[5] This soon results in the return of his son and the end of the film, but not before the wife has become so overcome with anxiety and grief that she is effectively ushered out of the film by a nurse. She is in no condition to discuss her husband's decision to gamble with the life of their child. In Ron Howard's 1996 remake, however, the wife Kate is compos mentis when Mullen decides to act entirely on his own and publicly refuses to pay the ransom. Kate and Agent Hawkins are flabbergasted to see Tom on the television broadcast, and they both look for ways to pay off the kidnappers with or without Tom's cooperation. In a conversation with Kate, Tom explains his decision: if the Mullens pay, they are likely to lose their son; but if the kidnappers know that a huge bounty has been put on their heads, they will return the child "in mint condition" and live the rest of their lives without being targets for bounty hunters. As an essential element in the gender and racial politics of the film, Tom's logic is meant to be more convincing to the audience than to the film's other characters. By daring the kidnappers to kill his son, Tom can resist the voice of the Other—in this case a woman and a black man—and remain the audacious, autonomous protagonist of his own narrative rather than a passive player in the kidnappers' drama.

As several critics pointed out, a crucial scene in *Ransom* recalls the final shots of *The Godfather* (1972): Tom and his advisors are photographed from his wife's point of view as she discovers that she has been excluded from Tom's deliberations. A major difference, however, is that *Ransom* does not, like *The Godfather,* characterize Tom's decision to exclude his wife from "family business" as a descent into evil. Quite the contrary. Tom's gamble pays off when Jimmy Shaker (Gary Sinise), a corrupt police detective who is the leader of the kidnappers, kills his co-conspirators and attempts to collect the reward money as if he were an honest cop who had stumbled upon the kidnappers' lair. Tom soon discovers Jimmy's deception and kills him in a long and bloody fight scene that climaxes the film. The credits role with the family reunited, the kidnappers destroyed, and the hero vindicated. Any suggestion that Tom has irreparably damaged his marriage by ignoring his wife and risking the life of his son is drowned out by the sound of bullets and by the cathartic drama of Tom's triumphant fight to the death with Jimmy Shaker.

A MORLOCK ASCENDS

The white hero in *Ransom* reestablishes his autonomous masculinity not just because he resists the feminizing effects of family and not just because he kills the mastermind behind the kidnapping of his son. As I have suggested, Tom Mullen also overcomes the attempts of a powerful black man to control his dealings with the kidnappers. Furthermore, Tom enhances his success by escaping the gaze and control of members of the American working class, both black and white.

The film begins at a party in the Mullens' penthouse in which well-heeled guests are served by caterers, one of whom wears a tattoo on her neck, a marker of lower-class status and ethnicity. This is Maris (Lili Taylor), later revealed to be one of the kidnappers. Also in a clearly subservient role is a Latina woman, Fatima (Iraida Polanco), the Mullens' housekeeper. Once the kidnapping plot is under way, Tom can no longer interact with members of the working class in so rigidly a hierarchical fashion. In order to deliver the money to the kidnappers, Tom must follow the elaborate orders given to him by Jimmy Shaker, who speaks into a masking device attached to the telephone that gives his voice a deep, demonic resonance. The odyssey on which Jimmy sends Tom takes him first to a swimming pool in a Harlem recreation center, where Tom must dive into the water fully clothed in order to retrieve a key. The key goes to a locker in which Tom will find a change of clothes. Jimmy has sent Tom into the water to disable the listening device that he is likely to be wearing and to change his appearance so that the FBI will have more difficulty following him. This plan also gives Jimmy the pleasure of imagining Tom as he confronts the startled black bathers in and around the pool. The film's construction of an ascendant white masculinity here explicitly contrasts the trim, well-dressed body of Mel Gibson with the dark, partially clothed bodies of Harlem residents, many of them aged and overweight.

After Tom Mullen has emerged from the recreation center, he listens on a portable telephone as Jimmy directs him to a stone quarry in New Jersey. As he drives along the same highway unnoticed by Tom, Jimmy overtly categorizes his relationship with Tom in terms of a class struggle by describing

George Pal's 1960 film, *The Time Machine.* Jimmy explains that *The Time Machine* foresees a world divided into two groups, the Eloi and the Morlocks. The beautiful, blonde, toga-clad Eloi live a carefree existence above ground while the ugly, ape-like Morlocks live beneath the surface. The Morlocks provide all the necessities of life for the Eloi, but the Morlocks occasionally ascend to the surface and bring back one of the Eloi for food. Jimmy explains that New York is like the world foreseen in *The Time Machine.* He is a Morlock and Tom is one of the Eloi: "Every now and then one of you gets snatched." Although Pal's film draws upon Cold War ideology of the 1950s and early 1960s and explains the Morlock/Eloi division in terms of a nuclear holocaust, Jimmy's reading of the film is more faithful to the 1895 H. G. Wells novel on which the film is based. A committed socialist, Wells projected a capitalist economy that would banish workers to underground factories, leaving the surface of the earth a vernal paradise for industrialists and their families. Eventually, the workers revolt and overpower the Eloi on the surface, but only after their long confinement by the forces of capital causes them to evolve into troglodytes who cannot survive above ground. *Ransom,* however, like Hollywood's *The Time Machine,* gives the working class little sympathy, consistently associating characters from the lower classes with predators and criminals while portraying the powerful and the elite as their victims.[6]

After finishing his exegesis of *The Time Machine,* Jimmy says to Tom, "See you at the Whitney, see you at the Four Seasons, see you at the Met," ultimately chanting only the mantra-like phrase, "See you." Jimmy's look at Tom is tinged with envy and class hatred, but it is only one of many looks that are directed at Tom from the lower classes. Tom is also watched by members of the press corps who camp outside his apartment building, as well as by African Americans at the swimming pool. The film even dwells on a medley of gazes in a scene that might otherwise seem gratuitous. Immediately after Tom announces on television that he is transforming the ransom money into a bounty, he is filmed in slow motion picking up the money he has dramatically spread out on the table before him. The music in James Horner's score becomes atonal and percussive, connoting confusion and disorientation. Slow motion shots of Mel Gibson's face are then intercut with three separate shots of employees at the television station staring at him with varying degrees of disbelief. The camera then shoots Gibson from behind so that the television spotlights are on either side of his body, emphasizing the extent to which he has become a media spectacle. Leaving the station, Tom's image is doubled as he walks past the mirror-like exterior of the building while a crowd shouts at him. Symbolically in danger of becoming fragmented by the plenitude of refracted images of himself, Tom is trying to seize control of the narrative so that he is once again the one who looks down on the people and not the one at whose multiple images the people can gaze.

The tension between Tom and the working class is also central to an important subplot. When Sean is first seized, Tom suspects the involvement of Jackie Brown, a union official who had accused Tom of bribing him to prevent a strike at Tom's company, Endeavor Airlines. We learn that Brown was imprisoned after a sting operation involving union deals at another airline. In negotiations with prosecutors, Brown offered to testify against Mullen in exchange for a shorter sentence. Tom denied offering a bribe, and after an extensive investigation, the FBI declared that Tom was innocent of the charge. When the FBI arrive at his home after Sean has been kidnapped, Tom reluctantly explains to Agent Hawkins that he did in fact arrange to give Brown a payoff. Tom attempts to justify the denial he made when Brown's accusations became public. "See, most guys at the top, they acquire their airline. Not . . . not me. I built Endeavor from the ground up, and it's mine. No bastard's taking it away from me. No union, no government, and no two-bit gangster like Jackie Brown. . . . I paid him off. I initiated the bribe. I had a business to run. I had two thousand employees, God knows how many customers, and I didn't have time for a goddamned strike."

Tom and Lonnie Hawkins then ask Jackie Brown in prison if he is involved in the kidnapping. Brown is played by Dan Hedaya, a rough-hewn actor who is more likely to play a scrappy schemer than a graceful aristocrat. Wearing bright orange prison coveralls, a bad haircut, and a day's growth of stubble, Brown is at first confused by a visit from his antagonist but soon becomes enraged when he hears Tom accusing him once again. He crawls over a table and strikes Tom on the face, loudly proclaiming his innocence. As he is dragged back to his cell, he shouts, "I got six of my own kids and I would die for every one of them, and I haven't seen them since I got locked up in here because of YOU. Why aren't you in here?" Whatever sympathy the audience may have for Jackie Brown at this point is left unexplored. He disappears from the film after this scene. We later discover, however, that Jackie Brown is at least indirectly involved with the kidnapping. During the same conversation in which Jimmy Shaker explains *The Time Machine* to Tom, Jimmy says that he had seen Tom on television professing his innocence in the Brown affair. Once again the gaze of the Other is stigmatized when Jimmy says that he looked into Tom's eyes and could tell that he was not telling the truth: "You're a lyin' ass dog, pal." Jimmy felt certain that Tom was the kind of man who would buy his way out of trouble.

Tom finds himself in a kidnapping crisis because he paid off Jackie Brown and then lied about it. But there are no other important repercussions, at least not in the film's basic story line. When Kate finds out that Tom had lied even to her about his innocence, she expresses disappointment in one brief scene. Like Tom's unilateral decision to withhold the ransom money from the kidnappers, his deception of his wife in the Jackie Brown affair is forgotten and presumably forgiven when the family is united at the end of the film. It can even be argued that Tom has learned from his mistakes—he paid off Jackie Brown, but now he knows better and will not pay off the kidnappers. The only other person who knows the truth about Jackie Brown is Agent Hawkins, but in a scene that seems awkwardly attached to the script, he tells Tom that he may never tell anyone what he knows about the affair.

The class issues raised by the Brown affair—and much else in the film—are further effaced by suggestions that Tom and his wife themselves come from the working class, or at least that they have only recently joined the ranks of the super rich. Kate was once a grade school teacher, and in a television commercial for Tom's airline that runs early in the film, Tom is dressed in a cowboy hat as a self-made man. It even seems that they have only recently moved into a Fifth Avenue penthouse that is still undergoing renovations. Although Tom and Kate are elegantly dressed during the initial party scene, they spend most of the film wearing blue jeans and, in the case of Tom, a T-shirt with a school insignia, the kind of "legible clothing" usually associated with the working class.[7] When Tom visits Jackie Brown in prison, he wears a black leather jacket. All these attempts to place the Mullens outside the moneyed classes fuzzes over *Ransom*'s important class dialectic and allows audiences to see Mel Gibson as another working-class action hero fighting for his family and not as a white-collar criminal.

NOT A LOVE STORY

The person in *Ransom* who seems most concerned about social and economic class is Jimmy Shaker. In the American cinema, as in much of American political life, members of the white haute bourgeoisie are seldom marked as possessing "class," just as they are almost never marked as having "race." A term such as "class warfare" inevitably suggests insurrections by the lower elements rather than measures taken at the top to eliminate opportunities for those on the bottom. When Tom Mullen argues that he wanted to prevent a "goddamned strike" at his company, Endeavor Airlines, there is no suggestion that he may have prevented his employees from winning better salaries and working conditions. The film takes the side of the attractive captain of industry, not that of his workers. So, Jimmy Shaker, who compares himself to one of H. G. Wells's Morlocks, is the one unattractively obsessed with class issues, not unlike black characters in many Hollywood films who cannot stop talking about race in the presence of white people who seem completely oblivious to racial distinctions. In *Die Hard with a Vengeance* (1995), for example, the constant harangues of Zeus Carver (Samuel L. Jackson) finally lead to the outburst by John McClane (Bruce Willis): "Just because I'm white, you don't like me. Have I oppressed you? Have I oppressed your people somehow?"[8]

Similarly, Tom Mullen is irritated by Jimmy Shaker's concern with class because he does not see himself involved in any class struggle. The American cinema has perpetuated the notion that the white ruling class is not itself a class but a legitimate element of the status quo. Like the members of that class, the American cinema often categorizes those who talk of race and class as, at best, misguided malcontents. The extent to which white American paranoia lies behind this pattern of representation is especially clear when films such as *Die Hard with a Vengeance* and *Ransom* foreground an obsessed Other full of anger about race or class.

FBI agent Hawkins briefly alludes to class difference when he is shown speaking sweetly to his wife on the telephone, urging her to hug their daughter and expressing satisfaction with his own middle-class status: "I'm so glad we're not rich. You just got to thank God for what you have." He then breaks off the conversation when Tom Mullen enters. Throughout the film Hawkins never once mentions race. Nevertheless, the central conflict in *Ransom* does not simply match Tom Mullen/Mel Gibson with a group of white kidnappers. Symbolically, Agent Hawkins is the *real* obstacle to Mullen's attempts to regain the manhood that is in danger of floating away like fragile balloons.

Hiring Delroy Lindo to play Hawkins was an inspired bit of casting. Very few actors, black or white, carry themselves with as much masculine power.

Fig. 27. Delroy Lindo at his most menacing in *Get Shorty* (1995, Jersey Films/MGM). Photofest Film Archive.

For *Ransom,* Lindo even adopts the look of many urban black males who have shaved their heads while retaining some facial hair. Because of the long association of hair with sexuality, baldness often symbolizes castration. Consequently, bald men face three choices: they can cover the tops of their heads with wigs or with elaborate combing strategies in hopes of denying their castration; they can leave the top of the head bare while grooming the hair on the sides in a conventional fashion, thus refusing to acknowledge the association of baldness with castration; or they can completely disavow castration by shaving off all of their remaining hair in order to *become* the phallus. White male stars such as Yul Brynner and Telly Savalas embraced this third choice in the 1950s and 1970s, but in the 1990s a completely shaved head was associated primarily with black men, most notably star athletes such as Michael Jordan and gangsta rappers such as Tupac Shakur. Because white men look to black men for images of masculinity, many young whites in the 1990s followed African American fashion by shaving their heads. Appropriately, Miles (Evan Handler), one of the white kidnappers in *Ransom,* sports a hairless pate.

In *Ransom,* the phallic head of Delroy Lindo bears a commanding, even threatening countenance. If you know Spanish, you know that Lindo is not *lindo.* But at the same time that Lindo can *look* extremely menacing, he can also be gentle and accommodating. In his public appearances, Delroy Lindo is good-natured and personable. Obviously a gifted actor rather than a "natural" performer, Lindo has given convincing performances as evil characters who seem at first to be reasonable men. In *Get Shorty* (1995) his Bo Catlett initially presents himself as a Runyonesque gangster and an aspiring screenwriter (fig. 27). He is soon revealed, however, to be a sociopathic killer. In a crucial scene, he holds the young daughter of his henchman Bear (James Gandolfini) on his lap, speaking sweetly to her while clearly implying that he is capable of crushing her if Bear does not do his bidding. Because of Lindo's engaging manner, the child is completely unaware that she is in any danger. In Spike Lee's *Clockers* (1995), Lindo plays the drug-dealer Rodney, who initially seems good-hearted, even functioning as a surrogate father for the young hero Strike (Mekhi Phifer). Once again, Lindo's character eventually reveals a murderous side, and as in *Get Shorty,* his violent death is obligatory. As Lonnie Hawkins in *Ransom,* Lindo never reveals a dark side, but he is assertive and forceful when necessary. For the ideological project of the film, however, he must carry a great deal of racial menace in his face and body, not to mention the intertextual baggage from earlier roles in films such as *Get Shorty* and *Clockers.*

In the narrative of *Ransom,* Agent Hawkins continually attempts to rein in the heroics of Tom Mullen, assuring him that he is only there to "get your

Fig. 28. Delroy Lindo's first attempt at taking charge in *Ransom* (1996). Photofest Film Archive.

boy back." Nevertheless, the tension begins early when Hawkins slams his own hand down on top of Mullen's when the phone first rings and Tom is anxious to speak with the kidnappers even though the FBI staff is not yet fully prepared to trace the call (fig. 28). Later, after Hawkins and Mullen visit Jackie Brown in prison, Mullen wonders if the same FBI that failed to catch him for the Brown payoff is capable of finding his son. Hawkins chooses a curious means of reassuring Tom: "Take a good look at me. Take a *real* good look at me. I got to be real good at what I do to be in the position I'm in. See, they didn't assign me to the Endeavor investigation. But if I had been, if it's any consolation to you, I'd have nailed you." It is not exactly clear why Hawkins asks Mullen to look at him. Alongside this powerful but unacknowledged registering of his race, Hawkins could be suggesting that a black man must be extremely talented in order to rise through the ranks of an organization with a racist past such as the FBI, or he could simply be asking that Mullen observe the determination in his face. Either way, Hawkins is saying that he would win in an adversarial relationship with Mullen. In the racial and gender dynamics of the film, this is a challenge that Tom Mullen accepts.

After the FBI intervenes and botches Tom's attempt to deliver the money to the kidnappers, Mullen feels sufficiently betrayed to strike Hawkins in the face as soon as he returns to his penthouse. Tom had insisted that he make the drop unassisted, but a small army of agents watched his every move. Although it is clear that Hawkins is not giving all the orders, Tom holds him personally responsible for preventing him from handing over the ransom money. In the narrative, Tom is simply taking out his anger on the person he feels is most guilty. But it is significant that the target of his anger is a black man seeking control. After Tom strikes him, Hawkins immediately immobilizes Tom by holding his arm behind his back and pinning him to the floor face down. This is the last time that Tom will find himself under the control of the black FBI agent.

When Mullen subsequently decides not to pay the kidnappers, he is not only overcoming the impotence brought on by his life as a family man. He is also overcoming the impotence he feels in the face of constant attempts by a black man to restrain him. Hawkins even works on Kate by telling her that Tom lied to her about Jackie Brown in hopes that she might dissuade him from withdrawing the ransom. Nevertheless, toward the end of the film, when Jimmy Shaker holds a gun on Tom and tells him to drive to the bank for the reward money, Tom surreptitiously finds a way to summon Hawkins. On one level, this is simply an obligatory moment in the American action cinema in which the purposes of the "outlaw hero" and the "official hero" converge. For Robert B. Ray, the reconciliatory finale is essential to the Western and various "disguised westerns." In *Shane* (1953), for example, the eponymous hero comes to the rescue of Joe Starrett; in *Casablanca* (1942) Rick saves Victor Laszlo; and in *Star Wars* (1977) Han Solo extricates Luke Skywalker from a near-death situation. As Ray points out, this narrative strategy is especially satisfying because it allows the audience to have it both ways, relieving them of the anxiety of choosing one hero over the other. The reconciliatory finale also functions ideologically by justifying the anti-social, even paranoid behavior of the more glamorous outlaw hero. According to this syntax, however, Tom Mullen should be rescuing Lonnie Hawkins and not the other way around.

Furthermore, the phallic male competition between Mullen and Hawkins continues right up until the last seconds of the film. Before Hawkins has arrived on the scene, Tom has taken charge once again and severely beaten Shaker with his fists. When Hawkins and the police finally do arrive, they hold Shaker at gunpoint and repeatedly tell Mullen to drop the gun he has acquired in the struggle. Mullen is still resisting, refusing to relinquish the pistol. As is almost always the case in this film, Mullen is vindicated: like most movie villains of recent vintage, Shaker is capable of one last murderous assault even after he appears to be near death. Just when Shaker seems on the verge of collapse, he reaches for a gun strapped to his ankle and takes a shot at Mullen. Although Agent Hawkins puts three bullets into Shaker's body, Mullen strikes first, quickly getting off a shot that hits Shaker in the heart. Tom wins again.

In many ways, Lindo's Lonnie Hawkins recalls the many black judges and police captains who regularly appear in Hollywood films. These figures are often allowed a great deal of anger and power as they deliver rebukes or bark orders at white defendants and subordinates. (The convention was even parodied in *Last Action Hero* [1993], whose black police superintendent is constantly shouting for no particular reason.) As Ella Shohat has written, black characters in movies are often "'guests' in the narrative" (240), placed there simply to give presence to African Americans rather than to serve the needs of the plot. Sharon Willis, however, argues that the ubiquitous black judge or police chief does more than just affirm a film's multicultural pretensions; as "the embodiment of legal authority or moral surveillance" these characters "operate as indexes of paranoid fantasies that situate African Americans as the ones who know the truth about race, while avoiding any occasion for a reciprocated gaze that would cause the dominant culture to look at itself through another's eyes" (Willis 5–6). But rather than efface the implied threat these characters must carry, *Ransom* brings the paranoid fantasy to the surface by allowing Agent Hawkins to confront the hero with his transgressions. Although the narrative displaces class and racial elements into purely legal conflicts, Tom Mullen does more than just refuse the "reciprocated gaze" that action heroes such as Bruce Willis usually avoid; Mullen actively works to triumph over the judgmental gaze of the black FBI agent. In this way, the film makes Hawkins the double of Jimmy Shaker, another figure associated with the law who gazes at Tom and passes judgment on him.

In fact, Jimmy Shaker and the other white kidnappers fill in many aspects of the film's paranoia about the empowerment of African Americans that are missing from actual black characters. As is often the case in *Ransom*, negative associations attached to blacks, women, and the working class slide together and overlap; like highly charged elements in the culture's dreamwork, they are displaced and condensed. One of the kidnappers has "boom" tattooed on his hand with one letter on each finger, recalling the "love" and "hate" on the hands of Radio Raheem (Bill Nunn) in Spike Lee's *Do the Right Thing* (1988) (a quotation by Lee of Robert Mitchum's hands in *Night of the Hunter* [1955]). While Agent Hawkins never uses ghetto language, the kidnappers regularly adopt speech patterns and slang associated with African Americans. Evan Handler's Miles, for example, says, "Hey, ya know what the brothers call this? 'Some more draaama.'" Lili Taylor's Maris refers at one point to the power of her lover Jimmy Shaker by saying, "My man is runnin' shit." When Shaker appears in Tom's apartment to claim the reward money, he holds a gun on Tom and at one point gestures with his arm and shoulder in the style of a black rap artist.

Of the many films in which white males face challenges from blacks, women, immigrants, and other previously disempowered groups, *Falling Down* (1993) is most often mentioned by critics. But this film asks audiences to take a critical look at the confusion of D-Fens, the white protagonist played by Michael Douglas. Viewers are invited to appreciate the irony in his final remark, "I'm the bad guy?" Films such as *Ransom,* however, invite almost total sympathy for the white hero and do not acknowledge his paranoia toward the Other. In this sense, *Ransom* has more in common with *Forrest Gump* (1994), another film with a sympathetic white hero and carefully coded racist sentiments. Early on, that film includes a clip from *Birth of a Nation,* surely the most important Angry White Male film ever made. As part of a catalogue of Forrest's ancestors, the old black-and-white footage from *Birth of a Nation* is doctored so that the face of Forrest/Tom Hanks digitally replaces that of Henry B. Walthall as he leads the charge of the Ku Klux Klan. Although viewers with a knowledge of film history may watch this scene with ironic bemusement, a later scene is meant to be taken much more seriously. John Groch has written that Forrest perfectly embodies the angry white male when he encounters his beloved Jenny (Robin Wright) with a group of student radicals during the Vietnam War years. Forrest watches Jenny being slapped by her white activist boyfriend at the same time that a black militant is directing a nonstop verbal harangue at Forrest. Seemingly oblivious to the African American man, Forrest runs to the side of Jenny and repeatedly punches the boy who had hit her. The voluble black man does not commit violence, and Forrest does not direct any hostility toward him, but as Groch argues, the black militant's contiguity to the violence and his aggressive participation in the same antiwar harangue as the abusive white peacenik suggest that Forrest might as well be beating up the black man.

Ransom adopts the same practice of racist displacement as *Forrest Gump.* While *Gump* finesses its racial thematics by having the angry white hero ignore the black militant while foregrounding his race, *Ransom* can allow its angry white hero to strike the black man because the narrative has *not* foregrounded his race. In both films, however, the violent outbursts allow audiences to see white men righteously asserting themselves over hypermasculine black characters. Although Mel Gibson has played opposite Danny Glover in all four of the *Lethal Weapon* films, his relationship with Lindo in *Ransom* does not suggest the homosocial, interracial romance of the *Lethal Weapon* films, not to mention the many other American narratives that allow white men to bond in significant ways with men of color. *The Last of the Mohicans, Moby Dick, Two Years Before the Mast,* and *Huckleberry Finn* are the most commonly cited American novels in this tradition. The familiar interracial relationship has been updated and conventionalized in the three *Die Hard* films (1988, 1990, 1995), the two *48 Hrs.* (1982, 1990), *Unforgiven* (1992), *The Last Boy Scout* (1991), *Se7en* (1995), *The Glimmer Man* (1996), *I Spy* (2002), and many others. All of these films find their own means of addressing the need among white people to imagine that they can be redeemed by winning the love and devotion of a single powerful, dark-skinned man.[9]

But unlike Danny Glover in the *Lethal Weapon* films, Delroy Lindo in *Ransom* has little in common with Queequeg, Chingachgook, or Nigger Jim. On the one hand, Lindo's Lonnie Hawkins superficially resembles Roger Murtaugh, the Glover character in the *Lethal Weapon* series, who is also a happily married family man whose failed attempts at constraining the Gibson character only add to the white man's luster. On the other hand, at no time in *Ransom* does Tom show even mild affection for the black FBI agent, while Hawkins himself is less concerned about the personal situation of Tom and much more concerned about the displeasure of his superiors at the FBI. Furthermore, Lindo's Hawkins is substantially more potent than the aging, frequently ineffectual Murtaugh in the *Lethal Weapons. Ransom* often speaks to male misgivings about the feminizing effects of family and child-rearing, but the film is more directed toward arousing and containing white male uneasiness about perceived threats from hypermasculine black men.

Although the vaguely racist underpinnings of the *Die Hards,* the *Lethal Weapons,* and the rest have been thoroughly unmasked by critics such as Fred Pfeil, Sharon Willis, and Robyn Wiegman, *Ransom* is an especially malign contribution to this tradition. The racial and gender dynamics of *Ransom* might be considered alongside the hypermasculine posturings in many of Mel Gibson's films (Luhr 227–246). But *Ransom* should be compared to other screenplays by Richard Price, who also wrote scripts for *Sea of Love* (1989), *Kiss of Death* (1995), and the aforementioned *Clockers* (1995). Price may have brought an urban, race-conscious style to the script for *Ransom* that became paranoid in the hands of Gibson and Ron Howard. The obsessions of director Howard surely play a role in *Ransom*'s desperate reinscription of discredited forms of masculinity. His earlier films, such as *Gung Ho* (1986), *Backdraft* (1991), *Far and Away* (1992), and *Apollo 13* (1995), are all driven by a fascination with male bravado and reactionary, unexamined notions of heroism. Howard may even have been seeking to revise the public's memory of him as the young Opie on *The Andy Griffith Show* and the nerdy Richie on *Happy Days.* After the release of *Ransom,* Bernard Weinraub wrote in the *New York Times,*

> Mr. Howard acknowledged that his acting persona, especially on "Happy Days," and his smiling, easy demeanor had helped shape the impression that he was a film maker without an edge. "I've always been involved in sort

of pop entertainment," he said. "You live with a little bit of frustration that that kind of work is not taken as seriously as other kinds of work. I mean, there's great feedback, but yeah, sure, I was sort of legitimately categorized and typed as the all-American guy." (Weinraub C11)

Howard also told the *Times* that he identified with Mel Gibson's character in the film: "He's a winning character but flawed" (Weinraub C11). But Gibson's flaws in *Ransom* are the kind that audiences can tolerate in an attractive action hero, especially when they complement qualities that speak to conscious and unconscious anxieties about social, racial, and gender hierarchies. Although the film seems to empower a black man by casting Delroy Lindo in a part that many actors, white and black, would have given their eye-teeth to play, the filmmakers may have intended—consciously or unconsciously—to give *Ransom* an extra degree of appeal to white viewers by allowing Gibson to triumph over Lindo at numerous points in the film. With a fantasy about a hard-working couple fighting their way to Fifth Avenue splendor, a climactic death struggle against an implacable villain, and the almost complete neutralization of a black man's attempts to control a white man, many whites would have had no difficulty identifying with a good-looking white man struggling to prevent his masculinity from floating away.

THE BIG WHITE-OUT

In some ways, *Fargo* deflates the myths that drive *Ransom*. White masculinity is treated as an invitation to disaster if not as a source of humor. Gunfighting in particular is deprived of any heroic dimension. The only character who righteously shoots down a murderous villain is Marge Gunderson (Frances McDormand), a pregnant policewoman with a bulky uniform and few of the heroic qualities attributed to male stars like Mel Gibson. Marge may not even belong in the film, in spite of the fact that her performance won her an Academy Award and surely made the film a hit. The idealization of Marge in *Fargo* undermines its grim satire of life in the upper Midwest, and does nothing to ameliorate the broad caricaturing of nonwhite people throughout the film. Like *Ransom*, *Fargo* has much to say about race, gender, and class as it spins out its kidnapping narrative.

Fargo's highly unstable irony is present from the moment the audience sees an opening title card flatly asserting that the film is based on a true story and that it is told exactly as it happened "out of respect for the dead." Because the filmmakers themselves have admitted that Fargo was not based on actual events, the title card can be seen as typically Coenesque—playful and ironic in the most deadpan fashion. But shortly after that opening title card disappears and a tiny bird suddenly flitters about on the pure white screen, the ominous music of Carter Burwell turns majestically fortissimo. (Burwell's score at this point reads "molto bombasto" [Adams 31].) The grandiose music promises something more earnest than the lighthearted genre parody of The Hudsucker Proxy (1994), the Coen brothers' previous film. Although Fargo does not always live up to the promise of Burwell's auspicious score, the film does provide what amounts to an anatomy of whiteness.[10] The story of Jerry, the kidnappers, and Marge begins in a pure, frigidly white environment and places people of northern European descent firmly at the center of a distinctly American landscape. Everything that is wrong with these people, the film seems to suggest, is what is wrong with white America, including the almost complete marginalization of people who can be called "non-white."

Fargo's improbably homogeneous cast of characters share Scandinavian surnames (Lundegaard, Gustafson, Gunderson) and vernacular expressions ("Oh, you betcha," "Thanks a bunch," "Kinda funny lookin'"). Their forced cheerfulness is epitomized by the painfully false smile in the photograph of Jerry Lundegaard (William H. Macy) displayed among those of the many other salespeople at Gustafson Motors in an early establishing shot. Even the two kidnappers, Carl Showalter (Steve Buscemi) and Gaear Grimsrud (Peter Stormare), who seem entirely incompatible (fig. 29), choose to enjoy a pair of prostitutes and then a broadcast of The Tonight Show side by side in the twin beds of a motel room. In the world of Fargo, Wade Gustafson (Harve Presnell) makes the rules, and Jerry Lundegaard tries to find ways around them; Carl and Gaear break the laws, and Marge enforces them. The snowy world that stretches from Fargo to Brainerd and then on to Minneapolis belongs to these white people. One of the pleasures in watching the film is its keen sense of how the principal characters have adapted—in both body and spirit—to the frozen plains of America's northern heartland.

A more problematic pleasure is following the Coen brothers' scrupulous catalogue of white masculinity and its failures. A key element in this project is the creation of a set of Others who, for better or worse, provide the outer limits within which whites can be themselves. The Native American Shep Proudfoot (Steven Reevis) displays more rage and ferocity than anyone else in the film, just as the Asian American Mike Yanagita (Steve Park) is by far the most pathetic character. Although Proudfoot plays a small role in the plot mechanics of the film—he told Jerry that he could vouch for Geaer as the right man to carry out Jerry's scheme—there is no comparable story logic behind the one scene in which the Asian American Mike pathetically attempts to woo Marge. Proudfoot and Yanagita recall the film industry's worst stereotypes of Indians and Asian men. They are sketchy characters made real primarily by the strong performances of Reevis and Park. We never learn, for example, how Proudfoot first ended up in jail or how Yanagita or his family came to live in Minnesota. Nothing in the film unites them with a history of oppression that might explain their separate pathologies. Neither, however, seems interested in moving to more hospitable regions. Proudfoot, of course, may have grown up in Minnesota, and Yanagita has become so much a part of that world that he speaks with the exact same upper Midwestern accent as everyone else in the film. The Coens may even have created the part of Mike Yanagita simply as a joke about an Asian man talking like a Minnesotan.

Fig. 29. Phony tough guys (Steve Buscemi and Peter Stormare) in *Fargo* (1996, Gramercy Pictures/Polygram). Photofest Film Archive.

In this context, it is significant that the secondary male victim of Proud-foot's furious assault on Carl should be the film's one and only African American character, drawn into violence when he innocently knocks on the door to request that Proudfoot make less noise in the room adjacent to his. Before the black man can finish a single sentence, Proudfoot knocks him unconscious by bouncing his head off the wall in the hallway and then returns to pummeling Carl. The film makes a further excursion into what might be ethnic politics by placing Carl and his female companion at a performance of the film's one and only Latino character, the entertainer José Feliciano, who foreshadows the violent arrival of Proudfoot at Carl's motel room by singing "Let's Find Each Other Tonight." Black and Latino people are not absent, but they have virtually nothing to do with the important events in *Fargo*. What are they doing there?

We can ask the same about the kitschy figures on the credenza in Jerry Lundegaard's office. Frequently visible behind people facing Jerry at his desk, the three figurines represent genre scenes for fanciers of golf. On Jerry's left is a mustachioed Scotsman wearing a tam, a figure from the early history of the game. The other two statuettes portray black people. At Jerry's right a caddy leans indolently on a bag of golf clubs. The central figure uses both hands to hold a driver directly out in front of his body just below waist level. The pose is entirely typical of the ancient minstrel tradition that both ridiculed and celebrated black male sexuality. In his book on minstrelsy, Lott reproduces an illustration from the 1820s in which a black man, anticipating the phallic display of today's rock guitarists, holds out a banjo to suggest a large penis (*Love and Theft* 118). Although we never see Jerry playing golf, we do see him scribbling on a notepad inscribed with "I ♥ golf," complete with an image of a golf ball replacing the letter "o." In spite of the triumphs of Tiger Woods, there are few sports so thoroughly associated with the white moneyed classes that Jerry aspires to join. Apparently, no one who has sat in Jerry's office has ever objected to his particular style of dramatizing his love of the game. Long after lawn jockeys disappeared from middle-class homes or were simply painted white, Jerry still prominently displays comparable images in his office. The Coens may be implying that Jerry's demented aspirations toward white masculinity and upper-middle-class leisure depend on the subjugation of African Americans, not to mention the Native American Proudfoot, who holds a low-level job at the automobile dealership where Jerry sells cars.

As the theorists of whiteness have written, the existence of minority groups in the United States has always been essential to the construction of whiteness. Native Americans were the first authentic Other against which Euro-Americans defined themselves, becoming central to the captivity narratives that inaugurated a uniquely American literary genre (Slotkin). Later, slaves from Africa were recruited as an essential contrast to white Americans, ultimately inspiring whites to blacken up and create the nineteenth century's most popular form of entertainment, the minstrel show. Significantly, many who performed under cork as minstrels were themselves recent immigrants; in the nineteenth century the Irish were central to minstrelsy, and Jews were prominent in blackface entertainments in the early twentieth century. Richard Dyer and Noel Ignatiev have thoroughly documented America's marginalization of the first Irish immigrants through association with Africans as well as the strategies by which the Irish subsequently "became white." Similar stories can be told about Italians, Greeks, Hispanics, and other ethnic minorities. Especially in the inner cities, the dominant culture's reaction to the arrival of African Americans—and to a lesser extent other non-western peoples—served to transform highly diverse groups from distinct European cultures into "white" people.

Although blacks, Latinos, and Asian Americans continue to make large and small steps toward full participation in American culture, the Hollywood cinema still turns out a huge body of films in which the characters that matter most are white. So long as this remains the dominant practice and thus an impediment to further progress toward social equality, film scholars must continue to demystify whiteness and analyze its construction in American culture. On one level, *Fargo* is involved in this demystification when it places racist caricatures in the office of a callow, manipulating white man such as Jerry. It is surely significant that the first scene in which the audience sees the small statues of blacks in Jerry's office is immediately followed by a view of the gigantic statue of Paul Bunyan, a hyperbolic icon of white masculinity if ever there was one. But on another level, the film seems to have little sympathy for its non-white characters. At best, the film can be considered Swiftian in its satire, practicing equal opportunity misanthropy. But the strongest defenses of *Fargo* have rested on its oddball humor and what Janet Maslin called "the uncharacteristic warmth" with which the Coens treat the principals (Maslin, C1). Paradoxically, *Fargo* may be the warmest, most hospitable film the Coens have made in spite of its frigid mise-en-scène. Apparently, these unusual aspects tended to conceal *Fargo*'s critique of white culture as well as its reinscription of ethnic stereotypes.

In perpetuating ethnic stereotypes, *Fargo* is not at all unusual in the context of mainstream cinema or even in the context of other films by the Coen brothers. Think of the grotesque caricatures of Jews in *Miller's Crossing* (1990), of Italian Americans in *The Man Who Wasn't There* (2001), and even of Germans in *The Big Lebowski* (1998). Among African American characters in the films of the Coens, the blues singer Tommy Johnson, based on the legendary Robert Johnson and played by the real-life blues artist Chris Thomas King, is a curiously undeveloped character in *O Brother, Where Art Thou?* (2000), a film that otherwise teems with flamboyantly eccentric white characters. The black bartender played by Samm-Art Williams in *Blood Simple* (1984) is somewhat less of a cipher, but it may be significant that his part was reduced so that he appeared in fewer scenes when the directors' cut of the film was released in 2000. The god-like but marginal Moses (Bill Cobbs), who tends to the gigantic supernatural clock in *The Hudsucker Proxy*, anticipates a set of later films with African American angels that will be the subject of the next chapter. Characters such as Moses suggest inflated versions of the familiar white fantasy of the loyal, asexual retainer who obligingly performs essential services for a powerful white man and then gets out of the way. Recall "the faithful souls" in *Birth of a Nation* (1914) who remain true to their virtuous white masters but who, as Linda Williams points out, are absent from the triumphant procession at the end of the film (116).

LOST SHEEP AND A WALKING BASS

If the majority of the films directed, produced, and written by Joel and Ethan Coen were too complex to please large audiences, *Fargo* showed that the brothers could make a much more successful film. *Fargo* won Oscars for its original screenplay and for Frances McDormand's performance, as well as awards in Britain, Australia, and France and a Best Picture award from the prestigious New York Film Critics Circle. If anyone other than the Coens deserves credit for making *Fargo* more mainstream, it is surely Carter Burwell. His music brings a stateliness to the white characters, even the most unsavory among them. Burwell's score for *Fargo* gives the film the kind of *gravitas* that most award-granting groups demand when they honor a film. The music also tells audiences that they are experiencing something more than light entertainment.

Burwell studied architecture at Harvard University before indulging a fascination with rock and electronic music. In the 1980s, he played keyboards in some of the rock groups that flourished in downtown New York at the Mudd Club, CBGB, and other venues. When the Coens met Burwell through mutual acquaintances, they were looking for a composer who would work within the extremely low budget for their first film, *Blood Simple*. Although they contacted other composers, the Coens were sufficiently impressed by the themes that Burwell first sketched out for them that they hired him in spite of his total lack of experience as a composer for films (Kenny 272). Burwell has since written music for every one of the Coens' films. He has also become an extremely sought-after film composer in his own right; his prestige projects now include *Conspiracy Theory* (1997), *The Spanish Prisoner* (1997), *Gods and Monsters* (1998), *Being John Malkovich* (1999), *Three Kings* (1999), Michael Almereyda's *Hamlet* (2000), *Before Night Falls* (2000), and *Adaptation* (2002).

Burwell has said that when a filmmaker comes to him with strong ideas about what he wants in a film, it usually means that he'll turn down the job. The Coens, however, seldom know what they want in the background score and have always given a great deal of freedom to Burwell. In addition, the Coens intentionally leave space for music during shooting and editing. A good example is Albert Finney's long gun battle with his would-be assassins in *Miller's Crossing*. When the film was released, the audience heard a newly recorded but carefully antiqued version of "Danny Boy" throughout the scene, both when the Finney character is listening to the recording in his bedroom and later when the music moves onto the full soundtrack and Finney fires a machine gun out on the street at the escaping car. The entire sequence was filmed with the idea that *some* type of music would dominate the soundtrack ("Carter Burwell in Conversation" 31–32).

In *Fargo* the Coens left spaces for the music to interact with their images when, for example, the audience is slowly introduced to the artifacts in the bedroom of Marge and Norm Gunderson and whenever cars drive past the altered statue of Paul Bunyan outside of Brainerd, Minnesota.[11] In filling these spaces, Burwell has said that he did not wish to emphasize the comic dimensions of the film because he wanted the audience to believe in the *truth* of the story. (He did not seem to be concerned that the Coens had de-liberately misled viewers with their claim that *Fargo* was based on truth.) Burwell also looked for ways to capture the "desperate cheerfulness" of many of the characters. Ultimately, he decided that "this music is going to say 'Yes, I am a crime drama and I am going to take myself seriously.' This allowed me to play the drama and make that believable, but, by the music taking itself too seriously, I was also able to push the comedy" ("Carter Bur-well in Conversation" 35). He compared the music he wrote for *Fargo* to the work of Miklos Rozsa, specifically the music for small orchestra that the classical Hollywood composer wrote for the low-budget crime drama *The Killers* (1946).

For an effect more appropriate to the locale of *Fargo,* Burwell listened to Scandinavian music, particularly *hardanger* fiddle music, which had an "icy" quality he found fortuitous. He chose an old Norwegian folk tune called "The Lost Sheep" that seemed exactly right for the character of Jerry, both in its sound as well as in its title (Kenny 276). "The Lost Sheep" is played on the fid-dle after the harp introduces the film and Jerry's car emerges from the white-ness. For me, Burwell's orchestration of "The Lost Sheep" recalls the Celtic music in Stanley Kubrick's *Barry Lyndon* (1975). Kubrick is an important in-fluence on the Coens, who often refer to his work in their own films.[12] Ancient folk music from England was historically appropriate for *Barry Lyndon,* but it also achieved the classic Kubrickian effect of bringing musical beauty to char-acters and situations that were, at best, corrupt.[13] Since the action of *Barry Lyndon* is set in England, the music had the proper Anglo-Saxon resonance. In the contemporary United States, however, the music of northern Europe has the effect of privileging the heritage of the white people, even if many other aspects of *Fargo* are highly critical of these people.

Although Burwell says he chose "The Lost Sheep" as a theme for Jerry, the same music played on the same mournful fiddle also becomes the music of Marge Gunderson. We first see her with her husband, Norm, after the camera pans across images of ducks and artist's materials and then arrives at the Gunderson's bed with its simple wooden headboard. The music contin-ues to play as the camera closes in on Marge sleeping on pure white sheets. At thirty-three minutes into the film, *Fargo* has arrived at its moral center. "The Lost Sheep" now belongs as much to its heroine as it does to Jerry Lunde-gaard. The theme lends dignity to both.

Burwell has not given a source for the other theme that dominates his orchestral score. Almost surely Burwell's own composition, it recurs throughout
the film, always in connection with the kidnappers Carl and Gaear. In the
notes to the soundtrack CD, the various versions of the theme are called
"Moose Lake," "The Ozone," "Dance of the Sierra," and "Paul Bunyon" [sic].
The music implies mischief within an overall ominous setting. Written in
waltz time, the music consists primarily of whole notes played by strings while
reeds, a harp, or a synthesizer develop more melodic material. In addition, it
always includes a "walking" bass line. This kind of bass pattern is not completely absent from European classical music. It can be heard in compositions
as diverse as Debussy's *Golliwog's Cakewalk,* Elliott Carter's *Cello Sonata,* and
Ralph Vaughan Williams's *Fourth Symphony.* Nevertheless, a walking bass
pattern is most typical of African American musics such as jazz, blues, and
boogie woogie. The walking bass is in effect the *only* sound that recalls blues
or jazz in a film that otherwise ignores black music. Intentionally or not, on a
subliminal level the film is associating the worst of its white characters with
African Americans. Burwell and the Coens have revised the practice of using
invisible black music to romanticize white people. While the blackness of
Miles Davis and "So What" turns the white teenagers in *Pleasantville* into adventuresome rule-breakers, the walking bass submerged in *Fargo's* soundtrack
seems to tell us simply that Carl and Gaear are up to no good.

   While James Horner's music for *Ransom* is entirely functional—what
Claudia Gorbman would call "invisible and 'inaudible'" (73)—almost all
of the music in *Fargo* has extra levels of signification, consistently calling
attention to the banality of the white characters' lives. Virtually none of
the popular music on the soundtrack references the black-inflected traditions that are now most typically American. Jerry's son, Scotty, even plays
the accordion, an instrument associated most readily with the insipid
music of Lawrence Welk, the polar opposite of the earthy traditions of
African American musics. Early in the film, after the first taste of Burwell's
"The Lost Sheep," Jerry walks into the King of Clubs bar looking for Carl
and Gaear while Merle Haggard sings "Big City." Although it would be unfair to read the lyrics as racist, the song begins with the line "I'm tired of
this dirty old city," and includes the singer's plea: "Turn me loose, set me
free, somewhere in the middle of Montana." Not exactly a celebration of the
glorious rainbow of multicultural life in the inner city, the song celebrates

the freedom available in the upper Midwest, revealed by *Fargo* to be in fact cold and oppressive.

The other bits and pieces of music that are heard in offices, restaurants, and garages throughout *Fargo* include Muzak-like versions of "Do You Know the Way to San Jose?" "Up, Up, and Away," "Feels So Good," and "Tie a Yellow Ribbon 'Round the Ole Oak Tree," all of which convey even blander versions of the American utopianism expressed in Haggard's song. When Marge meets Mike Yanagita at the Radisson, the music is "Sometimes in Winter," originally written by Steve Katz for the rock group Blood, Sweat, and Tears but played here in the style of cocktail piano. The song provides some contrast to the more upbeat songs such as "Up, Up, and Away" and "Feels So Good." The lyrics to "Sometimes in Winter" narrate the singer's painful memories of a lost love, thus making the song thematically apposite to the sad stories that Mike tells Marge. But the lyrics are absent in the version of the song the audience actually hears, and it becomes just another piece of musical wallpaper.

While Marge and Jerry are associated throughout with "The Lost Sheep," and while Carl and Gaear have their own theme with the walking bass, Mike Yanagita only has a bit of Muzak in the background. Similarly, when Jerry enters the garage for a desultory conversation with Shep Proudfoot, a distant radio is playing Nancy Sinatra's recording of "These Boots Are Made for Walking." The music playing behind both of the disenfranchised characters definitively places them within a world where Middle American mediocrity sets the tone. The presence of José Feliciano as the featured performer in the night club where Carl sips champagne with a prostitute has the ironic effect of casting him as a distinctly "ethnic" presence in *Fargo*, even though Feliciano left Puerto Rico at age five and grew up in New York listening to rock 'n' roll, blues, and jazz.[14] Although he has regularly recorded music that embraces his roots in Latino culture, Feliciano has built his career on reaching out to a mainstream audience in white America. His most successful recordings were "Hey Jude," "California Dreamin'," and "Light My Fire." In *Fargo*, however, Feliciano seems flamboyantly exotic.

MARGE AMONG THE OUTCASTS

As played by Steve Park, Mike Yanagita recalls Richard Barthelmess's "Yellow Man" in D. W. Griffith's *Broken Blossoms* (1919) and even Mr. Yunioshi (Mickey Rooney) in Blake Edwards's *Breakfast at Tiffany's* (1961). He is another weak Asian man aspiring unsuccessfully to connect with a white woman. For the sake of historical specificity, I should point out that *Fargo* appeared just before Asian actors began making their mark in Hollywood films as powerful leading men. When Hong Kong actors and directors migrated to the United States after the British departure from their former protectorate in 1997, the American cinema was quickly populated with Asian men deploying their martial skills. But one year earlier, in 1996 when *Fargo* was released, a taste for movies starring Asian action stars was still confined to a small circle of true believers in the United States. Even *Dragon: The Bruce Lee Story* (1993), which actually dramatizes the young Bruce Lee's disgust at Mickey Rooney's portrayal of an Asian man in *Breakfast at Tiffany's,* did little box office in the United States.[15] The regular presence of Asian action stars in American films probably begins with Chow Yun Fat's roles in *The Replacement Killers* (1998) and *The Corruptor* (1999). Jet Li would not appear as the indomitable kung fu expert in *Romeo Must Die* until 2000. Sammo Hung had a brief run as a martial arts master in the television series *Martial Law* in 1998. Also in 1998 Jackie Chan found a large American audience with *Rush Hour,* followed by the hugely successful *Rush Hour 2* (2001). The recent success of these films, however, should be contrasted with the box office failure of an earlier attempt to make Jackie Chan into an American star in *The Protector* (1985), not to mention *Big Trouble in Little China* (1986), John Carpenter's unsuccessful endeavor to dress up an American action film with Asian martial arts. Earlier, in 1969, Bruce Lee himself played an incompetent, easily destroyed assassin in the film *Marlowe*. Japanese Americans were virtually nonexistent in American films when *Fargo* appeared in 1996. As for Japanese imports, the poetic but strongly violent cinema of Kitano "Beat" Takeshi that found a cult audience in the United States at the tip end of the last millennium was almost completely unknown when *Fargo* was made. The early action films of Kurosawa, such as *The Seven Samurai* (1954), *Yojimbo* (1961), and *Sanjuro* (1962), were known primarily to art house audiences, although John Belushi regularly imitated Toshiro Mifune's samurai heroes on *Saturday Night Live* in the 1970s. Consequently, at the time of *Fargo*'s release, there were no well-known traditions of cinematic Asian heroics, certainly not of the Japanese variety, that cried out to be parodied or somehow revised with the character of Mike Yanagita.[16]

Mike is easily the weakest character in *Fargo*. Jerry Lundegaard is a miserable loser, but at least he has a family and a job. Mike has neither family nor job but insists that he works for Honeywell as an engineer (a stereotypical job for an Asian American man) and that he was married to Linda Cooksey. He adds that she has since died of leukemia. He then makes a pathetic attempt to romance Marge, even though he knows that she is married and can clearly see that she is seven months pregnant. And of course he has chosen to make a play for an idealized woman from his past rather than a woman in the present with whom he might be better acquainted. At the end of the scene he breaks down and cries, pathetically exclaiming, "I'm so lonely." In a subsequent scene Marge learns from an old friend that Mike never married Linda Cooksey but in fact harassed and "pestered" her, that Linda is still alive, and that Mike had "psychiatric problems" and is now living with his parents. Immediately after making these discoveries Marge drives wide-eyed to a fast food restaurant while "The Lost Sheep" plays on the soundtrack. The music could be referring to the lost soul Mike Yanagita as well as to the mood created within Marge by what she has learned about him. Marge's face, however, betrays no emotion at all, and she may only be thinking about food. We do not know if Marge has been touched by her experience with Yanagita, and he is never mentioned or seen again as *Fargo* moves toward its conclusion.

At the other end of *Fargo*'s racial continuum stands Shep Proudfoot. Just as Mike Yanagita makes Jerry look determined and capable, Proudfoot makes the killer Gaear Grimsrud seem relaxed and restrained. Marge has threatened Proudfoot with a return to jail because a call to his phone has been traced to a man (Carl Showalter) linked to the killing of a police officer. Shortly thereafter, a raging Proudfoot bursts into the motel room where an exceptionally purposeful prostitute sits atop Carl, coaxing him toward full erection. Earlier, at the performance by Feliciano, Carl was failing miserably to be a sophisticate with a glass of champagne and a beautiful woman. Now failing to be the phallic male in bed with a woman, Carl nevertheless berates Proudfoot for the interruption—"What the hell ya doin'? I'm banging that girl." Unfazed by Carl's claims, Shep beats him mercilessly with his fists and his feet. He throws Carl across the room and strangles him with a belt until his eyes bulge. He then uses the belt to whip Carl's naked back. Throughout the scene, Shep loudly utters an unending series of curses and insults. The masculinity of Carl, who appeared as the tough guy when first approached by Jerry and then as the debonair lover with the prostitute, is exposed as nothing but a performance during his encounter with Proudfoot.

Just as Proudfoot strips away the fake masculinity of Carl, Marge thoroughly strips away Gaear's when she shoots him in the leg as he attempts to escape across the white plain. Although Gaear is capable of murder, the film never shows him in a prolonged state of anger. With his studied indifference and a cigarette dangling from his mouth, Gaear could be channeling Marlon Brando, or at least the Johnny Strabler of *The Wild One,* a key figure in the masculine presentation of men who see themselves as hipsters and/or outlaws. In a typically Coenesque moment of humor, we even see that Gaear has a degree of sensitivity when he pauses in the middle of his meal after a character in a television soap opera tells her lover that she is pregnant. His face shows real concern. In spite of his menacing exterior, Gaear is a bit softhearted, and his masculinity too is merely a performance. The Coens may be telling us that hip, Brandoesque tough guys exist only in American mythology. By contrast, Shep Proudfoot never reveals anything other than anger or contempt. A malignant and savage force of nature, he is the true face of American toughness.

Like Yanagita, however, Proudfoot is also a racial stereotype. I find it revealing that neither character ever sits across a desk from one of the other characters. The placement of a desk between two characters in a sharply defined power relationship is an important image in *Fargo* as well as in virtually all of the Coen brothers' films. Think of Paul Newman sizing up Tim Robbins in *The Hudsucker Proxy,* Michael Lerner's studio boss with John Turturro in *Barton Fink,* Gabriel Byrne with Jon Polito's Italian crime boss in *Miller's Crossing,* James Gandolfini interrogating Billy Bob Thornton in *The Man Who Wasn't There,* or even Trey Wilson's Nathan Arizona with Randall "Tex" Cobb in *Raising Arizona.* In each case, white people from different levels of society jockey for control and play games of intimidation. In *Fargo,* Jerry has a crucial meeting with his father-in-law, Wade, while he sits behind a desk. Very much the self-made man and the pompous patriarch, Wade uses his authority to continue what appears to be many years of intimidating Jerry. Marge has two tense confrontations with Jerry at his desk, ultimately inspiring him to flee from the Twin Cities altogether. Shep Proudfoot is never on either side of a desk throughout the film, and although Mike and Marge sit across from each other in a restaurant booth, Mike makes the anomalous move to sit on the same side of the booth with Marge. He is politely but firmly rebuffed by Marge, who returns him to his "place." Just as she was not afraid to threaten Proudfoot with jail, Marge is surprisingly firm with Yanagita.

BROTHERS AND MOTHERS

If the Coens are in fact exposing myths of American masculinity by ridiculing attempts by white men to be tough and/or hip, it makes sense that Shep Proudfoot and Mike Yanagita should be completely unlike any of the white male characters. But it is not clear to me why both are so completely beyond redemption. The Coens themselves have probably not decided how seriously they wish us to regard the racial and ethnic stereotyping in *Fargo*. Obviously, they are not concerned about being "politically correct" and may even have taken a certain pleasure in confronting the audience with ethnic stereotypes so offensive that they were effectively proscribed by the mid-1990s and hence permissible again. Perhaps the Coens were looking for humor in the fresh appropriation of old stereotypes. What is lacking is some critique of that stereotyping, even if it is not as thorough as the film's critique of white masculine pathology. Once Marge has been introduced into the film, the Coens can no longer hide behind their usual deadpan irony. As the moral center of the film, Marge possesses so much virtue that the film can no longer paint everyone in the upper Midwest as hopeless. The film's idealization of Marge also suggests that the Coens do not see the sufferings of Yanagita and Proudfoot as the result of white political structures, in which Marge plays a significant role. Even if the Coens do not care about the non-white characters, Marge should. Instead, she seems to have little sympathy for either. Her brief statement to Proudfoot that she understands his problems is quickly followed by the threat of charging him as an accessory to murder. And her reactions to the sad truths about Yanagita never go beyond her initial reaction: "Jeez . . . , well, jeez. That's a surprise."

Nevertheless, we are asked to regard Marge as a sincere character, perhaps the most sincere and likeable character in the entire Coen canon. Her substantial skill as a crime-solving detective coexists with a complete lack of pretension. We are allowed to laugh gently at her pregnant body clothed awkwardly in police gear, her huge appetite for junk food, and her unusual ability to consume an Arby's roast beef sandwich in close proximity to a bag filled with night crawlers for her husband's fishing trip. The film also pokes gentle fun at her compulsive use of the vocabulary of law enforcement ("He's fleeing the interview!") and at her range of facial expressions that may or may not be a policewoman's guileful way of showing an exterior much less sophisticated than what is behind the face. The mild quirks in Marge's character actually humanize her and make her even more lovable for audiences. We are also invited to have warm feelings for Norm, Marge's balding, overweight husband, who nurtures her almost as much as she nurtures him. At the same time we can admire her independence or simply look the other way when we learn that she may not be telling Norm the whole story of her assignation with Mike Yanagita, including her purchase of a new dress for the occasion.

Joel Coen has of course been living with Frances McDormand since 1984, the same year in which she starred in the Coens' first film, *Blood Simple*. They were married in 1993 and subsequently adopted a child. McDormand has played relatively small roles in *Raising Arizona* and *The Man Who Wasn't There*. She also took a brief, uncredited part in *Miller's Crossing* while working regularly on her own in over twenty-five films by other directors. But the Coens handed her a plum part in *Fargo*. Few husbands have given their wives a gift as unique and rewarding as the part that Joel Coen gave to Frances McDormand.

The Coens' idealization of Marge is even more remarkable given the film's attitude toward its other female characters. Marge is the only woman in *Fargo* treated with any sympathy at all. We are invited to feel little or no compassion for Jerry's kidnapped wife, Jean, as when we learn almost in passing that she has been killed. The three prostitutes introduced in a few scenes are broadly caricatured. The other films of the Coens often follow this pattern of presenting one and only one idealized woman. Holly Hunter's Edwina in *Raising Arizona* is satirized, but like Marge in *Fargo,* she is the moral center of the film as well as an honest cop. Verna (Marcia Gay Harden) in *Miller's Crossing* is a prostitute, but she too has powerful convictions and is completely devoted to her brother. Even Jennifer Jason Leigh's character in *The Hudsucker Proxy* is a woman capable of compassion and feeling who hides desperately behind a tough, Katharine Hepburn-career-girl facade until she finds a man she can love.

A psychoanalytic reading of the Coens' female characters might involve the unconscious pressures on artists who share the same mother. When brothers talk about women, they tend to slip into a more guarded mode than do men unrelated by blood. The specter of the mother is present in the mind of any man who generalizes about women. To avoid the fantasied catastrophe that follows every male child into psycho-social development, the son must renounce the mother and assimilate the values of the father. But the sweet memory of the mother's body and the corresponding anxiety about the punishing father never really goes away; though pushed back into the unconscious, these feelings maintain their power in the inner life of the adult male. To prove that he has resisted the perilous return to the mother's body, the adult male is likely to disparage or degrade women both in his private conversations with other men and, as feminist critics have pointed out, in countless works of literature, art, and cinema. Most men maintain a rigid distinction between the mother and the whore, with the latter category most often representing women in the abstract. The man's mother remains the only pure woman, so completely has any contemplation of her sexuality become taboo.

The situation is different with brothers, who have experienced the oceanic feeling at the breast of the same woman, and whose most abstract statements about women take them back to the same idealized female. When brothers engage in artistic creation together, they may unconsciously suppress conventional male attitudes about women and join together in creating an idealized woman. Once that woman is in place, they are free to fall back on more traditional attitudes, as the Coens seem to have done when they wrote the other female parts in *Fargo*. Along these lines, we might consider the idealized freedom fighter played by Carrie-Anne Moss in *The Matrix* (1999), directed by the Wachowski brothers and the irresistible Carlotta (Isabelle Huppert) in *Elective Affinities* (1996), directed by the Taviani brothers. Consider also the resourceful and charming stewardess played by Julie Hagerty in *Airplane!* (1980), directed by the Zucker brothers and Jim Abrahams. Perhaps the purest example of an ideal woman created by movie-making brothers is Cameron Diaz's eponymous heroine in *There's Something about Mary,* directed by the Farrelly brothers in 1998. In a film notorious for its gross-out humor, Mary remains angelic from beginning to end. She alone is spared the humiliations, pratfalls, and ridicule directed at virtually every other character in the film.

If in fact the character of Marge in *Fargo* is inflected by the unconscious dynamics of fraternal co-creation, some of the film's more troubling aspects come into sharper focus. For me, the degree to which Marge appears unfazed by the evil and suffering in her world is the most implausible aspect of the film. Just as she seems to forget almost immediately the revelations about the painful life of Mike Yanagita, she seems merely puzzled by the carnage at the house by Moose Lake where Gaear has murdered both Jean Lundegaard and Carl Showalter and then forced most of Carl's body through a wood chipping machine. Once she has apprehended Gaear, she naively lectures him about the meaning of existence: "There's more to life than a little money, you know. Don'tcha know that?" Smiling slightly, she adds, "And here ya are. And it's a beautiful day." As the sad violin picks up "The Lost Sheep," she says, more to herself than to the taciturn Gaear, "I just don't understand it." As the perfect maternal imago, the sordid realities of life cannot violate her wholesome spirit.

The loving home of Marge and Norm has virtually nothing in common with the violent, hate-filled world outside. In this sense, *Fargo* perfectly accommodates Hollywood's familiar project of rigidly separating public and private spheres, with love completely confined to the private. As Anna Kornbluh has argued, Hollywood films encourage us to feel good about loving couples but do not acknowledge the unpleasant reality that love must be kept out of the public sphere if capital is to continue functioning smoothly. In the final scene, when Marge crawls into bed with Norm, he announces that his painting of a mallard duck will appear on a new three-cent stamp. He is upset because he did not get the twenty-nine center (for a typical letter in 1996). Marge consoles him by explaining the importance of three-centers when postage rates go up. As they cuddle, Marge says, "We're doing pretty good." The couple declare their love for each other, and as the film ends they each say, "Only two more months." Marge has apparently told Norm nothing about her discoveries at Moose Lake. She has also probably neglected to mention Mike Yanagita. But as the filmmakers are surely aware, these are the events and the people in the world where Marge and Norm's child will be born. Cultural conservatives might applaud the trinity of Marge, Norm, and baby that will stand firm against a corrupt world outside. But the film promises that they will be entirely alienated if they wish to carry their innocence anywhere outside their home.

Now, it is true that the stolidly cheerful parking lot attendants, waitresses, and prostitutes in *Fargo* are not meant to be taken seriously. There is a mismatch between the fallen world that the Coens so purposefully document and the ideal family tucked into bed at the end, just as there is a mismatch between the film's initial claim to truth and the generic disclaimer in the end credits that "all characters and events are fictitious," etc. By the time we hear "The Lost Sheep" for the last time after Marge and Norm have expressed unproblematized anticipation of their child's birth, the music absorbs the aura of domestic bliss that has preceded it. Just as Carter Burwell had made the music tell us that the film takes itself seriously as a crime drama, the music now says that the movie takes itself seriously as the depiction of two middle-class white people safe at home in their Middle American home.

Similarly, *Ransom* ends with a likeable white couple in each other's arms while the consoling, Coplandesque music of James Horner on the sound-track tells us that their crisis is over. We can assume that the Mullens' child is back home in safety, just as we can assume that the Gundersons' child will be lovingly nurtured after it is born. Typical of even the most traditional good guy/bad guy stories, the two films send out a variety of messages. We can find flaws in the character of the hero in *Ransom*, just as we can, like many of the people with whom I have discussed *Fargo*, find forebodings of trouble in that final conversation between Marge and Norm. For most audiences, however, the message is clear. Both couples, each with a beloved child, have done what is necessary to enjoy the privileges available to white people in the United States. The affluent domain where the Mullens prosper is not a place where Lonnie Hawkins is welcome, just as the warm, loving home of the Gunder-sons is no place for Mike Yanagita and Shep Proudfoot.

CHAPTER FIVE

Black Angels in America

Millennial Solutions to the "Race Problem"

I n an episode of *The Simpsons* broadcast in 2002, Homer, Marge, Bart, Lisa, and Maggie have nothing left to do after their television breaks down except disturb the peace. Arrested and confined to a singe cell, the family is visited by an African American social worker in a white suit. The voice of the social worker is provided by Delroy Lindo, whose soothing voice belies the menacing exterior he has projected in many of his film roles, including *Ransom* (see chapter four). Because of the voice and the white suit as well as the unmistakably celestial music that accompanies the social worker's entrance, Homer mistakes him for an angel. Although the visitor quickly turns off his pager with its sounds of heavenly choirs and introduces himself as a social worker, Homer is still convinced that the man is an angel. Marge apologizes, explaining that her husband has seen too many movies.

Even people who only saw a few movies at the end of the twentieth century might share Homer Simpson's conviction that African American men walk the earth as angels. While many of the films discussed in earlier chapters use the "magic" of African American romance and sexuality while keeping black bodies entirely off the screen, a substantial number of films prominently feature impossibly gifted black characters who only want to put their special powers at the service of attractive white people. Consider, for example, three films released in 2000 alone: in *The Legend of Bagger Vance,* Will

Smith carefully extracts Matt Damon from a life of despair and lays open the mystical truths of golf and life; in *Bedazzled,* Brendan Fraser receives heavenly wisdom from a black actor with the angelically correct name of Gabriel Casseus; and in *The Family Man,* Don Cheadle, a tough ghetto dweller with attitude and a gun, replaces cuddly old Clarence (Henry Travers) in a haphazard remake of Frank Capra's *It's a Wonderful Life* (1946).

The films in this chapter take the familiar conventions of Hollywood realism and shift them toward fantasy, where ideology is always more readable. When white filmmakers cast black actors as angels, they are free to displace the realities of African American history into more viewer-friendly narratives. They can also create scenes of easy and unproblematic black/white reconciliation, often providing the audience with an emotional, even cathartic moment. For most audiences, these reconciliation scenes are most effective when racial, social, and cultural formations remain unmentioned and unquestioned. Thus, the white protagonist inevitably remains the central figure, and the black angel unselfishly moves heaven and earth to keep it that way. The African American characters in these films are not necessarily placed below the central white people; they are simply placed outside the hierarchies dominated by whites. The result, intentionally or not, is that audiences are less likely to notice the old structures of power still standing just outside their field of vision. On one level, this basic narrative appeals to legitimate feelings among whites and blacks alike that the races can and should live together productively. On another level, it reflects a serious racial crisis in American life so unpleasant that it must be replaced by fantasy. Worse, the black angel films reinforce the same racist ideologies that continue to keep most white people in places where blacks are absent and unwelcome.

One place in which black people *are* welcome according to these same ideologies is the American prison system, where African American men are increasingly overrepresented. *The Green Mile,* based closely on a novel by Stephen King, directed by Frank Darabont, and released in 1999, provides an excellent introduction to the black angel phenomenon if only because its displacements of white anxieties about African American men are so transparent. The film even takes the extraordinary step of representing the execution of its African American angel (Michael Clarke Duncan). Although *The Green Mile* is set primarily in the 1930s in the southern United States, the film provides a virtual primer on white mythologies of blackness at the end of the twentieth century. As has long been the case with Hollywood films, especially those made after 1980, the fantasies that dominate a black angel film like *The Green Mile* are consistent with the "family values" that America's cultural right has so carefully constructed. Because these fantasy realms are especially hospitable to simple, even Biblical notions of Good and Evil, the films tilt heavily toward melodrama, which depends on purely good characters squaring off against purely bad characters.

As Linda Williams has argued in *Playing the Race Card: Melodramas of Black and White from Uncle Tom to O. J. Simpson,* white Americans tend to conceive of race relations primarily in terms of exaggerated virtue and villainy. In the white imagination, blacks tend to be either heroically suffering models of moral excellence, like Harriet Beecher Stowe's Uncle Tom, or vicious defilers of white women, like the renegade Gus in D. W. Griffith's *Birth of a Nation.* Williams designates these categories as Tom and Anti-Tom, both of which comfortably accommodate a large body of melodramatic books, plays, and films. Rather than demonize one and exalt the other, Williams sees Tom and Anti-Tom as two sides of the same melodramatic coin that feed off each other and are still with us today. Stepping outside the intensely mythological realm of twentieth-century American cinema, Williams argues that in the 1990s even the beating of Rodney King and the trials of O. J. Simpson were played out as Tom and Anti-Tom melodramas. Although the stories of both black men might have been written in shades of gray, King was at first portrayed as a suffering victim (Tom) until the defense team for the white police officers who beat him convinced at least one jury that King was a raging beast (Anti-Tom), appropriately subdued by officers of the law. Similarly, Simpson was characterized primarily as a dark monster (Anti-Tom) violently taking the life of a white woman, until *his* defense team argued successfully that he was the victim (Tom) of an insidious frame-up by racist cops.

Williams ends her book with a discussion of *The Green Mile,* which appeared just before the book went to press. For Williams, the story of the Christ-like African American behemoth John Coffey (Duncan) is an only slightly updated version of the Tom melodrama. Its representation of the intense sufferings of an innocent black man served the continuing need among whites to feel deep compassion for African Americans. (The extremes to which *The Green Mile* pushed this need may even have been partially responsible for winning Duncan an Oscar nomination.) But if the film displays a black man in pain so that whites can feel morally uplifted, it also assures white people that a huge black man who acts out forbidden moments of interracial sex is in fact put on earth to heal white people. The only time that John Coffey deploys his miraculous healing powers on something other than a white person is when he restores life to one inmate's pet mouse.

At a climactic moment toward the end of *The Green Mile,* John Coffey approaches the bed-ridden and dying Melinda Moores (Patricia Clarkson), the wife of the prison warden. Although Coffey has been unjustly imprisoned for the rape and murder of two little white girls, he has been brought to Melinda's bedside by a team of outrageously virtuous death row prison guards, led by Paul Edgecomb (Tom Hanks), who are convinced that Coffey can miraculously cure her cancer. As Linda Williams perceptively observes, many of the conventions of the Tom and Anti-Tom narratives overlap or are rearranged when Coffey approaches the white woman. To use Tania Modleski's phrase again, the film "arouses and contains" the audience's racial anxieties (77). At first, Coffey glimpses the white-clad Melinda through a crack in the door, as if he were a rapist about to steal into her room. The woman is lying on the bed moaning, her legs open and the hem of her nightgown lifted well above the knee. Coffey enters the room alone as she eyes him with suspicion. Deranged from the ravages of cancer, the woman taunts the giant with obscene sexual language—"Don't come near me, pig-fucker"— at the same time that she lifts one leg to expose her lower thigh.

But when John Coffey sits on the bed and brings his face close to hers, the film drops its generic forebodings of black-on-white rape, and Melinda speaks to him with tenderness. She asks his name and softly inquires about the many scars on his huge body.[1] The long, interracial kiss that she seems to accept willingly is quickly robbed of its erotic element by special effects teams from Industrial Light and Magic: viscous trails of light pass from her body into his as clocks stop, lights explode, and earthquakes rock the house. When Michael Clarke Duncan lifts his head after the long kiss, we can see that Patricia Clarkson's cancer makeup has been removed and that her movie-star face is glamorous once again. This moment in *The Green Mile* exploits America's unending anxiety about interracial sex at the same time that it reassures white Americans that a large black man kissing a white woman is in fact an enchanted moment of healing. The scene is played for maximum pathos and emotional effect, aided prominently by reaction shots of Melinda's husband and Thomas Newman's gushing background score.

Fig. 30. The gigantic but Christ-like John Coffey (Michael Clarke Duncan) wins the respect of prison guards in *The Green Mile* (1999, Castle Rock Entertainment/Warner Bros.). Photofest Film Archive.

Barely able to walk, presumably because he has taken Melinda's sickness into his own body, John Coffey is returned to his cell (fig. 30). Within moments, however, he does away with the film's two most unsavory characters. First, he breathes into the mouth of Percy Wetmore (Doug Hutchison), the only unsympathetic guard in the section of the prison designated "the green mile" because of a green floor stretching from death row cells to the electric chair. Percy torments even the most congenial prisoners, at one point rigging one electrocution so that the still-conscious victim bursts into flames. And true to his surname, Percy urinates into his trousers during a crisis. After receiving whatever it is that John Coffey has imparted with his breath, Percy marches zombie-like to the cell that holds "Wild Bill" (Sam Rockwell) and shoots him multiple times in the chest. It was Wild Bill, we soon learn, who raped and killed the two white girls, the crime for which Coffey was convicted. After shooting Wild Bill, Percy collapses into a state of permanent catatonia. True to the conventions of melodrama, these characters go to their fates in the same spirit of love and justice with which John Coffey heals white people. Because audiences have been rooting against these characters, they can feel good about themselves when Wild Bill is killed and Percy is confined to a mental institution.

But as Williams adroitly points out, audiences are also meant to feel good about themselves when Paul and the other lovable prison guards execute John Coffey near the film's conclusion. As in the Stephen King novel, Coffey's miraculous powers allow him to see and to feel the evil in the world. During an execution earlier in the film, Coffey cries out in his cell, his body jerking back and forth in unison with the man being electrocuted. And simply by touching Wild Bill, Coffey can see that he killed the two little girls. He is even capable of transmitting a well-edited short film about the crime into the mind of Paul, the prison guard played by Tom Hanks. The film cuts away from Paul, grimacing as John Coffey squeezes his hand, to a montage of images leading up to the moment when Wild Bill murders the two girls. Coffey insists that seeing and feeling the evil in the world has made him "tired" and that he seeks the release he will find in death. Paul and the audience are meant to take this statement at face value. We are not invited to enjoy the spectacle of an innocent man being executed, but neither does the film suggest that there is anything wrong with an American legal system that regularly executes innocent people and that has historically executed African Americans in much greater proportion than whites. Instead, the film ends with Paul as an old man, paying his penance for depriving the world of one of "God's great miracles." Paul understands that his divinely ordained punishment is a long life of seeing each new set of loved ones pass away. John Coffey and the forces that brought him to death in the electric chair are remembered in religious rather than political terms.

A touchstone film for placing *The Green Mile* more firmly in American political reality is *Monster's Ball* (2001), especially the early scenes that explore what is in effect the *etiquette* of capital punishment. The father-and-son team of white prison guards cannot agree on the proper amount of personal attention owed their African American prisoner, Lawrence Musgrove (Sean Combs). The older member (Billy Bob Thornton) of the team rigidly enforces a code of conduct that is incomprehensible to his son (Heath Ledger). The absurdity of carefully regulating the degree of humanity extended to a man about to be deprived of the most fundamental aspect of his own humanity is laid bare when the father upbraids his son for touching the prisoner and expressing interest in his drawings. But later, when the son collapses and vomits while Musgrove is being led to the electric chair (fig. 31), the father is even more outraged at the violation, striking the son and yelling, "You fucked up that man's last walk."

Fig. 31. Sean Combs goes for his last walk with Billy Bob Thornton (*right*) and Heath Ledger (*left*) in *Monster's Ball* (2001, Lee Daniels Entertainment). Photofest Film Archive.

Monster's Ball consistently foregrounds the power imbalances in race relations, not just in the execution of Lawrence by mostly white prison guards, but also in the final scenes in which Halle Berry, as Lawrence's impoverished widow, whose only child dies shortly after her husband's execution, comes to the sobering realization that she has few alternatives but to continue as the mistress of the man who carried out her husband's execution. Like most of the black angel films, *The Green Mile* elides all but the most superficial examinations of race in American life by placing its enchanted African American character outside the kinds of complex racial interactions we see in *Monster's Ball*.

SEXUAL HEALING IN BLACK AND WHITE

The Green Mile also belongs in the large group of late twentieth-/early twenty-first-century films in which African Americans enhance the sexuality of white people. In films as diverse as *Three Men and a Baby* (1987), *Se7en* (1995), *Jerry*

Maguire (1996), *That Thing You Do!* (1996), and *The New Guy* (2002), African American characters give authoritative advice to white protagonists about how to be better lovers, parents, and spouses. And of course, in *The Bridges of Madison County, Indecent Proposal* (1993), *Groundhog Day* (1993), and many others, whites make love onscreen while the music of black artists plays in the background. Early in *The Green Mile,* before John Coffey has performed his first miracle, Paul is suffering from a severe urinary tract infection. Late one night he staggers to the backyard in hopes of urinating in the outhouse but collapses in pain before he gets there. The next day, as Wild Bill is brought into the prison, he breaks loose from the guards and viciously kicks Paul in the groin. Left alone by the other prison guards, Paul collapses in front of Coffey's cell, immobilized by the overdetermined pain in his genital region. Speaking as always in Joel Chandler Harris English, Coffey calls Paul over to his cell and places his hand on Paul's groin. Just as audiences are distracted from the sexual elements of Coffey's kiss with the cancerous Melinda, the image of one man touching another man's penis is desexualized by the effect of light bulbs exploding and by the ominous music on the soundtrack.

After he releases Paul, John Coffey exhales a black cloud of what looks vaguely like swarming flies. Paul then wanders into the bathroom. The camera closes in on his face to reveal a look of blissful pleasure as the audience hears the unmistakable sounds of healthy urination. Quickly the scene changes to Paul arriving at his house, where his wife, Jan (Bonnie Hunt), is preparing dinner. He begins kissing her gently. Almost immediately the scene changes to an exterior shot of a bedroom window accompanied by the sounds of the couple making love. After a brief blackout to show that the couple's night of lovemaking has continued into the morning, Jan says, "Not that I'm complaining, but we haven't gone four times in one night since we were nineteen." These scenes with Paul and his wife take place less than four minutes after John Coffey has put his hand on Paul's penis. Equally significant is the invisible presence of the African American jazz singer Billie Holiday, whose 1937 recording of "I Can't Give You Anything but Love" plays on Jan's radio when Paul first looks at his wife and begins kissing her.

Although not at all unusual, this scene is a blatant example of how Hollywood uses black sexuality to raise the level of romance for whites. John Coffey has simply said that he wanted "to make it better," easing the pain in Paul's groin. He has, however, managed to accomplish much more, sending

Paul home with the sexual prowess of a teenager. As if Coffey's laying on of black hands were not sufficient, the sounds of a great African American vocalist are there to put the couple into the proper mood. In *The Green Mile,* however, the humanizing, sexualizing encounter between a black man and a white man literally takes place in the sphere of magic.

ANGELIC HISTORY

Black angels have appeared in American films at least since agents of the Lord came to rescue the soul of Little Joe (Eddie "Rochester" Anderson) after they heard "the powerful praying" of his wife, Petunia (Ethel Waters), in *Cabin in the Sky* (1943). In the 1940s, racial segregation extended even to the movie screen, and like many films of the era, *Cabin in the Sky* exists in a universe without white people. So black angels descend only to help black people. In more recent cinema, Harry Belafonte plays the title role in *The Angel Levine* (1970), based on a short story by Bernard Malamud. In the twenty-first century, *The Angel Levine* seems as ancient as *Cabin in the Sky*. It recalls a moment in American history when studio executives were willing to take chances on offbeat projects. With a startling, modernist score by William Eaton, the film features avant-garde effects like the black-and-white fragments that interrupt the color narrative to show what the Jewish tailor Mishkin (Zero Mostel) witnessed earlier in the day when a man died on the streets of New York. *The Angel Levine* was directed by the expatriate Hungarian Ján Kadár, whose most widely known film was *The Shop on Main Street* (1966). The film was written by Bill Gunn, who would later write, direct, and act in the extraordinary vampire/blaxploitation/art film *Ganja and Hess* (1972). Part of the financing for *The Angel Levine* was provided by Harry Belafonte's own production company. In many ways the film is even more complex than the brief story by Malamud. This was truly the "independent cinema."

As *The Angel Levine* begins, Mishkin has a fight with his bed-ridden wife, Fanny (Ida Kaminska), during which she convulses and appears to die. Moments later, Belafonte appears in Mishkin's kitchen wearing a black leather coat and claiming to be a Jewish angel named Alexander Levine (fig. 32). Although there is no laying on of hands, Fanny is soon fully recovered and even capable of rising from bed to make Matzoh Brei for her husband and Levine. Nevertheless, there is some question as to whether or not Levine is really an angel who has succeeded in bringing Fanny back to life. He begs Mishkin to

Fig. 32. Levine (Harry Belafonte) attempts to convince Mishkin (Zero Mostel) that he is in fact an angel in *The Angel Levine* (1970, Belafonte Enterprises/United Artists). Photofest Film Archive.

believe in him, claiming that only then can he perform a miracle. Mishkin, however, remains unconvinced. So does the audience, especially since Levine seems much more human than divine, especially as he tries to resurrect a failed romance with a sensual black woman named Sally. The part of Sally is played by the distinguished stage actress Gloria Foster (fig. 33), who began her film career with short but memorable roles in Shirley Clarke's *The Cool World* (1963) and Michael Roemer's *Nothing but a Man* (1964), and whose last role before her death in 2001 was an engaging performance as the Oracle in *The Matrix* (1999) and *The Matrix Reloaded* (2003). (I will have more to say about Foster and the *Matrix* films later in this chapter.) As Sally, Gloria Foster brings out levels of sexuality, contrition, and desperation in Levine that were not apparent as he tried to establish his angel credentials with Mishkin.

Although Mishkin never believes in him, and although no miracles can unambiguously be attributed to Levine's works, the two men share a moment of intimate conversation and bonhomie over a bottle of wine and Fanny's Matzoh Brei. Finally, however, Levine disappears into the shadows when Mishkin insists once again that he cannot believe in him. The theme of the film seems to be the inability of man to understand God's plan, or at least a plan that must be articulated by one human to another. The film becomes an allegory for black/Jewish relations if not for the highly vexed nature of any interaction between people from different cultures. Nevertheless, the film suggests that people can indeed cross racial and cultural boundaries to find a common human bond, at least for a moment or two, as when Mishkin and Levine enjoy their meal together. For my purposes, the film is exceptional for fleshing out the character of the black angel every bit as much as the white man to whom he offers his services. More importantly, the film is *not* interested in validating resurgent white masculinity or in staging African American suffering for the sake of white liberal compassion.

In John Sayles's *The Brother from Another Planet* (1984), Joe Morton plays an alien traveling through space to evade an interplanetary police force. Except for his feet, with their unusually large toes, Morton's alien resembles an African American man. After his space vehicle happens to land in Harlem, the film leans strongly toward allegory when the two aliens who arrive looking for him are played by white actors. In a joke that runs throughout the film, the

Fig. 33. Gloria Foster, thirty-five years before she would appear as the Oracle in *The Matrix*. Photofest Film Archive.

alien "brother" gets through his days in Harlem without incident even though he never speaks. Simply because he is black, most of the people he encounters in Harlem assume that he is in the same predicament as everyone else in the neighborhood. And in a sense, their assumptions are correct. Ultimately, however, *The Brother from Another Planet* has more in common with *Cabin in the Sky* than with the other films in this chapter, if only because Morton's black alien uses his special powers only to help other black people.

If we consider the *current* rash of magical Negroes, a key figure is Oda Mae Brown, the bogus medium played by Whoopi Goldberg in the 1990 film *Ghost*, directed by Jerry Zucker. After the audience has seen her bilking several neighbors who have come to her in hopes of contacting deceased loved ones, Oda Mae is as surprised as anyone to discover that she can actually speak to the dead when Sam (Patrick Swayze) uses her to communicate with his wife, Molly (Demi Moore). *Ghost* was a huge sleeper hit, grossing more than $500 million after an initial investment of $22 million. The film made Demi Moore a major star, and when Goldberg won an Oscar for her role as Oda Mae, *Ghost* showed filmmakers exactly how black magic could lead to huge box office and a golden statuette. The message did not seep in immediately, however, at least in part because Whoopi Goldberg did not play Oda Mae as the ahistorical, supremely benevolent figure more typical of magical Negroes in subsequent films. Oda Mae is firmly situated in an African American urban community and, perhaps as a result, is reluctant to become involved in the affairs of the two white yuppies, Molly and Sam. Nor is she at all comfortable with the notion that one of the people she is helping out is dead. Of course, part of the thrill the film offers its appreciative audiences involves Oda Mae's softening to the charms of Molly, even kissing her on the mouth while Sam occupies her body. The homoerotic charge that goes with this thrill anticipates the scene in *The Green Mile* when John Coffey touches Paul Edgecomb's penis. Although not every film in the black angel genre has equally explicit scenes of homoeroticism, there is no question that the films respond to the polymorphous interracial sexual fantasies that circulate among audiences. Calvin Hernton is surely right "that all race relations tend to be, however subtle, sex relations" (7). On its surface, of course, *Ghost* is firmly devoted to idealizing the lives of upper-middle-class white people, and Oda Mae's initial reluctance to help the two lovers gives dramatic force to this project (fig. 34).

Fig. 34. Demi Moore became a star, but Whoopi Goldberg won the Oscar for *Ghost* (1990,Paramount Pictures). Photofest Film Archive.

By contrast, five years later, in the Coen brothers' *The Hudsucker Proxy* (1995), the god-like clock keeper Moses (Bill Cobbs) is not at all reluctant. In fact, he saves the life of Norville Barnes (Tim Robbins) without making his acquaintance. A minor character in the film, Moses is occasionally shown working by himself amidst the gigantic gears that drive the clock atop a sky-scraper from which several characters, including Norville, plummet dramat-ically. At one point in a film that plays fast and loose with the supernatural, Moses stops the gigantic clock after a spectacularly extended series of shots in which Norville plummets past what seems to be several hundred stories. Although Moses has not been told what knowledge Norville takes with him as he descends to certain death, the film implies that he is both omniscient and capable of stopping time. After inserting a broom handle into the clock's gears, he leaves Norville frozen a few feet from the pavement. Moses then looks at the camera and says, "Strictly speaking, I'm never supposed to do this, but have you got a better idea?" As I argued in chapter four, the Coens like to keep their irony unstable and have little interest in revising Hollywood's racial stereotypes. It is thus unclear why Moses cares about Norville or how he comes by his special powers. On the one hand, as in *Fargo*, the protagonist of *The Hudsucker Proxy* is not at all the familiar white hero whose masculinity is ringingly reaffirmed at the film's conclusion. On the other hand, as in *Ghost*, a magical African American character provides an impossible service for a desperate white person. At least in *Ghost* Oda Mae is paid for her contributions. In the Coens' film, Moses saves Norville but does not even receive a thank you.

By 1997, the English director Danny Boyle was surprisingly prescient in laying the groundwork for the many black angel films soon to come. Shortly after his art-house successes with *Shallow Grave* (1994) and *Trainspotting* (1996), Boyle came to the United State to direct *A Life Less Ordinary* (1997), in which a highly bureaucratized heaven administered by a white angel (Dan Hedaya) sends down a pair of subordinates to create a match between Ewan McGregor and Cameron Diaz. A few years before he loaned out his voice for the animated social worker on *The Simpsons,* Delroy Lindo played a charming, white-clad angel joined by Holly Hunter, also clad entirely in white and also devoted to fulfilling orders sent down from heaven. Lindo's blackness is never mentioned in the film, and although Hunter brings a large measure of free-floating sensuality to her part, sex between angels (or between angels and humans) is never a possibility. Lindo's character is thus sexless and his masculinity entirely free of menace. He just happens to be black, and the interracial couple of which he is a part just happens to be devoted to looking after a white couple (fig. 35).

But Lindo does at least interact with other characters in *A Life Less Ordinary.* The magic deployed by Bill Cobbs's character to save the life of Tim Robbins's character does not keep him from being almost completely segregated from the other characters in *The Hudsucker Proxy.* The only character in the film who directly addresses the audience, Moses functions as the narrator of the film, recalling the African American actor Louis Armstrong, who narrates *High Society* (1956), and the African American actor Nat King Cole, who sang (with Stubby Kaye) the narration in *Cat Ballou* (1965). In 2002, Taye Diggs plays piano and serves as the master of ceremonies in Rob Marshall's *Chicago* but otherwise has no role in the narrative. As is so often the case, black characters—magical or not—can be *in* the film but *outside* the action.

There are, of course, innumerable films in which black people are distinctly unmagical. It would be difficult to imagine, for example, anyone less magical than the accountant played by Danny Glover in *The Royal Tennenbaums* (2001).

Fig. 35. Delroy Lindo at his most angelic with Holly Hunter in *A Life Less Ordinary* (1997, Channel Four Films/Polygram Filmed Entertainment/Twentieth Century Fox). Jerry Ohlinger's Movie Material Store, Inc.

Nor has there been an end to films which pick up where *Birth of a Nation* left off. Audiences can still pay to see armies of suicidally murderous black men attacking lovable whites (occasionally alongside a few "faithful souls") in films such as *Black Hawk Down* (2001), the 2002 remake of *The Four Feathers*, and *Tears of the Sun* (2003). While the armies of autochthonous monsters in the first two episodes of *The Lord of the Rings* trilogy are not played by Africans (they are instead mostly computer generated), since the films were shot in New Zealand, some of the monsters were probably played by the country's aboriginal Maori people, not unlike the villainous Jango Fett (Temuera Morrison) in *Star Wars: Episode II—The Attack of the Clones* (2002).[2] The spectacle of dark-skinned, undifferentiated hordes attacking sympathetic white warriors has long been familiar to American audiences, and is probably best understood as the flip side of the black angels phenomenon.

"THE PACKAGE DOESN'T COUNT"

My primary concern in this chapter is the sudden appearance of a distinctly *magical* Negro in the predominantly white Hollywood of the late twentieth century. The character assumes a wide variety of guises, and whenever he— and occasionally she—appears, the film displays great ingenuity in separating the character from any real connection with African American culture. In Vincent Ward's *What Dreams May Come* (1998), for example, Cuba Gooding Jr. first appears in a white, V-neck sweater, looking very much the preppie as he welcomes Chris Nielsen (Robin Williams) to a heaven that resembles a child's fantasy more than Dante's Paradiso. Even when Gooding adopts body language and vernacular speech that suggests black culture, he seems to be playing at being black (fig. 36).

In a film that goes a long way toward validating official church dogma about suicide and its consequences in the afterlife, we learn that Gooding's character is not actually black and that the souls in heaven can choose how they wish to appear to newly deceased loved ones. Gooding is in fact playing the part of Chris's son, who had died in an automobile accident. Chris's daughter, who died in the same accident, first appears to him as an Asian woman (Rosalind Chao) before revealing her identity. When she finally identifies herself to her father, the daughter says that she was once with her father when he flew to Singapore and remarked how the Asian stewardesses were "lovely and graceful." She says that as a girl she thought, "When I grow up, I want to be that." The film is explicit about how a young white woman might regard Asian women as exemplars of exotic beauty and feminine submissiveness. But no one in the film suggests that a young white man might look to black men as models of masculinity or some other desired quality. Gooding explains that he has chosen to look like the doctor with whom his father, also a physician, had once interned. The son remembers that the black doctor was the "only guy you ever listened to."

Consistent with Hollywood's *faux* multiculturalism, *What Dreams May Come* argues for the complete irrelevance of skin color. The actual black doctor impersonated by Chris's son turns up later in the film played by the Swedish actor Max von Sydow. He too is there to help Chris adjust to heaven and eventually to bring his wife (Annabella Sciorra) back from hell, where she landed after committing suicide. In effect, the white protagonist is welcomed by a white man in blackface and a black man in whiteface. Nevertheless, Chris seems uninterested in why his son and his old friend should reverse colors. The old mentor first raises the subject, asking Chris if he knows why he has chosen to be white. Chris responds innocently and dismissively, "The package doesn't count. One's as good as the other." But the mentor replies, "The old baggage, the old roles of authority, who's the teacher, who's the father, gets in the way of who we really are." The film bypasses any confrontation with racial hierarchies by suggesting that boundaries within a profession pose a greater obstacle to self-actualization than does skin color. Furthermore, the

Fig. 36. In heaven, Cuba Gooding Jr. wears a V-neck sweater because he is not really black. With Robin Williams in *What Dreams May Come* (1998, Interscope Communications/Polygram Filmed Entertainment). Photofest Film Archive.

film suggests that colors are detachable from everything that goes with them and are in fact interchangeable. Thus, when Gooding speaks with the rhythms of an African American dialect, he could simply be deploying speech patterns that anyone—black or white—might adopt in a moment of enthusiasm. When Gooding speaks to Robin Williams in serious tones, he speaks without the African American accent and inflections. And when Max von Sydow talks to Williams, he sounds like an old actor with a Swedish accent, which in fact he is. Significantly, we are never told who welcomed von Sydow's black doctor to heaven when he first arrived.

In Brett Ratner's *The Family Man,* however, when the black angel played by Don Cheadle first appears in a small greengrocer's in urban New York, he immediately activates white fears about working-class black men. He wears a thick gold chain around his neck and a baseball cap with the bill turned backward. He uses gestures that many white Americans would associate with rap artists and other seemingly menacing types. Although he begins the scene in a jovial tone, claiming that he has a winning lottery ticket, Cheadle's character quickly turns sinister and brandishes a handgun. Cheadle is a versatile actor, capable of playing dangerous psychopaths (*Devil in a Blue Dress, Out of Sight*) as well as dignified patriarchs (*Rosewood*). When he portrayed Sammy Davis Jr. in the made-for-television film *The Rat Pack* (1998), he brought so much pathos and intensity to the role that he eclipsed the other performers as they attempted to re-create the personae of Frank Sinatra, Dean Martin, and Peter Lawford. Cheadle convincingly dramatized the pain that Davis suffered performing with white stars for whom the mere act of sharing the stage with a black man was a constant source of humor. In *The Family Man,* Cheadle puts all of his talents to work as he creates an angel who, for no particular reason, transforms the life of a prosperous white man.

A title card at the beginning of *The Family Man* tells us that it is 1985 as Jack (Nicolas Cage) and Kate (Téa Leoni) embrace passionately at an airport. Jack is leaving to begin an internship at Barclay's Bank in London. But Kate, brimming with the sincerity of an idealistic young woman about to enter law school, urges him not to go. She pleads with him to stay and begin a life with her immediately. Although Jack assures her that he is coming back and that a year in London will not change the love between them, a quick cut to thirteen years later shows him in an expensive apartment sharing a post-coital moment with a young red-haired woman who possesses few of Kate's wholesome qualities. In spite of his promises to Kate, Jack is now a wealthy finan-cier living alone and clearly enjoying the most expensive pleasures available to a single man in Manhattan. About twelve minutes into the film, Jack stops by the greengrocer's to buy eggnog. In the store, Cheadle's character (the credits refer to him as "Cash") is begging and cajoling the Asian counterman to give him cash for his winning lottery ticket. (We will later learn that Cash is testing the counterman to see if he is entitled to a miracle.) But although the action takes place on Christmas Eve night (part of the attempted con-nection with *It's a Wonderful Life*), the counterman is not in a holiday mood. Consistently hostile, he threatens to call 911 if Cash does not leave immedi-ately. Finally, the black man brandishes his gun and orders the counterman to look at what he continues to insist is a winning ticket. At this point, Jack offers to buy the ticket. Sensing that he can prevent violence, he says that he and Cash can make "a little business deal."

Cash responds to Jack's offer by pointing the pistol directly at his heart, holding the gun sideways in true gangbanger fashion. Adopting his most threatening tone, Cash says, "Stupid ass white boy in two-thousand-dollar suit gets capped trying to be a hero. News at 11:00. That's what you want to see?" Moving closer to Jack, cocking his gun, and speaking in measured tones, Cash twice asks, "Do you want to die?" When Jack softly replies, "No," Cash immediately becomes highly affable and agrees to sell the ticket. Out on the street in front of the store, Jack takes the ticket and gives Cash two $100 bills in exchange (fig. 37). Even though the gratified Cash has begun to walk away with the money (and the eggnog), Jack calls after him, asking him why he needs the gun. In one of the film's more preposterous ex-changes, Jack asks him if there is not some kind of program or "opportunity" that could change the life of an indigent black man, even one who had threatened murderous violence just moments earlier. Cash is amused, asking loudly, "Wait a minute. Are you actually trying to save me?"

It is never clear precisely why Jack wakes up a few moments later in total surprise, living the middle-class life with Kate in suburban New Jersey that the film suggested was once in store for him. But before he goes home to bed and wakes up in his alternative life, Jack tries to convince Cash to seek help. After Cash insists that he does not need to be saved, Jack says, "Everybody needs something." No longer speaking in the urban vernacular we heard in his first exchanges with the Asian counterman, Cash asks ingenuously,

Fig. 37. Nicolas Cage and Don Cheadle share a moment on Christmas Eve in *The Family Man* (2000, Beacon Communications/Saturn Films/MCA/Universal Pictures). Jerry Ohlinger's Movie Material Store, Inc.

"What do you need, Jack?" Although Jack replies, "Nothing," and insists that he already has everything he wants, Cash says, "But you just said everybody needs something." Cash then appears to make a decision. Perhaps he simply does not believe that Jack is totally satisfied with his current life. The angel may also be impressed by the sincerity with which Jack tells him, "with some honest hard work . . . *(pause)* . . . and possibly some medicine," he could have a better life. Or perhaps Cash wishes to reward a man who heroically and in-geniously found a way to stop another man from committing mayhem with a gun. Regardless, Cash clearly knows what the film knows—having a loving wife and children in a middle-class New Jersey suburb is superior to even the most affluent existence in Manhattan. Laughing, he says, "I'm really going to enjoy this." As the scene comes to an end, Cash says, "You just remember that you did this, Jack. OK? You brought this on your self. Merry Christmas."

If Cheadle played a down-and-out, potentially murderous homeboy in his first appearance in *The Family Man,* he resembles a well-heeled version of Shaft or Superfly when Jack next encounters him. Jack has had the pre-dictable confusion and panic as he first appears in the rambling house he is suddenly sharing with Kate, two small children, and a large dog. After no one recognizes him at his "old" apartment and office, he encounters Cash driving a fancy sports car on Park Avenue. It is in fact the car that once belonged to Jack. Wearing a handsome black leather coat, a white turtleneck, and no headgear, Cash explains to Jack that he must create his own solutions now that he is being given a "glimpse" of what might have been. Throughout their conversation, during which Jack tries to find a way back to his old life, Cash wheels the car aggressively through the New York streets. Cheadle's character is superficially as rooted in black culture as before, although at no time does he express any interest in anyone except Jack. Nor does he bother to explain why he is trying to convince Jack that his life would be better with a mortgage, a messy home life, and a drastically reduced income. For this, the screenwriters were clearly intent upon appropriating dominant "couple" ideology and connecting with audiences who can feel proud that they handle their own lives with children, pets, and a mortgage better than Jack as he tries to adjust to his new circumstances.

After sampling his new life, even his job selling tires, Jack inevitably discovers that this is what he wants. On the third and final occasion when Jack sees Cash, the angel is a clerk in a convenience store, wearing a red, short-sleeved polyester jacket over a white T-shirt. For once he resembles a man holding down a job rather than a Hollywood fantasy of black masculinity. At the convenience store, Cash takes a $1 bill from a white teenage girl who has purchased a bottle of Coke for 99 cents. He says, "Outta ten" and hands her nine dollars and a penny in change. He watches carefully as she slowly walks to the door, suppressing her surprise at receiving more money than she deserved. Cash expresses disappointment when she continues out the door without turning back. Like the Asian counterman in the earlier scene, the young white girl has apparently missed an opportunity to do the right thing and perhaps even receive a magical gift from a black angel. The film never raises the possibility that Cash might offer a similar opportunity to an African American.

By the time Jack approaches Cash in the convenience store, he has become so enamored of his new life that he begs not to be sent back. Cash explains, however, that he was only being given a glimpse of what might have been. Jack knows that he will soon be returned to his old identity, just as the audience knows that he will then seek out Kate and try to regain what he once had in his glimpse of bourgeois family life. As Jack leaves the store, Cheadle looks after him with benevolent satisfaction. Like Clarence in *It's a Wonderful Life,* he has succeeded in putting a white protagonist at the center of a highly idealized American family. Cash may even have earned the kind of promotion that Clarence received in Capra's film, although the orders of angels is a subject never broached in *The Family Man*.

A character who has much in common with Cheadle's Cash in *The Family Man* is the young black inmate (Gabriel Casseus) with corn rows and the beginnings of a goatee who counsels Eliot (Brendan Fraser) in Harold Ramis's 2000 remake of *Bedazzled*. Casseus makes the first of his two brief appearances after Eliot has been seeking a consultation with God. Eliot has been repeatedly duped by the Devil, played here by Elizabeth Hurley. He entered into the conventional sale-of-soul agreement when he decided there was no other way to get close to his dream girl, Allison (Frances O'Connor). Realizing that he may soon be going to hell without even living out his fantasies with Allison, the beleaguered hero wanders into a large Catholic church. A priest (Brian Doyle-Murray) tells him that there is nothing he could say that a priest would not understand. When Eliot begins complaining that the Devil has granted him seven wishes and that he has used up five although the Devil claims that he has actually used six, there is a quick cut to Eliot being led away in handcuffs by two policemen. To his surprise, the policewoman who leads him to his cell is Hurley's Devil. In *The Family Man*, Don Cheadle calls Nicolas Cage's character "Jack" before they have been introduced, but then disavows any special knowledge, insisting that he calls all white men "Jack." Similarly, in *Bedazzled*, Casseus is first heard leaning out of the shadows on his lower bunk and saying, "She's the Devil, that one." But when Eliot says, "What?" Casseus brushes off the remark by saying that the policewoman who brought him to the cell is a devil, as if to change the case of the "D" from upper to lower.

Evidently, Eliot's request to speak with God has been heard. The young man in his cell gives him crucial advice. Casseus wears the conventional prison-issue blue denim jacket and trousers, and when he begins his conversation with Eliot, he lights up a cigarette and takes a deep drag. He tells Eliot that he cannot in fact *sell* his soul because it does not belong to him. It belongs to "that universal spirit that animates and binds all things in existence." As he continues to give Eliot familiar religious advice about keeping his mind and heart open to God's plan, he could be any prison inmate who has found solace in Christian belief. Nevertheless, Eliot seems moved by his cellmate's words and the assured, measured cadences with which he delivers them. Eliot asks, "Who are you?" The reply: "Just a friend, brother. Just a really good friend." The black man then disappears back into the shadow beneath the upper bunk from which he originally emerged. Cutting back to Eliot on his own bunk, the film sets up a montage of Eliot in deep thought as the light changes to night and back again to day.

Released from prison, Eliot tells the Devil that he wants out of their agreement. In an elaborate show of special effects, conventional images of hellfire flash before Eliot. Hurley appears as a giant towering over him with a huge pitchfork. When she demands that he make his seventh and final wish, Eliot says simply that he wants Allison to live a happy life. In an awkward finale, the Devil immediately gives up, informing Eliot that an escape clause in his contract takes effect if he performs one selfless act. Eliot is then free to return to his old life, a changed man. Although Allison subsequently turns him down once he finally summons the courage to ask her to join him for a cup of coffee, he immediately meets her exact double, also played by Frances O'Connor but with a different hairstyle. In the last moments of the film, as the two lovers walk through Golden Gate Park, the audience gets its only other glance at Gabriel Casseus. He and Hurley, both dressed in white, are playing chess at a table near the sidewalk as Fraser and O'Connor stroll by. Once again a black angel is multiply removed from African American culture and deploys his powers only when a white person's soul is endangered.

In 2003, Hollywood took the black angel story to a new level and cast Morgan Freeman as a strangely attentive anthropomorphic god in *Bruce Almighty*. Primarily a vehicle for Jim Carrey, the film suggested that God not only listens to prayers but that he can be personally offended when Bruce (Carrey), a second-rate television reporter down on his luck, shakes his fist at the heavens and insists that he could do a better job of running things. God hands over all his powers and lets Bruce run the universe for a few days, presumably in order to teach him about humility and compassion. As God, Morgan Freeman is just about the only black person in a film that never explains why a god with the flesh and speech patterns of an African American man would waste his and the world's time on a middle-class white man like Bruce. Jim Carrey's need for a box office hit may be the most compelling explanation. At its conclusion, *Bruce Almighty* recycles the ending of the 2000 remake of *Bedazzled* when Bruce asks God to relieve him of the awesome set of responsibilities, of which he has begun to tire. Just as Brendan Fraser in

Bedazzled found an escape clause by asking that a beautiful young woman have a good life, Bruce pushes the right buttons with God when he declares that the one thing he most wants is a worthy husband for the lovely Grace (Jennifer Aniston), his estranged girlfriend. Thanks to God, Bruce has become that man. All the havoc randomly wreaked by Bruce during his tenure as God has become irrelevant.

RESEXING THE BLACK ANGEL

Although Whoopi Goldberg's Oda Mae in *Ghost* is surely the mother of Hollywood's black angels, almost all of the other movie angels have been male. The only exception I have been able to locate is in *The Matrix* (1999). In that film Gloria Foster plays the Oracle as a plainspoken old matriarch. When the audience first sees the Oracle, she is baking cookies while the Duke Ellington Orchestra's 1944 recording of "I'm Beginning to See the Light" plays in the background. Although she has many other superficial connections to African American culture, and although *The Matrix* does not fit comfortably with the pleasant fantasies offered by *The Family Man* and *What Dreams May Come,* the Oracle's purpose is consistent with those of her male peers in the other films. Her function is to prepare the white hero for his impending success, in this case over the nearly omnipotent "Agents," who resemble Mormons with dark glasses.[3]

The plot and premises of *The Matrix* are confusing if not incoherent, but it is clear that Neo (Keanu Reeves) will, after some spectacular special effects and slow-motion violence, lead the rebellion against malevolent forces that have somehow enslaved the human race. This alone makes the film wildly inconsistent with the other films to which Gloria Foster had previously contributed her talents. About halfway through the film, Neo is brought to see Foster's Oracle so that she can muster her precognitive powers and determine whether or not he is the One. White Americans have long regarded blacks as highly spiritual, at least since slaves first embraced Christianity. More recent versions of white mythology present African Americans as more secure in their beliefs and able to speak (and sing) with great authority in situations where whites are less emphatic (Griffin). And because they and/or their ancestors have endured greater hardships than the typical white person, blacks are represented as more effective at coping with misfortune and with dispensing soul-healing advice.

All of these notions are in play in *The Matrix* when Neo enters the Oracle's apartment. As we later learn from Morpheus (Lawrence Fishburne), the film's most important black male character, the Oracle is about to tell Neo "exactly what he needs to hear." In a sequence that seems designed to anchor the film more securely in the Asian martial arts genres from which it takes much of its action sequences, Neo is introduced to something entirely unlike African American spirituality before he is ushered into the Oracle's kitchen. Waiting in the living room, he briefly joins the other "potentials," a group of children with serious expressions on their white—occasionally Asian, but never black—faces. On the one hand, the children represent an assortment of Eastern religions as they occupy themselves in the Oracles's Western apartment. One child sits behind a book with Chinese characters that can be translated as "esoteric" and "wisdom." A child who is occupied telekinetically with bending spoons has a shaved head, a saffron robe, and a British accent as if to suggest Gandhi. He instructs Neo in the art of spoon-bending, explaining that the trick is to remember that there is no spoon. This is a piece of advice that Neo will rely on later when he realizes that the ferocious Agents are not real and that their bullets cannot harm him. On the other hand, the amount of firepower and physical violence that Neo will initially deploy to defeat the Agents and their armies seems well beyond the capacities of the fragile young candidates for his job in the Oracle's apartment.

The location of the Oracle's apartment on a narrow hallway with abundant graffiti on its cinder block walls places her firmly in an urban black working-class milieu. Grounding the Oracle in this setting further enhances · her image as a no-nonsense woman who can size up a person—especially a ᵊ white one—and then deliver whatever wisdom is needed at the time. That she · pulls no punches when she tells Neo that he is *not* the One while offering him a freshly baked cookie suggests that she is as maternal and nurturing as she is down to earth. In the logic of the film's narrative, all of this is an illusion and has been presumably constructed to give the right impression. But the film relies much more on white mythology than it may have intended as it places the Oracle in surroundings that would verify the film's tolerance for minorities as well as its blending of Eastern mysticism and African American spirituality. Hong Kong action meets Blaxploitation.

But, of course, the white hero really is the One. It's right there in Neo's anagrammatic name. The Oracle has told him that he will have to decide whether he or Morpheus, the leader of the resistance, will eventually have to die. Morpheus has already told Neo that the Oracle has said he "would find the One." We know this is true after Morpheus has suffered mightily for the rebellion. When he is apprehended by the Agents, a group of policeman with billy clubs flying surrounds Morpheus in a scene that strongly recalls the Rodney King beating. When Neo arrives to rescue him, Morpheus is manacled to a chair and wears the stupefied expression of a man who has experienced mental and physical torture. Although Linda Williams does not discuss *The Matrix* in *Playing the Race Card,* the sufferings of the resolute black man place these scenes firmly within the genre of "Tom melodrama." They also give white audiences additional reason to cheer the righteous violence of both the white hero and the powerfully adept white heroine (Carrie-Anne Moss) as they battle the Agents and their army to rescue Morpheus. Ultimately, the heroine reports to Neo that everything the Oracle told her has come true, presumably that Neo will save the resistance and that she will fall in love with him. Both the Oracle and Morpheus—not to mention all other black characters—are absent from the final moments of the film when the camera circles Neo on a busy street populated entirely by whites. Nevertheless, Morpheus and the Oracle have done their job in bringing the white lovers together and in establishing that Neo is the One.

The Matrix ends with the triumph of a white male, one who first appeared as an alienated and beleaguered office worker. Christopher Sharrett compares *The Matrix* to a pair of films also released in 1999, *Fight Club* and *End of Days,* all of them built around "male self-absorption" and a nostalgia for a better time before feminism and affirmative action. For Sharrett, *The Matrix* is "the *locus classicus* of neoconservative apocalypticism," ultimately relying on "a well-worn and incomprehensible messiah narrative to carry a jumble of special effects" (326). Although the sequels to *The Matrix* bring several new black characters into the story, even granting a few of them some degree of power, Sharrett's description is as accurate for the other films in the trilogy as it is for the first *Matrix.*

Neoconservative apocalypticism is also in play, although with tongue somewhat more firmly in cheek, in Kevin Smith's *Dogma* (1999). This is also the only Hollywood film in which a black angel has assisted a white *female* protagonist. Like *What Dreams May Come,* which also takes its theology more seriously than its irreverent surface might lead one to believe, Bethany

(Linda Fiorentino) is told that she alone has been chosen to save the world from an imminent apocalypse. Two rebel angels (Matt Damon and Ben Affleck) hope to exploit a loophole in supernatural law and return to heaven cleansed of a long list of sins they have been studiously acquiring for several thousand years. Meanwhile, the demon Azrael (Jason Lee) has managed to imprison God (played by the Canadian pop singer Alanis Morissette) in the body of a comatose man in a hospital. We are told that if God remains constrained while the angels return to heaven, it will somehow "negate all existence." In order to help Bethany accomplish her vital tasks, heaven sends down Rufus (Chris Rock), the thirteenth apostle of Christ. Rufus makes his first appearance in the nude, falling vertically onto the road where Bethany is attending to her disabled automobile.

   Dogma may go further than any other film in its attempts to disassociate an African American character from urban black culture while connecting him concretely with ahistorical religious fantasies. Although we do not know the past histories of John Coffey, Cash, or the Oracle, their daily participation in African American culture is less important than their miraculous connections with divine forces. With Rufus, however, we are told in no uncertain terms where he has spent the last twenty centuries prior to his abrupt appearance. Nevertheless, Rufus speaks in contemporary African American dialect, complains bitterly about the racial prejudice that has kept him out of the Gospels, and insists at one point that Jesus was black. He tells Bethany that he has come to help her stop the rebel angels in return for her help in getting the word out about serious omissions concerning race in the Gospels. At first, he is consistently angry with his situation and with the two foul-mouthed "prophets," Jay and Silent Bob, who have already joined Bethany (fig. 38). Since this is, after all, Chris Rock, it is easy to associate his anger with the outrage at mainstream white culture he usually expresses in his standup comedy routines.

   But in *Dogma*, Rufus's mission on earth is to help a white woman stop two white male angels and one white male demon from destroying the plans of a white female god. Once he has been traveling with Bethany for a while, Rufus becomes substantially less angry and soon delivers most of the film's religious messages. He is also the one who explains why Bethany has been chosen to stop the rebel angels. According to Rufus, she is "the Last Scion," the only surviving descendant of Christ's younger siblings. When Jay (Jason Mewes) asks if this means that Bethany is part black, Rufus simply glares at him, and the subject is dropped. But if Rufus is right, and if Christ did walk the earth as a black man, then questions about the extreme whiteness of Linda Fiorentino's skin are perfectly legitimate. At the conclusion, when Bethany succeeds in discovering the key to freeing God from the body of the comatose man and thus prevents an apocalyptic conclusion, Rufus is happy to return to the side of Jesus, once again outside of history and culture. He even appears to have abandoned his campaign to rewrite the Gospels by inserting himself and a black Christ.

NO LYNCHING ON THESE LINKS

Although all of the films in this chapter abandon credibility as they play out their fantasy scenarios, they faithfully observe certain conventions of Hollywood naturalism. In *The Family Man* or *Dogma,* for example, the audience would never see a character boarding an airplane with the name of an airline company that had gone bankrupt twenty years earlier. Nevertheless, these films contain much grosser anachronisms that audiences are not invited to notice, such as the color-blind deference with which Depression-era prison guards treat John Coffey in *The Green Mile.* Like *The Green Mile,* Robert Redford's *The Legend of Bagger Vance* takes place in the South in the 1930s and ignores the racial segregation that was so rigidly enforced during those years. Just as Paul Edgecomb and the other prison guards accord John Coffey the same courtly respect they pay to white inmates, Rannulph Junuh (Matt Damon) and the many other whites with whom he interacts seem completely oblivious to the fact that Bagger Vance (Will Smith) is black. But while John Coffey is mostly taciturn, never speaking up even to proclaim his innocence, Bagger Vance is not at all bashful about saying whatever is on his mind, even if it means insulting the dignity of Junuh. Somehow, both black men manage to escape lynching, a common practice in the southern United States that continued into the 1950s but that both films do not in any way acknowledge.[4]

Like Gabriel Casseus in *Bedazzled,* Bagger Vance emerges from the shadows and speaks directly to the problems confronting the white hero. For reasons that are never explored, Bagger takes a personal interest in absolutely nothing except helping Rannulph Junuh play a better game of golf. As a young man among the elite of Savannah, Junuh had been a world-class golfer prior to his induction into the army and his experiences on the bloody battlefields of the First World War. The film suggests that the war made him

Fig. 38. The last surviving descendant of Christ (Linda Fiorentino) with Rufus, the Thirteenth
Apostle (Chris Rock), and the two prophets (Kevin Smith and Jason Mewes) in *Dogma*
(1999, View Askew Productions/Lions Gate Films). Photofest Film Archive.

incapable of living among civilized people for several years, but that he is
fully capable of moving past the trauma once Bagger helps him focus on golf
again. Immediately after the war, Junuh disappeared from Savannah social
life as well as from the life of Adele (Charlize Theron), to whom he had been
engaged. He turns up much later, unshaved, shabbily dressed, and keeping
company with a group of heavy-drinking African American gamblers. When
Adele invites him to participate in a golf tournament with Bobby Jones and
Walter Hagen, the two greatest golfers of the day, he protests that he cannot
because he has "lost his swing."

In a film that goes to absurd lengths to find mysticism in golf, losing
one's swing takes on portentous meanings. Most notably, losing one's swing
means losing touch with white masculinity. Hoping to seduce the reluctant
Junuh into returning to the links, Adele strips down to her underwear and
prepares to have sex with him while Duke Ellington's 1930 recording of
"Mood Indigo" plays softly in the background.[5] Junuh, however, is either unwilling or incapable of accommodating her desire. The film provides a

closeup of his hand reaching up to touch her body. Before the hand makes contact, it goes limp and falls away, a metonym for Junuh's impotence. Within moments after Adele has expressed her disappointment and left, Junuh begins slugging away at golf balls in the dead of night. Moments later, Bagger Vance makes his first appearance and immediately starts providing Junuh with life-changing advice. Once again, a black man provides lessons in manhood to a white man. In fact, Bagger tells Junuh very little about how to swing a golf club. Instead, he points to mystical meanings in the most mundane aspects of golf, such as how the grass on a putting green responds to the movements of the sun. Bagger usually delivers lessons in vernacular sports philosophy, such as "The rhythm of the game just like the rhythm of life." At his most prolix, he has lines such as "See the place where the tides and the seasons and the turnin' of the earth all come together, where everything that is becomes one. You got to seek that place with your soul, Junuh. Seek it with your hands. Don't think about it. Feel it."

In spite of what is soon revealed to be his complete devotion to the salvation of Junuh, Bagger is not at all obsequious. At their first encounter, after Bagger has seen Junuh shank a few balls and then offered his services as a caddy, Junuh asks, "You a caddy?" Bagger replies, "Well, that depends. You a golfer?" When Junuh gets off to a bad start in the first days of his match with Jones and Hagen and says, "This is becoming embarrassing," Bagger smiles and answers, "Oh no, sir. It's been embarrassing for quite some time now" (fig. 39). Nevertheless, Bagger continues to pass on abstract but somehow effective bits of wisdom to Junuh, who eventually wins the tournament with a long putt on the final hole. Junuh has also, of course, regained his masculinity and once again become the lover of the beautiful Adele. Having restored Junuh's potency and swing, Bagger strolls off along a beach and out of the film. And as the two men agreed earlier, Bagger has provided his services for a mere five dollars. A white man has triumphed again, and the black man who made it possible does not even seek remuneration.

PARANOIA AND LONGING

The fact that so many Hollywood films have introduced an African American angel to a white protagonist is a testament to the film industry's ability to tell the same story from innumerable angles. The black angels in these films cut across the borders of class, gender, physical type, and conversational style.

Some suffer mightily in the traditions of the most intense Tom melodramas, and some invoke, at least at first, the extremes of Anti-Tom hysteria. The degree to which they are connected to some divine force also varies widely, running the gamut from Chris Rock falling directly out of heaven to Will Smith inexplicably sauntering in and out of Matt Damon's field of vision. All these beings share an overriding desire to participate beneficently in the lives of white people while pursuing no connection whatsoever with other African Americans. The films suggest that white Americans can like individual black people but not black culture.

I am not, of course, the only person besides the writers of *The Simpsons* to notice this similarity among recent films. The "Magical Negro" is regularly discussed in Internet chat rooms. In addition, Spike Lee has expressed strong sentiments on the subject. He told interviewers at *Cineaste,* "Michael Clarke Duncan tongue-kisses cancer out of a white woman and cures her. And in the end Tom Hanks offers to set him free, but guess what? He refuses to leave Death Row. He'd rather die with Hanks looking on. Get the fuck outta here! That's that old grateful slave shit." Lee also pointed out that lynching is never mentioned in *The Legend of Bagger Vance.* "If this magical black caddy has all

Fig. 39. Junuh (Matt Damon, *right*) refrains from lynching Bagger Vance (Will Smith, *left*) when he criticizes Junuh's golf game in *The Legend of Bagger Vance* (2000, Wildwood Enterprises/Dream Works Distribution). Photofest Film Archive.

these powers, why isn't he using them to try and stop some of the brothers from being lynched and castrated? Why is he fucking around with Matt Damon and trying to teach him a golf swing? I don't understand this! That is insane. What world was that?! Please tell me" (Crowdus 5).

Lee's candor is refreshing, especially since the fantasy of black angels assisting white characters seems to be as persistent as it is unremarked upon by the vast majority of working movie reviewers. The films surely appeal to some · unconscious wish among white people that must be repeatedly fantasized and ⸝ refantasized. On some levels, it is a very old wish. The black angel films of the 1990s could be updated versions of the many American stories in which a dark-skinned man is the loyal retainer to a white male hero. The list extends well into the past, long before Mel Gibson and Danny Glover began making interracial buddy films. As I suggested in chapter four, celebrated examples include Natty Bumpo and Chingachgook, Huck Finn and Nigger Jim, Ishmael and Queequeg, the Lone Ranger and Tonto, Jack Benny and Eddie "Rochester" Anderson, Tom Doniphon and Pompey in *Man Who Shot Liberty Valance* (1962), Rick Blaine and Sam in *Casablanca* (1942), Robin and Azeem in *Robin Hood: Prince of Thieves* (1991), and William Munny and Ned Logan in *Unforgiven* (1992). We could include a film such as *Dave* (1993), toward the end of which a black Secret Service agent played by Ving Rhames assures Kevin Kline's false but benevolent president that he would "take a bullet" for him. In *NASA/Trek,* Constance Penley adds Captain Kirk and Mr. Spock to the list.

The story of a white male and his dark male companion has even been subjected to genderbending in *The Long Kiss Goodnight* (1996), in which Geena Davis plays a female secret agent on the run assisted by Samuel L. Jackson's private detective. In general, however, these stories are about men. ⸝ Despite the implicit homoeroticism in the narratives, the pure, asexual love · between a white man and a colored man living outside the laws of Ameri- · can culture is a common fantasy. As Penley suggests, the long list of books · and movies about a white man bonding with a Native American or a black ⸝ man reflects a dream among whites that they can be redeemed by winning ⸌ the love and devotion of a single powerful, dark-skinned man. All those ⸌ centuries of hatred and oppression can be wiped clean by this one pure act · of love. If only it were so. ⸌

Needless to say, the people who run the Hollywood studios do not want to exclude a large paying audience of African Americans. Nor do they want to enrage this audience with the old appeals to white racism. In the 1970s, the studios used various strategies to lure African American audiences away from blaxploitation films, including the release of conventional Hollywood films starring interracial couples, like Richard Pryor and Gene Wilder. By the late 1990s, the studios were finding juicy roles for the large contingent of talented, often glamorous black actors. With few exceptions, the most successful in this group ended up primarily working in conventional films about white people. Most of these actors were surely delighted to have good parts in high-profile films. As Hattie McDaniel said to those who raised questions about her stereotypical role as a mammy in several films, including *Gone With the Wind* (1939), for which she won on Oscar, "I'd rather play a maid than be a maid."

At best, these films reveal a yearning among white Americans for reconcil-iation with their black brothers and sisters. Ella Shohat and Robert Stam make this case convincingly in *Unthinking Eurocentrism*. They argue that the appeal of films such as those addressed in this chapter touches "something deep within the national unconscious, a historically conditioned longing for interracial har-mony" (236). After cataloguing the daily manifestations of this yearning in places such as the "multiethnic camaraderie of Eyewitness News," Shohat and Stam recognize the challenge of translating "the utopian energies behind these consolatory representations of ethnic harmony into the necessary mobilization for structural change that alone can make racial equality a quotidian reality" (236). The fantasy of apolitical, enchanted blacks saving white heroes may ac-tually stand as an obstacle to structural change, reassuring audiences that there is nothing wrong with the old racial hierarchies.

Ultimately, these films provide a sad commentary on the hopelessness that surrounds race relations in the United States today. They suggest that on some levels white Americans are incapable of living comfortably with black Americans in the workplace, the school, the church, and the neighborhood. But because whites are no longer entirely comfortable with the old racist mythology, and because they are almost entirely dependent on blacks for their sports and popular music, they have latched onto these silly dreams about black angels. As Sharon Willis has pointed out, the glut of films that feature black judges and police superintendents is not just a sop to "political correctness" or an attempt to protect the cinema from charges that blacks only appear in the popular media as criminals. Willis sees black characters with legal authority as part of "paranoid fantasies that situate African Americans as the ones who know the truth about race, while avoiding any occasion for a reciprocated gaze that would cause the dominant culture to look at itself through another's eyes" (6). If Willis is right—and I think that she probably is—Americans suspect on various conscious and unconscious levels that blacks have a great deal of insight into white behavior and that they are judging us. The more recent, more pleasant fantasy is that even if African Americans are in fact judging us, they nevertheless find us to be worth saving. If only it were so.

PART THREE

UNREPRESENTABLE SUBJECTS

Evidence

Thelonious Monk's
Challenge to Jazz History

I n America, the mainstream cinema and even "independent" films such as
Dogma and *The Hudsucker Proxy* have no difficulty creating magical black
characters who use their special powers to save white people. For audiences
unnerved by the sight of a black person but uplifted by their voices, the film
industry regularly addresses their joys as well as their anxieties. And ever
since Griffith immortalized the Klan in celluloid, the American cinema has
specialized in demonstrating the many ways that white characters are superior to black characters. When it comes to representing the lived experience
of African Americans, however, only a handful of filmmakers seem interested, and most of them are black. (Chapters eight and nine in this book are
about Spike Lee's *He Got Game* and Robert Altman's surprisingly thoughtful
Kansas City. Both films attempt to get below the surface of America's racial
mythologies.) Although there are a handful of small-budget films and documentaries on figures as crucial to American history as Duke Ellington, Paul
Robeson, and Jackie Robinson, serious attempts at telling the stories of important African Americans are rare indeed.

But even if most filmmakers tend to regard eminent blacks as unrepresentable, the brilliant jazz composer and pianist Thelonious Monk has been

the subject of several documentaries in spite of (or perhaps because of) his almost dazzling inscrutability. In this chapter I am concerned with three films that arrive at strikingly different conclusions about Monk. The title of Matthew Seig's 1991 documentary is itself significant; *Thelonious Monk: American Composer* presents a dedicated artist and family man who created a spiritually rich music rooted in a great tradition. In Charlotte Zwerin's *Thelonious Monk: Straight No Chaser* (1988), Monk is bizarre and unpredictable, functioning as an artist primarily because of the highly professional support of sidepersons, the steadfast dedication of his wife, Nellie, and the patronage of the Baroness Pannonica de Koenigswarter. For Jean Bach, the Monk prominently featured in *A Great Day in Harlem* (1995) is a trickster who carefully choreographed how the world would see him when he appeared in the famous 1958 photograph of important jazz artists posing in Harlem.

THE LIFE AND THE MUSIC: MEDITATIONS ON INTEGRATION

Although writers of biography would like to turn their prose into a window with an unobstructed view of their subjects, they can never deliver the semblance of *truth* that is available to the documentary filmmaker.[1] Biographers in general and jazz biographers in particular face additional problems as they attempt to integrate the work into the life of the subject. Writers who examine a collection of biographical material eventually produce nuanced language to explain how the art relates to the life and vice versa. If documentary filmmakers are to justify the inevitable truth claims inherent in their work, they must rely on some combination of voice-of-God narration, archival footage, and talking heads to present their subjects. In the "classical" and "modernist" documentary, narration is scrupulously avoided. John Grierson, perhaps the father of documentary cinema, simply turned his camera— and later his sound equipment—on his subjects in the 1920s and 1930s and recorded their activities (Winston). In the modernist documentary, which probably begins with *Point of Order* (1964), Emile de Antonio's careful selection of early television footage to expose the malevolence of Joseph McCarthy, narration has been written out as pretentious and awkward. In the jazz documentary of the 1980s and 1990s, we are likely to watch people being interviewed, often in front of carefully composed backgrounds and with no real evidence that anyone is doing the interviewing. When the documentary subject is a living person, filmmakers will train the camera on the subject and hope for moments of self-revelation. Even if there is no self-revelation, the actual appearance of the subjects on film makes them at least seem to be transparent. When the documentary subject is a black jazz musician, transparency is much less inevitable, and the task of revealing the life through the work and vice versa becomes more complicated. For one thing, jazz archives are not nearly so full as Civil War and baseball archives, to pick two examples from Ken Burns's mammoth portfolio. Although Burns tracked down virtually all of the most important films and photographs of his favored jazz artists for the 2001 miniseries on jazz, he had clearly taken on a deeply vexed subject that could not be accommodated even in seventeen and a half hours. In the minds of many important critics, Burns failed to create an accurate account of jazz history, especially for the last thirty years of the twentieth century. Jazz filmmakers without the prestige or the budget of Ken Burns often have to improvise with a limited amount of stock footage, stills, and interviews. The Cotton Club Dancers filmed for *Black and Tan,* Dudley Murphy's 1929 film with Duke Ellington, appear again and again in films that make reference to the Jazz Age. Throw in some well-chosen recordings from the period, add a few interviews with survivors and/or journalists, and the result is your generic documentary about Harlem, jazz, or the Jazz Age. (The segment on the 1920s in Ric Burns's ten-hour *New York: A Documentary Film,* shown on PBS in November 1999, is an especially good example of this practice.)

Attempts to yield the "truth" about black subjects are further complicated by a technology that was designed by and for white people. As the African American director and cinematographer Ernest Dickerson has pointed out, white filmmakers assume that they have the proper lighting if white faces show up clearly in the frame, often at the expense of clarity for the black faces (Dyer 98).[2] With the standard technology and technicians, black subjects are problematic from the outset. Clint Eastwood's *Bird* (1988), with cinematography by Jack N. Green, offers a telling example of how mainstream cinema finds visual metaphors for the inscrutability of black Americans. As I have argued elsewhere (*Jammin'* 88–90), the irrational behavior of Charlie Parker (Forest Whitaker) in *Bird* must be clarified for the audience by white characters, such as Parker's sideman Red Rodney and his common-law wife, Chan Richardson. For example, when the institutionalized Parker attacks a white inmate for no apparent reason, the audience must wait for Chan to explain to a psychiatrist that Parker has given up drugs and alcohol and

thus needs to feel something, even if it is the pain of a fight. The dark, impenetrable surface of Parker/Whitaker is made all the more opaque by lighting
and camera work that keeps him almost constantly in the shadows.[3]

But as all jazz scholars know, many of the most important black artists *are*
notoriously opaque, often speaking in their own metalanguage and scrupulously avoiding the kind of self-revelation the interviewer seeks. An emblematic moment occurs in Lester Young's famous 1959 interview with François
Postif when Young asks permission to speak freely with his "nasty" words
(Porter, *Reader* 177). Young's hesitancy to use the language with which he is
most comfortable is typical of jazz musicians who have perhaps sought out
musical expression in order to *avoid* certain kinds of verbal communication.
Accordingly, some films about jazz artists resemble ethnographic films that
construct "an exotic whose culture is open to inspection by the invisible camera and its scientist/operator. The truths displayed produce an order, a history,
and thus a narrative about the relationship of the 'primitive' to 'progress,' self
to other" (Rabinowitz 12).

The evasive, "signifying" style of self-presentation exhibited by black
artists in "ethnographic" films and in interview situations is often typical of
white jazz musicians as well. Consider Chet Baker in Bruce Weber's 1988 documentary, *Let's Get Lost,* in which the trumpeter often seems to be putting
on an act to charm the infatuated filmmaker. In general, however, the kind
of symbiosis between documentarian and subject we see in *Let's Get Lost* seldom happens when the director is white and the subject is black. The gulf is
too great to cross, whether the cause is technology, the different worlds of
the filmmaker and the musician, the preconceptions of the filmmaker, or the
self-presentation of the jazz artist. In some cases the relationship between
the music and the life is simply impossible to fathom, no matter how close
the biographer gets to the subject, and no matter how hard the filmmakers
work to bring specific sets of meaning to carefully arranged bits of film and
music. I am referring here to works about Monk, but also to works about
Charlie Parker. Let me address Parker for just a moment, if only because the
scholarship on him is a bit further along than it is for Monk.[4]

John Gennari has written an intriguing essay on the work of Ross Russell,
the man who recorded Charlie Parker for Dial Records in the late 1940s and
who subsequently made two attempts at interpreting Parker's life, first in the
novel *The Sound* (1961) and then in the biography *Bird Lives* (1973). In "Race-

Fig. 40. Jazz pianist
Thelonious Monk in
one of his many hats.
Jerry Ohlinger's Movie
Material Store, Inc.

ing the Bird: Ross Russell's Obsessive Pursuit of Charlie Parker," Gennari bril-
liantly reveals how the cultural upheavals that took place between the two
works help to explain the vastly different ways in which Russell accounts for
the life and art of Parker. Whereas Red Travers, the character carefully modeled
after Parker in *The Sound,* is a manipulative but self-destructive hipster king of
the 1950s, the Parker of *Bird Lives* is a "black power hero" consistent with the
racial politics of the early 1970s. More importantly, Gennari shows how Russell
was obsessed by the gap between the brilliance of Parker's music and the
wretchedness of his personal life. (Gennari quotes Ralph Ellison, who characterized Parker as "one whose friends had no need for an enemy, and whose en-
emies had no difficulty in justifying their hate" [Ellison, *Collected Essays* 263]).
Russell was never able to bridge this gap except by falling back on readily available discursive practices during the two eras in which he was writing.

Stanley Crouch, who is writing his own biography of Charlie Parker, has
said that the relationship between Parker the man and Parker the musician
is mysterious to him. He quotes pianist Lennie Tristano, who said that Bird

would have been a brilliant musician if he had been born in China hundreds of years ago. Few jazz scholars would agree with Crouch's assertion that the life experience of the musician does not necessarily shed light on the music. I recommend Mark Tucker's biography of the young Duke Ellington, Robert O'Meally's book on Billie Holiday, and Scott DeVeaux's work on Coleman Hawkins and Howard McGhee (DeVeaux, *Birth*), exemplary texts that show how an artist's music and life interrelate. Documentary filmmakers have also sought this integration in biographical accounts of artists such as Parker or Monk. For better or worse, however, the filmmakers ultimately rely on well-established discourses that have long been available to jazz biographers.

THELONIOUS MONK: AMERICAN COMPOSER

Matthew Seig's *Thelonious Monk: American Composer* is part of what might be called "The Lincoln Center Project," with its goal of establishing a canon of African American genius composer/musicians all linked by a history of apprenticeships and direct influences. Although Jazz at Lincoln Center is relatively young, the canonizing practices it has promoted were already present in the late 1950s in the journal *The Jazz Review* and in subsequent books, such as Gunther Schuller's *Early Jazz* (1968) and Martin Williams's *The Jazz Tradition* (1970). Embryonic signs of the project appeared in the popular media as early as 1957, when Monk was invited to perform on the CBS television broadcast *The Sound of Jazz*. Although Monk appeared as a remote figure concealed behind dark glasses, the producers at CBS placed an appreciative Count Basie as a privileged spectator at the opposite end of the piano, thus associating Monk with an important (and beloved) figure from the early history of the music.[5]

In Seig's 1991 film, Monk's music is linked with great predecessors from the outset. We are told that James P. Johnson lived in the same neighborhood as the young Monk and functioned as an inspirational figure. Duke Ellington and Coleman Hawkins, two of the most celebrated artists in the jazz canon, appear in still photos with Monk and are held up as key influences on the younger musician. Monk's work at the Five Spot with John Coltrane in 1957 is meant to show that the pianist had a major effect on the next generation of geniuses just as the earlier geniuses had inspired him. Comparable to the Vergil of T. S. Eliot's "What Is a Classic?" who looks backward to Homer and forward to Dante, Monk is an essential link in a chain of great musicians, his art inconceivable without them. There is danger, however, in placing Monk in this type of his-

torical pattern, if only because it is a profoundly Eurocentric way of looking at
a music that ought to be approached with more complex methodologies.

Seig's treatment of Monk is consistently reverential. In one of several appearances, Thelonious Monk Jr. speaks of a strong tradition of education, re-
ligion, and respect for elders that formed part of his father's upbringing and
made him a serious artist. We see footage of Monk walking gracefully past
the camera, pausing patiently to indulge the questions of a reporter. The
dominant "authenticating voices" throughout the film are the two African
American pianists Randy Weston and Billy Taylor.[6] Weston is the voice of jazz
authenticity, speaking eloquently of the spirituality in Monk's music and the
values it embodied. Taylor, who holds a doctorate in music education and is
often referred to as "Dr. Billy Taylor," is the articulate intellectual who designates Monk as a unique artist and a central figure in the history of jazz.[7] As
with the symbolic appropriation of Basie in *The Sound of Jazz,* moments in
Seig's film attempt to domesticate the music, insisting that Monk was much
more in the mainstream than some have supposed. Footage of Monk playing
the familiar pop song "Just a Gigolo" is offered as evidence.

Not until Seig's sixty-minute film is half over does the narrative turn to
the less wholesome aspects of Monk's life and describe his arrest for possession of drugs. Taylor tells the camera in no uncertain terms that the arrest
and the subsequent suspension of Monk's cabaret card was a racist act: "Too
many black people [in New York] were working downtown." T. S. Monk Jr.,
however, is more reassuring, reminiscing about his father playing "Mr.
Mom" while Nellie Monk supported the family during the years that her
husband could not work in New York clubs. We hear that Monk used the
time to write music and to play games with his two children. Mention of the
family's financial problems serves as a cue to introduce Baroness Pannonica
"Nica" de Koenigswarter, the wealthy European jazz enthusiast who be-
friended and gave financial support to Monk, Parker, and other musicians in
New York. Orrin Keepnews compares her to a Medieval patron of the arts,
and Weston praises her for recognizing Monk's genius. There is no discussion of her personal relations with Monk. After less than a minute of discussion, the baroness is never mentioned again.

Drummer Ben Riley appears in the film shortly after the halfway mark
and recalls the strange circumstances under which he suddenly became a
member of the band during what he thought was a brief job at a recording

session. Although Riley says that Monk never once spoke to him during the session, at the end Monk turned to Riley and astonished him by telling him to get his passport ready because "We're leaving on Friday." But even this incident appears to show how tightly Monk focused on his music to the exclusion of mundane affairs. Riley also explains that Monk's dancing was his way of enjoying the music while his sidemen performed. According to Riley, Monk always knew exactly when it was time to return to the piano no matter how involved he became with his dancing.

Throughout Seig's program there is no mention of Monk's affection for unusual hats, although we see many of them. Weston refers to his lurching dance style as "ballet." The program winds down with a few statements on Monk's refusal to play during his last years. Weston says that Monk should have lived in a place where an artist's needs were completely fulfilled, but because he never had such a place he simply gave up: "I felt spiritually that he just shut the door." In order to further emphasize Monk's role in a thriving tradition, the penultimate moments of the program are devoted to the music of Sphere, a quartet consisting of two former Monk sidemen (Charlie Rouse and Ben Riley), plus two musicians who had clearly listened closely to Monk even though neither had ever worked with him (Kenny Barron and Buster Williams). The group began its career by recording only tunes by Monk, who died—coincidentally and poignantly—on the group's first day in the recording studio. The program ends with stirring video footage of Monk playing "Oska T."

The creation of a jazz canon with a list of great artists in a coherent tradition has been a necessary step in the growth of jazz studies as a legitimate discipline (Gabbard, "Introduction"). And as DeVeaux has argued in "Constructing the Jazz Tradition," it is probably unfair to deconstruct a canonical view of jazz history so soon after it has been constructed. On the one hand, African American artists have made monumental contributions to music even though they have been neglected, marginalized, and exploited throughout the first century of jazz history. There is also no question that jazz musicians have been profoundly influenced by earlier jazz musicians. Seig's Monk film is a valuable collection of personal reminiscences and performances that would not have been possible without the canonizing practices of grant-giving agencies and a growing audience of serious and devoted listeners.

On the other hand, Seig's film and the project it represents borrow a template from traditions of European art music that have almost always excluded the music of the Other. In *Early Jazz,* for example, Gunther Schuller used a European model to construct Jelly Roll Morton as "The First Great Composer" even though this model inadequately describes a music that grows out of improvisations and group interactions and is seldom performed as a stabilized text. Much the same can be said about the implications of the title *Thelonious Monk: American Composer.* Furthermore, both Morton and Monk surely learned a great deal from musicians outside the world of jazz, as have many of the artists in the jazz canon. And by concentrating only on the great soloists and composers, the canonizing project ignores contributions from crucial figures in jazz and other musics and thus distorts jazz history. As Sherrie Tucker and Lara Pellegrinelli have convincingly demonstrated, the entrenched practice of writing women out of jazz history throws all received notions of the music's history into question. Although it was originally broadcast on the Bravo cable channel, Seig's Monk film is one of several programs produced primarily for PBS titled, appropriately, "American Masters." These programs presented artists such as Duke Ellington, Charlie Parker, John Coltrane, Sarah Vaughan, Billie Holiday, Louis Armstrong, and Thelonious Monk as significant figures whose lives are consistent with their achievements as artists. As with the title of Seig's Monk film, Kendrick Simmons and Gary Giddins say a great deal at the outset by naming their 1987 Parker documentary *Celebrating Bird: The Triumph of Charlie Parker.* The programs in this series do not actually conceal troubling incidents in the biographies of Monk, Parker, or Holiday, but they often border on the kind of hagiography that was, until the last decades of the twentieth century, afforded only to canonical figures from classical music.

THELONIOUS MONK: STRAIGHT NO CHASER

Although hardly an anticanonizing film, Charlotte Zwerin's *Thelonious Monk: Straight No Chaser* contains material that might have been purposefully omitted from Seig's film. The same T. S. Monk Jr. who had spoken so warmly of a caring father to Seig's camera soberly tells Zwerin how it feels "when you look your father in the eye and you know that he doesn't exactly know who you are." From the outset Monk is a much different figure than the one presented by Seig. Zwerin does not hesitate, for example, to confront the close relationship between Monk and Nica de Koenigswarter. Harry Colomby, Monk's personal manager from 1955 to 1967, explains that Nellie never felt threatened by

Fig. 41. Thelonious Monk performs in *Thelonious Monk: Straight No Chaser* (1988, Malpaso
Productions/Warner Bros.). Jerry Ohlinger's Movie Material Store, Inc.

her husband's dependence on Nica: "They were splitting duties." We also see
a good deal of Monk at his most difficult, first at a 1967 recording session for
Columbia records and later when he and an octet are on tour in Europe.[8]

At the record date Monk arrives wearing a three-cornered hat that resembles a mortar board. He also sports a set of wire-rimmed glasses without
lenses. Monk explains that the hat was given to him in Poland and that he is
wearing "invisible glasses." The quartet plays "Ugly Beauty" until producer

Teo Macero stops them. Monk becomes querulous, cursing and complaining because Macero did not record the band as it was rehearsing.[9]

In the segment devoted to the European tour we learn that Monk neglected to write music for his large ensemble until the last possible moment. We see him awkwardly stopping trumpet soloist Ray Copeland in the middle of a solo while a confused audience looks on. In footage presumably shot backstage after the concert, Monk paces nervously and eventually strikes some metal furniture in an angry gesture. Later we see members of the octet struggling to understand what Monk wants; the most satisfying performance footage in the segment is not by the collective ensemble but by individual soloists. Although Bob Jones's voice-over tells us that audiences were highly appreciative as the tour continued, a great deal of the footage presents Monk at his most bizarre. At one point he wanders in an airport and continually spins completely around for no discernible reason except perhaps to amuse the camera crew tracking his every move. Other moments show that Nellie has taken over the daily responsibilities of travel so that her husband can be free to concentrate on his music. But even Nellie is presented as somewhat eccentric when Bob Jones, the band's road manager, reports that she brought back empty Coke bottles in her suitcase so that she could redeem them for the deposit.

In addition to Colomby, the most favored witness in Zwerin's footage is Charlie Rouse, who spent many years playing tenor saxophone in Monk's groups. In contrast to Randy Weston and Billy Taylor in Seig's film, Colomby and Rouse speak more openly of a Monk who was difficult and enigmatic. Rouse is not a natural raconteur like Weston, but his terse comments tend to be more revealing than the latter's grand statements in *Thelonious Monk: American Composer*.

Zwerin begins her film by showing Monk dancing and spinning while the other members of the quartet perform "Evidence." When it is his time to solo, Monk runs to the piano a bit late, in contrast to Ben Riley's claim in Seig's documentary that Monk always arrived at the piano at exactly the right moment. Monk plays with great animation, perspiring profusely, pounding his foot, and bouncing on the piano bench, still very much the strange figure who was spinning and cavorting a few seconds earlier. After the opening performance footage, Monk speaks, something he does in only one brief scene in Seig's film. Bob Jones reads from an encyclopedia that gives

Monk's vital statistics. When Jones says, "It appears that you're famous, The-lonious," the pianist mutters, "What does that mean?" Jones tells him that the book also lists popes and presidents, to which Monk says, "I'm famous. Ain't that a bitch?"

The placing of Monk in a great tradition that is the principal goal of Seig's film is handled with much greater dispatch by Zwerin. After the intro-ductory performance footage and the conversation about fame with Jones, the voice-over narration of Samuel E. Wright (who appeared as Dizzy Gilles-pie in Clint Eastwood's *Bird*) is heard for less than five minutes. Wright pro-vides a few details on Monk's childhood, his connections to James P. Johnson and jazz history, his apprenticeship with Coleman Hawkins, and his role in the birth of bebop. When Rouse tells the camera that many of Monk's compositions have become classics, the statement is confirmed by footage of Tommy Flanagan and Barry Harris playing a two-piano version of "Well, You Needn't." In this ninety-minute documentary, Monk's troubles are intro-duced early: the arrest for drugs and the loss of the cabaret card are men-tioned before the first fifteen minutes have elapsed. In the next few minutes Colomby talks about Monk's gig at the Five Spot with Coltrane, and the his-tory lesson is effectively over. We then see black-and-white footage of Monk spinning around while Nica sits on a set of stairs in the background, chatting with someone off-camera. Finished with his spins, Monk looks at the cam-era and says, "Someone else did that, they'd put 'em in a straitjacket. People say, 'Oh, that Thelonious Monk. He's crazy.'" Hearing applause somewhere off camera, Monk then bows slightly and says, "Thank you." The rest of the film features a good deal of performance footage, but Monk's eccentricities and psychological problems are consistently foregrounded.

Most of the black-and-white footage that dominates Zwerin's *Thelo-nious Monk: Straight No Chaser* was shot by director and cinematographer Christian Blackwood in 1967 and 1968 for a Monk documentary that was never completed. Coproducer Bruce Ricker first located the footage and dis-covered that it was in excellent condition. He and Zwerin brought it to the attention of Clint Eastwood, who bankrolled the film and served as its ex-ecutive producer. Although portions of Zwerin's film are compatible with the canonizing tendencies in recent jazz writing, most of it derives from the familiar narrative of the revolutionary jazz artist laid low by prejudice, con-trolled substances, and an audience of philistines. Dorothy Baker, author of

Young Man with a Horn (1938), can probably take the lioness's share of the credit for first finding the proper balance of pathos and tragedy in the life of a neglected jazz artist. The inspiration for Baker's novel was the white trumpeter Bix Beiderbecke, who drank himself to death in 1931. The same narrative has dominated accounts of the lives of Holiday, Parker, Young, and others.[10] The jazz documentaries of Seig, Toby Byron, Gary Giddins, and their collaborators would not be so relentlessly positive if they were not responding to this older narrative.

Designed for the high-brow aesthetics of Bravo and PBS, the documentaries of Seig and the others inevitably celebrated jazz as a great American art form. Charlotte Zwerin, by contrast, was working in the tradition of independent cinema, with its refusal to be slick, demure, or self-congratulatory. She is not afraid, for example, to show us Monk when he is angry, child-like, and even incoherent. *Straight No Chaser* may be most disturbing when it chronicles Monk's mental illness. The psychologist Martin Margulies quotes T. S. Monk Jr., who said that doctors wanted to administer electroconvulsive therapy to his father but that the family would not give permission. Although the psychiatric reports on Monk have never been made public, Leslie Gourse has interviewed a psychiatrist who observed Monk for a month but found no convincing evidence of either manic depression or schizophrenia (Gourse, *Straight, No Chaser* 117). Gourse reports that several authorities suggested that Monk may simply have taken too many drugs, only some of them by design. On at least one occasion Monk was given LSD without his knowledge, and Timothy Leary may have shared peyote with him in the early 1960s (120). Gourse also quotes a doctor who believes that Monk was misdiagnosed and probably suffered brain damage from various drugs administered to him during his several periods of hospitalization (278).

Speaking to Zwerin's camera about his father's episodes, T. S. Monk Jr. says, "He would generally close up, introvert, and then he would get excited. And he may . . . pace for four days, or something like that. Then eventually he would get exhausted." For the Monk family these episodes must have been heartbreaking and financially devastating. But romantic myths of mental illness are also available to anyone wishing to tell Monk's story in a different fashion. Christian Blackwood began filming Monk during the same year as the release of Fred Wiseman's extraordinary documentary *Titicut Follies* (1967), shot inside a state mental hospital in Massachusetts. The mid-1960s

was a period of extreme reaction against the psychiatric profession, dramatically reversing a period of largely uncritical acceptance of Freud and the industry that grew up around his work.[11] The message of Wiseman's 1967 film
about life inside a mental hospital is that the keepers are as crazy as the patients.[12] Although Wiseman did not exactly romanticize mental illness, much
of the popular entertainment of the mid- to late 1960s did. Think of books
such as R. D. Laing's *Sanity, Madness, and the Family* (1965) and Ken Kesey's
One Flew over the Cuckoo's Nest (1962). Or think of films like *King of Hearts*
(1966) and *A Fine Madness* (1966). To one degree or another, Christian Blackwood undoubtedly succumbed to this revisionist view of mental illness as he
pursued Monk. In this context, the Monk of Blackwood's black-and-white
footage is a free-spirited eccentric whose music is a natural expression of
what the psychiatric establishment might call mental illness. In 1967 it was
not just the jazz cognoscenti who would have regarded Monk's behavior as
something other than insanity.

Zwerin, who both directed and edited *Straight No Chaser,* scavenged
among the many hours of Blackwood's footage. On some level she, too, was
fascinated by Monk's strange behavior and saw it primarily as part of a complicated artist's temperament. (And she undoubtedly tried to create a compelling narrative that would appeal to an audience beyond jazz fans.) By
1988, American culture had a much less romantic view of mental illness.
Zwerin has tried to place Monk's madness in a larger context in which the
beauty of the music tends to mitigate if not justify his weird deportment. For
example, she has included a scene in which Monk lies in a hotel bed trying to
order chicken livers from a baffled European waiter. The scene is immediately
followed by Monk's beautiful performance of "Ruby My Dear." Zwerin's tolerance for Monk's eccentricity is not at all incompatible with the familiar
liberal humanist account of a black artist destroyed by a corrupt American
culture. In the footage she herself brought to the film, Zwerin shows T. S.
Monk Jr. attributing Monk's emotional problems to the internalization of
pain from years of critical misunderstanding and popular neglect. Clint Eastwood embraced a version of this narrative in his well-intentioned but dreary
film about Charlie Parker that was released in the same year that Eastwood
made Zwerin's Monk film possible. For Zwerin and Eastwood in Hollywood
in the late 1980s, the paradigm shift toward the Lincoln Center Project was
still a few years away. If Matthew Seig's documentary presents the music as

the triumphant achievement of a beautiful man steeped in a great tradition, Zwerin's *Straight No Chaser* suggests that the music came from a tortured soul who found beauty in spite of his sufferings.

But Monk does not always appear to be suffering in Zwerin's film. Some of his most bizarre conduct seems to take place for the sake of the camera. After spinning about in an airport, Monk smiles broadly and knowingly as Blackwood's camera closes in on his face. Similarly, one wonders if Monk wore the "invisible glasses" to the recording studio only because he knew that he was being filmed. Macero and the recording engineer at the session treat the fashion statement as highly unusual even for Monk. One might also speculate about the extent of Monk's naïveté early in the film when he expresses surprise at the news that he has become famous. Although he was suffering breakdowns during this period, Monk does not appear irrational in his terse exchange with Jones. He was probably feigning ignorance. Appropriately, Zwerin's film ends not with the most moving example of Monk's lyricism but with the pianist knocking out a delicately ironic version of "Sweetheart of All My Dreams" on an out-of-tune piano. In these last moments when Monk is on camera, Zwerin shows him simultaneously serious and playful as he explores the ancient tune on what sounds like a child's toy piano.

A GREAT DAY IN HARLEM

It is the more knowing, more playful Monk of *Straight No Chaser* who emerges as an important character in *A Great Day in Harlem,* the documentary about the famous photograph of fifty-seven jazz musicians posing in front of a Harlem brownstone in 1958. Jean Bach, who produced and directed *A Great Day in Harlem,* appears to be uninterested in either of the two master narratives that drive the films of Seig and Zwerin. She focuses instead on the stories of several musicians and what happened when they showed up one summer morning to have their picture taken. The resulting photograph, captured by Art Kane for *Esquire* magazine, has become a unique document in the history of jazz. Although Bach's film devotes a few moments to the authenticating voice of Nat Hentoff (perhaps because Matthew Seig served as coproducer), the jazz artists are usually portrayed not so much as genius composer/musicians but as tricksters. As Burton Peretti has observed, when allowed to speak for themselves jazz artists are often fond of spinning tales about how they resourcefully overcame danger and humiliation or took advantage of some quirk in the protocols of American racism. W. O. Smith, who played bass with Coleman Hawkins on the great 1939 recording of "Body and Soul," tells a story that is emblematic. In his autobiography he writes of the time he and his fellow band members feasted at a nightclub after it was raided. The white managers and all the customers were taken to jail, but the local police force saw no point in arresting a group of black musicians, leaving them free to consume all the succulent food left behind (W. O. Smith 65). Other musicians, like most of us, just love a good story. In *A Great Day in Harlem,* Milt Hinton, Dizzy Gillespie, Benny Golson, Eddie Locke, and Johnny Griffin all have moments of screen time in which they display great wit and comic timing. With Bach directing and Susan Peehl editing *A Great Day in Harlem,* even the dour Hank Jones becomes a jokester, pointing out who in the photograph has or has not put on weight since 1958.

Monk probably receives more attention than any other artist in the photograph. Within the first ten minutes of the sixty-minute film we meet Robert Altschuler, the publicity man at the Riverside record company, where Monk was making most of his recordings in the late 1950s and early 1960s. Altschuler was assigned the complicated task of bringing Monk to the photo session. Before Altschuler can begin his story, however, Johnny Griffin appears and compares Monk to Jomo Kenyatta, saying that the pianist wore such an imposing facade that people were afraid to speak to him. In partial explanation of Monk's unapproachability, Art Blakey says that he loved and admired Monk because he had "higher morals than any man I ever met. . . . He always told the truth. If you wanted to know something, and you asked him a question . . . , he's going to tell you the truth, and that's what people don't like. That's why they were afraid of him."

Throughout Bach's film, stories about one figure drift seamlessly into stories about others. The narrative itself has a trickster quality. The subject of Monk is dropped shortly after Blakey's testimonial, but the story of his trip to the photo shoot is picked up again about five minutes later. After we see Monk performing "Blue Monk" from *The Sound of Jazz,* Altschuler reappears and continues his story of driving to the West Side to find Monk. Once again, however, the story is interrupted by various participants who talk about the complicated logistics of getting everyone into position. When Altschuler appears once again, he says that Monk made him wait for over an

hour, leading him to worry that they would miss the shoot. When Monk finally came down to the car, Altschuler tells us, he made no explanation for
his tardiness, but made a striking appearance in a yellow sports jacket. The
camera then picks up Dizzy Gillespie talking about how Monk seldom spoke,
in part because Nellie often did his speaking for him. On one occasion, after
Nellie had answered a question addressed to her husband, Gillespie told her,
"Nellie, Monk speak English . . . in a weird way, but he speak English." Griffin comes back to say that Monk could listen quietly to a group of musicians
gossiping and "running their mouths" and then destroy everything they had
said with "three or four words."

Finally, Altschuler explains why Monk was late. Gigi Gryce, who had accompanied Monk uptown for the occasion, later told Altschuler that Monk
had been trying on different clothes in order to stand out as much as possible among the other musicians. As Altschuler speaks, the camera shows a
montage of photographs displaying the wide variety of distinctive outfits that
Monk wore in public over the years. When the camera cuts back to the main
photograph, Altschuler points out that Monk made himself even more con-
spicuous by standing next to the two beautiful pianists Marian McPartland
and Mary Lou Williams. This is surely not an act from the out-of-control figure in Zwerin's film or from the high priest of bebop in Seig's documentary.

In directing *A Great Day in Harlem*, Bach joins a surprisingly large group
of women who have directed jazz documentaries. Practically a genre unto itself, the list includes *But Then . . . She's Betty Carter* (Michelle Parkerson,
1980), *Maxwell Street Blues* (Linda Williams, 1980), *Bix: Ain't None of Them
Play Like Him Yet* (Brigit Berman, 1981), *Toshiko Akiyoshi: Jazz Is My Native
Language* (Renee Cho, 1983), *Mary Lou Williams: Music on My Mind* (Joanna
Burke, 1983), *Ernie Andrews: Blues for Central Avenue* (Lois Shelton, 1986),
Ornette: Made in America (Shirley Clarke, 1986), *The International Sweethearts
of Rhythm* (Greta Schiller and Andrea Weiss, 1987), *Tiny and Ruby: Hell Divin'
Women* (Greta Schiller and Andrea Weiss, 1988), and *Listen Up: The Lives of
Quincy Jones* (Ellen Weissbrod, 1989), as well as Charlotte Zwerin's Monk
film.[13] We might speculate that the neglected art of jazz coupled with the neglected art of the documentary provides the path of least resistance for a woman
seeking to break into the patriarchal industry of filmmaking. We might also
risk comparing these unusual women's films to the "official" jazz biographies
that appear on PBS and Bravo, virtually all of them written, produced, and

directed by men, and virtually all devoted to elevating the stature of favored jazz artists. Susan McClary is surely right when she argues that music has historically been regarded as feminine and that male musicians have retaliated by, for example, insisting upon the "objectivity, universality, and transcendence" of certain music (17). Male critics, musicologists, and filmmakers have also tended to make lofty claims for jazz artists that women may not feel obliged to echo. Jean Bach has brought a playful, noncanonizing tone to her film, but I will not insist upon gender-specific explanations for why this is the case. I will, however, point out that Bach was a serious jazz devotee in New York City for many years and that she has portrayed the musicians in *A Great Day in Harlem* not as abstractions but as men and women she has come to know firsthand.

Even though Bach tells her stories with a light touch, there remains a solemn, almost ceremonious air about the photograph around which she builds her film. It may have been there from the beginning. The weathered faces of older jazz artists, such as Willie the Lion Smith, Miff Mole, Zutty Singleton, Luckey Roberts, and Red Allen, give the photo a distinctly austere look, in spite of Monk's bright sports jacket and the clowning of Gillespie and Roy Eldridge in the right-hand corner. With few exceptions, the artists in the photograph represent the music's past rather than its future. John Coltrane and Miles Davis, busy changing jazz history in 1958, are absent. So are the larger-than-life figures Duke Ellington, Louis Armstrong, and Benny Goodman, who might have given a "timeless" dimension to the photograph. But the carefully composed black-and-white photography and the nineteenth-century brownstone in Harlem where the musicians were posed make even jazz modernists like Charles Mingus, Gerry Mulligan, Sonny Rollins, and Thelonious Monk seem part of an ancient tradition. To her credit, Bach does not exploit the corresponding sense of loss that is built into the photograph. Necrophilic listing of deceased artists is virtually absent from the narration. Only Art Farmer raises the subject, and even then the tone is affirmative rather than nostalgic when he tells us, for example, that "Lester Young is here now."

A Great Day in Harlem is fond of its tricksters, crucial figures in the African American literary and cultural criticism of the 1990s. In his seminal book, *The Signifying Monkey,* Henry Louis Gates Jr. has explored the roots of trickster mythology and the central role the character has played in both

African and African American cultures. But producer/director Bach probably took the image of Monk as trickster from musicians rather than from
scholars. After all, she knew Monk and many of the other important figures
in jazz history. Her personal acquaintance with musicians and the trust she
has won with them over time is evident in many of the interview segments in
A Great Day in Harlem. Perhaps because of her ability to put her subjects at
ease, a different Monk emerges in her film, one who carefully chose how and
when to exercise control, entirely capable of guile and a false facade of madness. Miles Davis, too, has described Monk in this way: "He was a great put-
on artist, too, and that's the way he kept people off of him, by acting crazy
like he did" (*Miles: The Autobiography* 187). Whether or not the trickster
Monk produced trickster music is never explicitly addressed by Bach in *A
Great Day in Harlem*. On the three occasions when the subject of Monk
comes up, the film presents the scene from *The Sound of Jazz* in which he
plays "Blue Monk" wearing dark glasses and a sporty cap, very much the eccentric jazz musician. Simply through this juxtaposition, the stories told by
Altschuler, Griffin, Blakey, and Gillespie can be conceptualized as attempts
to link Monk's character with his music. But this does not seem to be Bach's
goal. She seems much more interested in reproducing the warmth, humor,
and human immediacy she has experienced among jazz artists. Nevertheless,
the image of Monk as a trickster feigning craziness must be tempered by the
knowledge that, on more than one occasion, Monk *was* crazy and entirely
unaware of his appearance.

In *A Great Day in Harlem*, Monk receives abundant praise from those
who knew him, much of it for his wit as well as for his morality. Only
Altschuler makes a brief reference to Monk's reputation for being "difficult."
The subject of mental illness is never raised even though Monk had already
been hospitalized no later than 1955. It is also true that the film's trickster
narrative applies only to one day in Monk's life. The films of Seig and Zwerin
are much more ambitious in attempting to account for virtually all of
Monk's life and music. But all three films adopt narratives for Monk that are
as different as they are easy to trace through other texts about jazz artists.
Obviously there is sufficient truth in all these narratives to have kept them
alive and eminently available for filmmakers interested in Thelonious Monk.
There is no denying that Monk *was* a unique artist influenced by other important artists, that he *was* a sensitive man crippled by racism and critical

neglect, and that he *was* sufficiently clever to orchestrate his own image. But in spite of the compelling ways in which these three films present Monk's life and music, as a group they may tell us as much about the theory and practice of jazz documentary as they do about Thelonious Monk himself. Because of his brilliance, his madness, and his playfulness, not to mention his opacity, Thelonious Monk could be a blank slate on which his observers have written much of what they themselves brought to the work of observation.

CHAPTER SEVEN

Revenge of the Nerds

Representing the White Male Collector of Black Music

Whether they favor compact discs, LPs, 78s, cassette tapes, or mp3 downloads, serious collectors of jazz and blues are not like other collectors. For one thing, they are almost always men. As Susan Stewart has suggested, women tend to collect souvenirs and mementos while men tend to collect *serially* as completists. A woman who collects postcards, for example, can pull an item out of a box and tell you all about the person who sent it and the circumstances under which it was received. By contrast, a man who collects baseball cards probably cannot tell you how he acquired most of the items in the box. For him, what is most important about his set of cards from 1958 is that he has them all. When it comes to recordings, a woman is likely to have only that music to which she is emotionally attached. Serious male collectors will seek a complete inventory, often based on some kind of list that gives order to the collection. On the shelves of a serious jazz and blues devotee, a "Volume One" is not likely to be next to a "Volume Three" with nothing in between. *(I have been a serious collector of jazz recordings since 1964. Several walls in my apartment are covered with LPs, CDs, and tapes. Close by my records I keep my discographies with their complete listings of recordings by specific artists. These discographies have been carefully* annotated, and I take great pride in those volumes in which I have put a little dash next to each and every one of the recordings listed in the book. Although I enjoy hearing new recordings, I am constantly frustrated that the unending flow of new releases on CD quickly makes a discography obsolete. Indeed, collecting any single artist complete is difficult because there are so many rare and out-of-print records, not to mention bootleg recordings, that circulate among collectors and can be acquired only through elaborate networking. Nevertheless, I have what I consider to be "complete" collections of recordings by Charles Mingus, Clifford Brown, Charlie Parker, Billie Holiday, John Coltrane, Eric Dolphy, Lester Young, Thelonious Monk, Bud Powell, Roy Eldridge, Fletcher Henderson, Betty Carter, Jimmy Lunceford, Johnny Hodges, Woody Shaw, Rahsaan Roland Kirk, Bix Beiderbecke, and Lee Morgan. For aesthetic and personal reasons, there are artists whose works I have not attempted to collect in their entirety. For example, I have most but not all of Miles Davis's records from the years after 1968, when he let influences from rock 'n' roll creep into his music. As much as I admire David Murray, I have stopped collecting his CDs because he is still alive and recording so frequently that it is difficult [and expensive] to keep up with him. Then there is Duke Ellington, the greatest of them all, whose entire works are virtually impossible to acquire since he performed almost every day of his life, and someone was probably running a tape recorder when he played a high school prom in Jamestown, Pennsylvania, on May 16, 1959, thus presenting the likelihood that sooner or later a tape will turn up in the circle of "advanced" collectors seeking the holy grail of a "complete" Ellington collection.)

A psychoanalytic explanation of the completist's behavior might suggest the persistence of the "anal stage," when children take special pleasure in holding on to material that should have passed out of their bodies. For me, a more plausible explanation of both the collector's pathology and the dominance of men among serial collectors can be based in Lacanian theories of the body within the Symbolic Order. The man whose collection is complete has no gaps and thus no anxieties about what is not there. In seeking plenitude, the serial collector is essentially warding off castration. At least in this way, collectors of jazz and blues share some qualities with other serial collectors, such as philatelists and numismatists, who also labor at filling gaps. (My friend Perry has compiled all the releases of certain pre-modern artists on 78 rpm discs but never listens to them, preserving them in carefully arranged volumes that resemble the albums of stamp and coin collectors.)

Jazz and blues completists who do not listen to their records are not typical, however. Most immerse themselves in the music in order to acquire expert knowledge of the history and styles of canonical masters. When Baudrillard writes that the collector prefers the "formal" aspect of objects to their reality (147–148), he may be right for most collectors, but probably not for collectors of jazz and blues. *(The fetishist's pleasure in a complete and well-ordered collection is in fact richly available to jazz and blues devotees, but most would say that they are acquiring something entirely separate from the mere vinyl on which it has been preserved. To those who are puzzled by the way I fill up my apartment with LPs and CDs, I patiently explain that the music is lighter than air and full of moments of transcendence unrelated to the spectacle of shelves groaning under the weight of discs.)*

In spite of the preponderance of men among the ranks of completists, and in spite of the Lacanian thesis that connects completism with the male anatomy, it is always better to think of serial collecting as masculine rather than male. After an early version of this chapter appeared in print, one male friend told me that he collected records like a woman. I am sure that other men who read the article had similar moments of self-reckoning. Indeed, if collectors did not initially have some strongly emotional, "unmanly" connection to the music, the prospect of obsessively compiling stacks of records would make little sense. But more than a few women approached me to say that they or a female acquaintance collected jazz and blues as completists. I have met several women with extensive collections and with great knowledge of specific jazz artists. At least two have sat with me at jazz clubs and conscientiously written down the title of every tune they heard, even if the musicians did not bother to announce what they were playing. To my horror, both have much more skill than I do when it comes to identifying tunes by minor jazz composers, such as Tom McIntosh and Hank Mobley.

Sherrie Tucker, the author of *Swing Shift,* the compelling study of women who played in all-female jazz bands in the 1930s and 1940s, has spoken passionately about her love for the music and her careful acquisition of discs: "I felt pleasure in collecting jazz recordings and in gaining mastery of knowledge about them because jazz was the most profound thing I had ever heard, and the conversations about the music were the most stimulating dialogues I had ever heard. I wanted to be a part of them" (Tucker, Conversation with the author). In a world where women are seldom respected for their knowledge, Tucker found that her impressive record collection earned her a degree of respect among other jazz enthusiasts, the same people whose opinions and ideas mattered most to her.

I also spoke with Lara Pellegrinelli, a graduate student in ethnomusicology and one of the smartest jazz journalists working in New York at the turn of the century. She told me that she never had a desire to build a record collection and engage in the usual jazz talk with her male friends: "I made a very conscious decision that I didn't want my knowledge to be judged on my ability to list the personnel off albums or on the size of my record collection. I knew I couldn't compete, and that frankly, I didn't want to. . . . It has always seemed to me that record collecting is not only about defining masculinity but a particular kind of male competition and one-upmanship" (Pellegrinelli, Conversation with the author). She also pointed out that the dusty, cluttered stores where completists are likely to seek out rare discs are seldom the kinds of places where women wish to congregate. Moreover, both Tucker and Pellegrinelli argued that record collecting among women ought to be historicized. Earlier generations of female fans surely built de facto societies around sharing and listening to records, even if women's disadvantaged financial situation would have limited their ability to compete with the more serious (and affluent) male collectors. Tucker pointed to Jean Hay as a heroic figure among female record collectors. As a disc jockey during World War II, she gained a substantial following among GIs and became the inspiration for the 1943 film *Reveille with Beverly* (fig. 42). Although Ann Miller played her in the film as "bubbly and cute and devoted to the servicemen," Hay was in fact the music supervisor for the film and had to fight with the white male producers to place the black bands of Count Basie and Duke Ellington in the same film with popular white artists, such as Bob Crosby, Freddie Slack, and a very young Frank Sinatra. Having two black bands in a mainstream film was seldom the practice at the time, but Hay was able to convince the producers that both bands were great and that they were suitably different from one another to be included. She later succeeded in making sure that all the band numbers were performed uncut and in their entirety. Thanks to Hay, we have rare and wonderful footage of the Ellington orchestra playing an extended verison of "Take the A Train," complete with a vocal by Betty Roche and a few of the dance steps with which the unique trumpeter/violinist/vocalist Ray Nance regularly delighted audiences.

Fig. 42. Disc jockey Beverly (Ann Miller) contends with an unsympathetic boss (Franklin Pangborn) in *Reveille with Beverly* (1943, Columbia Pictures). Photofest Film Archive.

Tucker also told me that in her early days as a jazz enthusiast she would share her collecting habits exclusively with a group of male friends. They went to the same jazz clubs, frequented the same used record stores, and listened to the same handful of radio stations. It was only after she became an academic that she took a special interest in the female jazz artists who were almost completely overlooked by jazz historians. She ruefully observed that if she had begun collecting female instrumentalists earlier, she would have had to move away from the masculinist construction of jazz discourse with which she was most familiar. Indeed, she might have lost some of the "mastery" over the music she had acquired by adopting this discourse.

For many men, and surely for a few woman, mastering the discourse of record collecting has always been a way of establishing a masculine identity. It is no wonder that young men often acquire a taste for record collecting when they turn fourteen or fifteen. The masculine identity that the young man seeks may be subversive, as is often the case with men who collect opera

(Koestenbaum); it may be self-consciously hypermasculine, as with those who listen to heavy metal (Grossberg); or it may be normative with a tinge of masochism, as seems to be the case with men who are devoted to country and western (Ching). The male collector makes conscious and unconscious connections to the masculine codes in the music, but he also works at acquiring a commanding knowledge that can be carefully deployed in the right surroundings. The display of authoritative information, especially when it has been acquired outside of "bureaucratized institutions of knowledge," is a well established sign of masculine power in contemporary American culture (Straw 7). The anti-institutional cachet of jazz and blues separates its devotees from those who collect classical music, a more profoundly institutionalized music without the phallic power of black masculinity. I await anecdotes about changes in male display among jazz fans now that formerly outré musicians such as John Coltrane and Clifford Brown are increasingly institutionalized and can even be experienced as musical wallpaper in chic restaurants. *(Most of the completists I know will probably be unfazed by this turn. Most likely they will continue to feel that they own the artists they collect and that the market has nothing to do with it.)*

Of course, as I hope I have already established, masculinity is anything but monolithic. In chapter two I mentioned Jonathan Goldberg's piquant observation that Arnold Schwarzenegger's celebration of "the pump," with its feeling of orgasms all over his body, recalls the sexual pleasures of a woman more than the vigorous body-building regime of an Übermensch. Race, sexuality, class, and nationality must all be included in any useful discussion of masculinity. Arnold Schwarzenegger's masculine self-presentation bears little resemblance to that of Donald Rumsfeld, which bears little similarity to that of Charles Barkley, who would never be confused with a member of the Village People. And do not forget that women from different social classes, gender orientations, and age groups have found their own ways of adopting any masculine quality that is traditionally associated with men, whether it be driving fast, building biceps, or collecting every record on which Lee Morgan performs. The fact that in the popular imagination a man like Schwarzenegger possesses a complete inventory of masculinity reveals the success with which the culture industry has concealed the contradictions in familiar constructions of masculinity. As Steven Cohan has written, American masculinity is built upon the great contradiction that it is performative at the same time that, at least for familiar middle-class white versions, it must present itself as "natural" and not at all as a performance.

HOMOSOCIALITY AND ITS DISCONTENTS

The man who bases his masculinity on the knowledge acquired through record collecting is hardly entitled to mainstream models of masculinity. *(By far the most aggressively devoted record collector I have ever known is Ken, who once told me that when it came to Miles Davis's recordings, he was not a completist, he was an "absolutist." In other words, if a Bulgarian record company re-leased the zillionth re-issue of* Kind of Blue, *Ken would buy it and file it in with every other incarnation the music has ever taken. Forgive me, Ken, but I'm guessing that you have never been a babe magnet.)*

Like all homosocial activities, a serious devotion to collecting may even hinder a man from acquiring the regular company of a sympathetic woman, and not just because so many record collectors end up with the unkempt look of the nerd. The collector's conundrum is central to Nick Hornby's 1995 novel *High Fidelity.* The connoisseurs of soul, rock, and pop who work in the South London store Championship Vinyl feel superior to the many people who do not share their refined tastes in music. But as the novel also suggests, this feeling of aesthetic purity coexists with a romantic streak based in a certain credulousness about what Al Green, Solomon Burke, Neil Young, and the rest are saying in their songs. At least for Rob, the protagonist/narrator of *High Fidelity,* real-life romantic encounters never measure up to the fantasies so compellingly inscribed in his favorite records, and he is not fortunate enough to meet a woman with the same rarefied but crucial attitudes about music that he shares only with his fellow collectors, all of them male. Throughout the novel, Rob joins Barry and Dick, the two misfits he employs at Championship Vinyl, in passing immediate and merciless judgment on anyone with conventional tastes in music. A serious interest in Stevie Wonder's "I Just Called to Say I Love You" is a death sentence. Barry specifically refuses to sell this record to a customer, sending him away with a little speech about how the record is "sentimental, tacky crap" (53).

The novel ends when the thirty-five-year-old Rob attends a dinner party with his girlfriend, Laura, with whom he is still involved even after a few breakups. Rob discovers that Laura has arranged for him to meet people he is sure to like, in spite of their tastes in music. Toward the end of an evening during which Rob has in fact enjoyed the company and the conversation, Laura urges him to take a look at his hosts' collection of CDs. He sees a "CD collection that is so poisonously awful that it should be put in a steel case and shipped off to some Third World waste dump. They're all there: Tina Turner, Billy Joel, Kate Bush, Pink Floyd, Simply Red, The Beatles. . . ." (Hornby 279). And yet Rob finds that he cannot muster his usual contempt for the people who have actually purchased this music. Rob realizes that "it's not what you like but what you're like that's important" (280). He does not intend, however, to explain this newly acquired bit of wisdom to Barry, his implacable colleague at the record store. *High Fidelity* associates Rob's change of heart with a maturation process that also leads him to nest comfortably with a woman for the first time in his life. *(Paula and I have been married since 1973, when I was twenty-five. I am happy to say that she shares my tastes in music and patiently tolerates my passion for collecting. Sometimes when I come home earlier than expected, I have actually found her listening to jazz. But Paula also loves classical music, and although she has no desire to pile up a collection of Mozart, Britten, Bach, Stravinsky, and her other favorites, I am always happy to join her in listening when she chooses to play these records.)*

Stephen Frears's film of *High Fidelity* (2000) starred John Cusack as Rob and was surprisingly faithful to the novel even though the action took place in Chicago rather than in London. For my purposes, however, an important difference between novel and film is a shift from mostly black to mostly white music. Rather than primarily favoring the recordings of soul artists, John Cusack's Rob listens to mainstream pop with a special interest in avant-garde rock. Perhaps as a result, the movie strives neither to masculinize him nor to demasculinize him as we might have expected if he collected jazz or blues. And in a scene that clearly separates him from the serial collectors on which this chapter concentrates, Rob is shown rearranging his huge record collection "autobiographically," placing each disc in an order coherent only to him. In the film, Rob explains his new system to Dick (Todd Louiso): "If I want to find the song 'Landslide' by Fleetwood Mac, I have to remember that I bought it for someone in the fall of 1983 pile but didn't give it to them for personal reasons." Dick may or may not be impressed (he seems more concerned about the potential damage to unfiled records lying on top of each other in large stacks on the floor), but there is no question that Rob's collecting habits exhibit a free and idiosyncratic spirit completely alien to most of the collectors who run in my circles. This scene in *High Fidelity* recalls a moment in Richard Powers's novel *The Time of Our Singing* when the character Teresa, who introduces one of the young classically trained protagonists to jazz and pop, says that she arranges her music "by happiness."

At least for me, the movie version of *High Fidelity* thus loses an important dimension by not giving its protagonist a taste for African American music, something created well outside his cultural domain. I am reminded of a sad remark by the British poet and jazz enthusiast Philip Larkin about the people he assumed were reading the jazz record reviews he published in the *London Daily Telegraph* in the 1960s: "sullen fleshly inarticulate men, stockbrokers, sellers of goods, living in 30-year-old detached houses among the golf courses of Outer London, husbands of aging and bitter wives they first seduced to Artie Shaw's 'Begin the Beguine' . . . in whom a pile of scratched coverless 78s in the attic can awaken memories of vomiting blindly from small Tudor windows to Muggsy Spanier's 'Sister Kate'" (Larkin 28). Muggsy Spanier and Artie Shaw were white, not black, but as an Oxford-educated librarian and poet living well north of London, Larkin was much more than an ocean away from the world in which these strange American musicians plied their trade.

In *High Fidelity*, the novel, Rob's constant failures at heterosexual bonding parallels his passion for a black musical culture from which he too is more than an ocean away. In the film, however, Rob, Barry, and Dick live in Chicago and are scarcely alienated from the world of alternative rock, produced in the garages and rec rooms of white people very much like themselves. At Championship Vinyl, the exceedingly nerdish Dick can even slip into a relationship with Anna (Sara Gilbert) after the two exchange knowing glances over a customer's inability to distinguish Stiff Little Fingers from Green Day. The film acknowledges that a woman can have an aficionado's command of alternative rock, but then the population of male and female fans of this music is much larger than the population of men and women who follow jazz and blues.

As many reviewers pointed out, the movie of *High Fidelity* looked back to Barry Levinson's debut feature *Diner* (1982), which featured a young white collector of black music but seemed more attentive to his pathological edge. In *Diner*, Shrevie (Daniel Stern) is one of six young men facing adulthood in the 1950s who regularly participate in male bonding rituals at a local diner. The only married man in the group, Shrevie clearly prefers the diner to life at home with his wife, Beth (Ellen Barkin). Nevertheless, Shrevie reveals a profound romantic streak when he talks about why his record collection is so important to him. In a memorable scene—in fact, the one scene that most people who saw the movie more than twenty years ago are likely to recall—Shrevie becomes enraged when he finds that Beth has filed one of his James Brown albums under "J" rather than "B" and in the rock 'n' roll section instead of in R&B.[1] He then explains to her the logic of his filing system.

> SHREVIE: I mean, you're not going to put Charlie Parker in with the rock 'n' roll, would you? Would you?
>
> BETH: I don't know. Who's Charlie Parker?
>
> SHREVIE: *(In a rage)* JAZZ. JAZZ. He was the greatest jazz saxophone player that ever lived.
>
> BETH: What are you getting so crazy about? It's just music. It's not that big a deal.
>
> SHREVIE: *(Still angry)* It is. Don't you understand? This is important to me.
>
> BETH: *(Near tears)* Shrevie, why do you yell at me? I never hear you yelling at any of your friends.

The comparison between Shrevie's homosocial bonding and his treatment of his wife makes explicit an unresolvable tension in the film. Accordingly, Shrevie expresses great regret that Beth never asks him about what is on the flip sides of records.

> BETH: Who cares what's on the flip side of a record?
>
> SHREVIE: I do. Everyone of my records means something. The label, the producer, the year it was made. Who was copying who's styles, who was expanding on that. Don't you understand? When I listen to my records, they take me back to certain points in my life, OK?

Like the protagonist of *High Fidelity,* Shrevie is disastrously overcommitted to the ordering of his records. But at least he is able to recognize that the music connects him with idealized moments from the past, even if it frustrates romance in the present. Although Marcel Proust is not mentioned in either

Fig. 43. Shrevie (Daniel Stern) makes a go of marriage with Beth (Ellen Barkin) in *Diner* (1982, MGM). Photofest Film Archive.

Diner or *High Fidelity*, the record collectors in both films somehow know that our only paradises are the ones we have lost. *(I'll never forget the extraordinary moment when I first began dating Paula. I put on the recording of Duke Ellington and John Coltrane playing "In a Sentimental Mood," and we danced alone in my apartment. But then everyone has a story like this.)*

After Shrevie abuses his wife for misfiling his beloved records, he goes for a drive with his friend Tim (Kevin Bacon), who shouts out the names of pop tunes so that Shrevie can recall the song on the flip side of the original 45 rpm release. Shrevie glows with delight during an experience that can only be shared with another male. Beth, meanwhile, feels so injured by Shrevie's rage that she is on the verge of an extramarital affair. Unlike *High Fidelity*, however, *Diner* does not show a way out of the record collector's obsessively homosocial behavior. At film's end, little has changed in the lives of the principal characters, including the marriage of Shrevie and Beth. Writer/director Levinson may have been after a critical view of men permanently trapped in late adolescence, but twenty years later the film seems more like a nostalgic if conflicted view of masculinity in the 1950s.

THE ROMANCE OF BLACK MUSIC

Although most of the music favored by the collectors in the novel *High Fidelity* and the film *Diner* is performed by African American artists, the race of musicians is never mentioned in either. Serious jazz and blues collectors, by contrast, are richly aware of race and develop a unique relationship with African American masculinity. As I have argued throughout this book, white males have historically based much of their gender identity in the performative masculinity of African American men. Working-class white men at the minstrel shows could indulge their contempt for African Americans at the same time that they took vicarious pleasure in the supposed transgressiveness, carefree abandon, and unlimited sexual license of black men. Eric Lott argues that many white men are so accustomed to taking their masculine cues from black men that they are for all intents and purposes unaware of it (*Love and Theft* 53). Just as *High Fidelity* and *Diner* never explicitly link race and gender, the importance of black masculinity to white men is seldom discussed in contemporary American culture, at least in part because it has become so unremarkable. The reluctance among white men to acknowledge their fascination with black masculinity may be reinforced by the widely held conviction that ignoring race is, as Toni Morrison has suggested, "a graceful, even generous, liberal gesture" (9–10). Nevertheless, white attention to black masculinity is now more intense than ever. Virtually every syllable of body language with which white athletes and white rock musicians exhibit their masculinity is rooted in African American culture. White men seek black masculinity even where it seems to be absent, as when they imitate the young Elvis Presley, an ideal figure for channeling blackness (Lott, "All the King's Men").

Some collectors of black music may bear a certain resemblance to the Elvis imitator. I am thinking in particular of men who primarily collect the music of white jazz artists, on one level keeping blackness at arm's length while embracing the work of white men who have built their careers on appropriating the styles of black musicians. Woody Allen's *Sweet and Lowdown* (1999) creates a white jazz guitarist from the 1930s named Emmett Ray (Sean Penn), who plays in the style of the Belgian Gypsy guitarist Django Reinhardt. As in *Zelig* (1983) and *Broadway Danny Rose* (1984), Allen includes talking heads or "witnesses" who speak in the style of documentary realism about the fictional guitarist. As is so often the case in jazz films, the handful of black musicians in *Sweet and Lowdown* are only there to validate the superiority of the white artist (Gabbard, *Jammin'* 76–82). And like many of the heroes of jazz films, Emmett Ray is so immersed in his art that he is incapable of making a serious commitment to a woman. As Ray, Sean Penn proves himself to be an extraordinary mime as he moves his fingers over the guitar, looking very much as if he is actually playing the solos that guitarist Howard Alden dubbed in for the film. On the one hand, Ray is one of the many disguises that Woody Allen has created for himself in his vaguely autobiographical films. Both Allen and his character Emmett Ray have disastrous relationships with women, but as Allen is at pains to demonstrate in *Sweet and Lowdown,* an artist's achievements serve to insulate him from any real blame. On the other hand, as a jazz musician Ray is the familiar white Negro, drinking to excess and even working as a pimp when he is not playing jazz. Along with Nat Hentoff and Douglas McGrath, Allen makes a playful appearance as himself in the film, very much the nerdish jazz fan, obsessed with the legend of the fictional Ray and able to speak with great authority about his career as a recording artist. It would not be fair to refer to Allen himself as a mere fan of white jazz, if only because his own clarinet style recalls Sidney Bechet, the canonical Creole clarinettist and soprano saxophonist from New Orleans. Allen even named his daughter after Bechet. Still, many jazz purists have contempt for enthusiasts like the character in *Sweet and Lowdown* played by Allen, who can only appreciate the music of white men imitating the music—and the perceived lifestyles—of black jazz artists.

Jazz purists often take pride in denouncing successful white musicians, such as Paul Whiteman, Glenn Miller, Stan Kenton, Stan Getz, and Dave Brubeck. White artists have made essential contributions throughout jazz history, and some have even made profound impressions on black musicians, the most commonly cited examples being the influence of the white saxophonist Frankie Trumbauer on Lester Young (Porter, *Lester Young* 33–35) and Gil Evans's extensive impact on the career of Miles Davis (Stein Crease).

But insisting on the superiority of "black" over "white" styles allows the jazz fan to claim the moral and political high ground in a racist culture. Many jazz purists were delighted when Miles Davis declared that Oscar Peterson, a black jazz pianist who grew up in Montreal, played like a white person (Lees 174). Peterson has maintained a large following for several decades, but at least since his authenticity as a black artist was questioned by Davis he has never regained the full favor of the jazz cognoscenti.

Those collectors most devoted to black artists will insist upon the superior musical abilities of African American musicians and repress what is, at base, a very strange relationship with black masculinity. One could argue that the white fan of black music is a race traitor who turns his back on the mainstreams of Euro-American culture. Both whites *and* blacks can then charge the white fan with any number of transgressions. A short list would include bad taste, snobbery, slumming, colonizing, voyeurism, and even a form of racism. But the white fan will insist that jazz and blues are simply great art musics and that he is sufficiently free of racial and cultural prejudice to be capable of recognizing the achievements of distinguished black artists. The well-established myth of jazz as an autonomous art is especially useful here because it shifts the debate into primarily aesthetic territory (DeVeaux, "Constructing" 542). As long as he stands by these claims, the white fan need not concern himself with the homoerotic and voyeuristic elements of his fascination with black men as they enact their masculinity with saxophones, trumpets, guitars, and other phallic instruments.

Nor does the white collector need to consider the inferior self-image he creates by insinuating his pale, relatively talentless body next to the African Americans he admires; although the collector possesses the manly power of extensive knowledge and although his gapless record collection provides him with the soothing feeling of masculine plenitude, none of this can compete with the masculine power of the real live black artist. When white collectors seek to justify their pursuits, they engage in massive acts of repression. *(But then all serious fans repress homoeroticism, voyeurism, and much else that is superficially forbidden in mainstream culture, whether they adulate a saxophonist, a coloratura soprano, a baseball player, a politician, or a classical composer. When Franz Schubert was "outed" in the 1990s by musicologists who found evidence that he may have been gay, I overheard one Schubert devotee saying, "But I was moved by Schubert's music. How could he be gay?")*

As is usually the case, the American cinema is where the repressed returns. A devastating portrait of a white jazz collector, including a dramatization of his masculine crises, appears in a 1955 film directed by Richard Brooks
and bearing the ironic title *Blackboard Jungle*. One of the first things we learn
about the bespectacled mathematics teacher Josh Edwards (Richard Kiley) is
that he collects "Swing." After several drinks in a bar with the film's hero,
Richard Dadier (Glenn Ford), Edwards listens admiringly to Stan Kenton's
1952 recording of "Invention for Guitar and Trumpet" on the jukebox, referring to Kenton as "Stan the Man." As Maynard Ferguson's hyperphallic
trumpet solo builds to its piercing climax, Edwards says that he has decided
to play his records for his students. When Dadier cautions him that the students may not like his music, Edwards responds, "Why not? Listen. It took
me fifteen years to collect those records. Half those records can't even be replaced." The stereotypical nerdish collector, Edwards lets his enthusiasm for
acquiring records determine how he conceives the tastes of his students.

Later, when he plays Bix Beiderbecke's trumpet solo on "The Jazz Me
Blues" for his class, Edwards begins by displaying his mastery of musical
knowledge, differentiating Beiderbecke from later stylists, such as Harry James.
Almost immediately, however, the film's principal villain, the tough-talking
delinquent Artie West (Vic Morrow) (fig. 44), takes over and throws the
records into the air while Edwards makes pitiful attempts at preventing them
from shattering on the floor. Unlike the heroic Dadier, who ultimately over-
powers the most malevolent students and wins the respect of the others, the
record collector has control only over his acquisition of musical information.
(*In spite of my current profession, I am like anyone who spent a large portion of his
or her youth locked in classrooms with mediocre teachers, and so I found myself identifying with the hoodlums in* Blackboard Jungle *as they smashed the records.
And seeing the film for the first time in the 1960s as a young jazz aficionado with
contempt for those who collected white artists such as Beiderbecke and Kenton, I
forged no identification with Kiley's Josh Edwards. When Vic Morrow reads off the
titles on the discs just before he throws them into the air, one is "Cow Cow Boogie."
Although the tune was written in part by Benny Carter, the great African American
composer, arranger, and multi-instrumentalist, the most successful version of
the tune was the 1942 recording by Freddie Slack, a Swing Era bandleader who
bleached and rusticated a music associated with urban blacks. This was surely the
record in Josh Edward's collection, and in the 1960s I applauded its destruction.*

Fig. 44. Juvenile delinquents led by Vic Morrow (*center*) are not impressed by Richard Kiley's record collection. *Blackboard Jungle* (1955, MGM). Photofest Film Archive.

Today, however, I am no longer so staunch a purist. An immersion in the critical theory of the 1970s and 1980s—with its battle cry "Problematize, problematize, problematize!"—has helped me develop an ironic distance from the old purism. Although I have never written on Freddie Slack, I am surely the only person born after 1945 who has written on his equally white, equally successful, and equally forgotten peer, Kay Kyser. See Jammin' at the Margins *19–33. I even conclude that Kyser's bands were not so bad when compared with other swing orchestras from the era.)*

The contradictory relationship between record collecting and masculinity is even more explicit in *Young Man with a Horn* (1950). The eponymous hero Rick Martin (Kirk Douglas) idolizes Art Hazard (Juano Hernandez), an aging black trumpeter who effectively adopts the orphaned hero as a child and instructs him in the art of the jazz trumpet. The young white acolyte's monkish devotion to Hazard and the discipline of the trumpet keeps him innocent until he marries the socialite Amy North (Lauren Bacall), who neglects Rick and, according to the logic of the film, turns him into an alcoholic. On the day that Rick returns from Art Hazard's funeral, he finds Amy in the beginnings of what the film darkly suggests is a lesbian affair. As if this blow to Rick's male ego were not sufficient, Amy tells him that she hates the sound of brass and then breaks his records by throwing them on the floor. Rick begins a downward slide that culminates when he falls in the street and a car flattens his trumpet, a sure sign of castration in the film's phallic discourse of the trumpet. *Young Man with a Horn* only allows Rick Martin to regain his masculinity when he abandons the jazz life and forms a liaison with Jo Jordan (Doris Day), a much more submissive and attentive woman than Amy North (Gabbard, *Jammin'* 67–75). We can also assume that a remasculinized Rick has no need for his record collection and the access it once gave him to his black mentor and the *jouissance* of the jazz trumpet.

BODY SNATCHERS

Unlike the Elvis imitator, and unlike Josh Edwards/Richard Kiley in *Blackboard Jungle,* the Rick Martin of *Young Man with a Horn* pursues black masculinity more directly by acquiring the music of a favored African American artist. So does Francis (François Cluzet) in *Round Midnight* (1986). But whereas the interracial erotics in *Young Man with a Horn* are moderated by allowing Art Hazard to function as both father and mother to Rick Martin, the romance is more overt in *Round Midnight,* in which Francis, a French jazz enthusiast, literally collects the body of the black jazz artist Dale Turner (Dexter Gordon). *Round Midnight* was inspired by the lives of Lester Young and Bud Powell, highly respected black American jazz artists who were plagued by substance abuse problems. Powell spent a great deal of time in Paris, where he was looked after by Francis Paudras, the commercial artist and jazz devotee who was clearly the model for the Francis of *Round Midnight.*

In *Round Midnight,* Francis first meets saxophonist Dale Turner when the latter is most interested in drinking himself into oblivion. Francis competes with Turner's black female companion, Buttercup (Sandra Reaves-Phillips), for possession of the lumbering saxophonist, who would spend most of his time in jails and hospitals without the constant interventions of Francis. Eventually Francis wins the struggle with Buttercup and relocates to a larger apartment that can hold both his young daughter and Turner, not to mention his record collection. Once he has moved in with Francis, the jazzman stops drinking and becomes a contented bourgeois, at one point preparing an elaborate dinner for Francis and his daughter. Turner also begins "composing," a familiar trope in jazz films that constructs the jazz musician

on a European model as a writer of music rather than as an improviser or con-
ceptualist. Turner only slips back into his old drug-taking habits when he returns to the United States, far away from the watchful eyes of Francis. The
Frenchman expresses his passion for the black jazz artist in a conversation
with his estranged wife midway through the film. Francis awkwardly asks his
wife to loan him money so that he can rent the larger apartment to accommodate Turner. He says, "If I'm anything today, it's on account of guys like
him," "I would do anything for him," and "Nobody inspires me like him."
The film may grant Francis's wife more pathos than it intends when she poses
a question that is crucial to *Round Midnight*'s interracial male romance: "And
I never inspired you?" Francis does not answer.

But Francis has taken his love of the music to unusual extremes by collecting a musician's body. Most jazz and blues collectors are content to fill
their lives only with the sounds of black musicians, although a few let their
collections expand in other directions. *(My friend Herbert is a good example of
the obsessed collector. In building what is surely the most extensive Charlie Parker
collection I have ever seen, he has filled his study not just with records, CDs, and
rare tape recordings of unissued material. He also owns a copy of every known
photograph of Parker, including several overlooked photos in which the alto saxophonist is not holding his horn. His vast collection of Parker memorabilia also includes documents such as record contracts with the saxophonist's signature and a
giant poster of Forest Whitaker as Charlie Parker in the 1988 film* Bird. *Herbert's
goal seems to be to re-create the body of Parker within his study.)*

As an "art" film by the French auteur/director Bertrand Tavernier, *Round
Midnight* could take on the subject of interracial male romance without fear
of intervention from nervous studio bosses. In the Hollywood cinema, by
contrast, white jazz collectors are more likely to pursue black women than
black men. In *Corrina, Corrina* (1994), Manny Singer (Ray Liotta) is a recently
widowed advertising executive living in the suburbs of Los Angeles in the early
1960s. He hires Corrina (Whoopi Goldberg) to be the caregiver for a young
daughter still traumatized by the death of her mother. Goldberg has frequently played a black woman with real devotion to white people, which may
explain why she has appeared in more than one hundred films and made-for-
television movies since 1985. While the earthy Corrina gradually brings both
the handsome father and the charming daughter out of their shells, she
bonds with the father as they listen to the jazz and black music in his collec-

Fig. 45. Francis (François Cluzet) brings home Dale Turner (Dexter Gordon) in
Round Midnight (1986, Little Bear/Warner Bros.). Photofest Film Archive.

tion, especially Louis Armstrong and Oscar Peterson's 1957 recording of "You
Go to My Head." The film suggests that the same open-minded approach to
life that made Manny a jazz collector has led him to make the daring but entirely appropriate decision to take the wise and warm Corrina as a lover.

Zack (Michael Rapaport), the teenage hero of *Zebrahead* (1992), comes
from three generations of jazz record collectors. He and his father run a
record store in Detroit that was established in the 1940s by his grandfather.
The walls are plastered with the photos of canonical jazz artists, and at one
point the grandfather boasts that he "broke bebop in." Although Zack also
has a passion for the most popular black music, and although he often
speaks in the cadences of a rapper, he reserves jazz for the more important
moments in his life, as when he seduces Nicky (N'Bushe Wright) with the
sounds of John Coltrane playing "Say It Over and Over Again" from the extraordinary *Ballads* LP from 1962. Nicky is a black teenager at the same high
school as Zack, and although their love affair has tragic results, they are
closer than ever at the film's end. Like *Corrina, Corrina, Zebrahead* is extremely generous about the white man's intentions, linking his love of black

music with feelings for a black woman that are not, as in Spike Lee's 1991 film, simply a case of "Jungle Fever." Nor does Michael Rapaport's Zack in *Zebrahead* look forward to the character that Rapaport plays in another Spike Lee film, *Bamboozled* (2000). Thomas Dunwitty (Rapaport) is the director of programming at a television network who encourages the black protagonist (Damon Wayans) to put old-fashioned minstrelsy on prime-time television. On several levels, *Bamboozled* recalls Ralph Ellison's *Invisible Man*, most notably when Dunwitty echoes the dogmatic white leader of the Brotherhood who exploits Ellison's nameless hero. Like Ellison's Brother Jack, Dunwitty points to his black wife and children to argue that he knows more about African American culture than does the black, Harvard-educated protagonist.[2] Rapaport's two turns as a white Negro show how a man's passion for black music and black women can be construed in radically different ways by two different filmmakers.

REDEEMING THE NERD

Hollywood's compulsory heterosexuality aside, it would be simplistic and obtuse to say that white male collectors are only attracted to black masculinity, which is every bit as variegated and complex as white masculinity. Fans of jazz and blues tend to be less interested in black athletes or in the more provocatively masculine music of African American youth culture, such as rap and hip hop. The favored form of black masculinity for jazz and blues collectors can be understated, ironic, instinctual, learned, witty, slightly transgressive, and maybe even a bit pathetic, as in the delicate tenor voices of some early blues singers. The most admired jazz artists can be regal like Duke Ellington, ebullient like Roy Eldridge, angry like Charles Mingus, or sublimely lyrical like Clifford Brown. Like Charlie Parker and John Coltrane, they can display great reserve in their nonmusical personae while playing with astounding intensity. By means of short musical quotations an accomplished improviser like Dexter Gordon can make sly references to other musical traditions, always maintaining a poker face so that only the most sophisticated listeners even know that a joke has been cracked (Gabbard, "The Quoter"). In short, the revered black jazz artist is hip.

Will Straw has developed a typology for understanding collectors of rock and popular music that is also useful for conceptualizing black artists and the white men who follow their recording careers. Straw differentiates the dandy, who has little substantial knowledge but complete mastery of how to appear poised in public, from the nerd, whose knowledge "stands as the easily diagnosed cause of performative social failure, blatantly indexed in the nerd's chaotic and unmonitored self-presentation" (8). To help theorize these types, Straw adds the figure of the brute, who is all physical, instinctual power but with little knowledge or grace. While jazz and blues enthusiasts may look to the black musician for a certain degree of instinctual, almost brutish energy, the most revered artists are likely to present a rich store of knowledge just beneath a seemingly intuitive, even crude exterior. This aspect of the jazz artist's self-presentation is surely what drives the allegory in Rafi Zabor's novel, *The Bear Comes Home,* the story of an anatomically complete Kodiak grizzly bear with the mind of a sensitive human and the ability to play the alto saxophone in the styles of Ornette Coleman and Jackie McLean.

Straw's typology provides the beginnings for one of those Greimasian squares so beloved by early semioticians. Ignoring the dandy's social graces for the moment, we can construct a square with one axis for exteriorized masculinity and another for knowledge. The dandy presents little in the way of either masculinity or knowledge; the brute is all masculine exterior without knowledge; the nerd has so much knowledge that it seems to prevent any conventional masculine display; but the hipster musician is able to balance a powerful masculine presentation with solid knowledge of a rich tradition.

THE JAZZ NERD AND HIS CIRCLE
(with apologies to Will Straw and Algirdas Greimas)

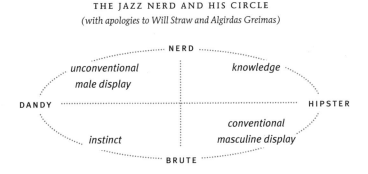

It might be argued that every white jazz nerd secretly desires to be a black jazz artist. Bill Moody has written a series of detective novels about a jazz pianist named Evan Horne that takes the idealization of the jazz connoisseur to new extremes. The dust jackets of Moody's books say that he is a jazz drummer, but he has not left much of a trail in the various jazz discographies. In each of Moody's five books, Evan Horne uses his insider knowledge of jazz to solve crimes that baffle the police. In *Bird Lives!* (1999), for example, he tracks down the murderer of commercially successful "jazz-lite" artists for whom both Evan *and* the killer have nothing but contempt. The killer, a devout fan of canonical jazz musicians, throws out clues that only a serious collector of jazz records can decode and eventually begins communicating directly with Horne through haikus constructed from titles of jazz recordings, such as

> On Coltrane's Soultrane
> Jazz is always great Good Bait
> Tadd's Long Gone—Delight! (Moody, Bird Lives! 98)

Although we are told that Horne is a fine jazz pianist, during large stretches of the novels he is either injured or preoccupied with chasing criminals and thus unable to work regularly as a musician. And although women find him attractive, he has difficulty maintaining a stable relationship. He is in effect a jazz nerd made heroic thanks to a fantasy in which a vast knowledge of music can save lives and bring criminals to justice. *(The more common fantasy among male collectors is probably that the energy expended in acquiring the music and the knowledge that goes with it pays off in getting him laid. But that fantasy has been thoroughly exploded in more than one film. Read on.)*

Straw writes, "Collecting is an important constituent of those male character formations, such as nerdism, which, while offering an alternative to a blatantly patriarchal masculinity, are rarely embraced as subversive challenges to it" (Straw 10). Record collecting in the Evan Horne mysteries does not allow for a subversion of patriarchal masculinity so much as it offers the heroic collector an opportunity to one-up the patriarchs on the police force. But a few American films involving jazz and blues collectors may in fact offer examples of nerdism as subversive challenge. First, there is the rare image of an African American jazz collector, Mr. Moses (James Earl Jones) in *The Meteor Man* (1993), directed by Robert Townsend, the famously resourceful black director who once financed a film by maxing out a stack of credit cards. *(Are there black jazz nerds in real life? I know, for example, African American computer nerds, but I have never met a black jazz nerd, and I doubt that any African American man will self-identify as such. My friend Maurice, for example,*

is a devoted African American collector of jazz recordings who also possesses an al-
most complete inventory of social graces and worked his way through college on a
baseball scholarship. The ontology of the nerd would seem to be unthinkable with-
out some distance from black masculinity.) Townsend probably found the name
for James Earl Jones's character *not* in the Old Testament but in the term
"Mose," African American slang for an older, more submissive black man.
(See, for example, the regular appearance of the term in the letters of Ralph
Ellison and Albert Murray collected in *Trading Twelves.*) Costumed throughout *Meteor Man* in nerd mufti, Mr. Moses reflects more than just Townsend's
desire to create a greater panorama of black culture than Hollywood usually
offers. Mr. Moses even takes on a heroic quality at a crucial moment when
he uses his beloved 78s as weapons against a gang of thugs.

Steve Buscemi plays a less dynamic but certainly more nuanced collector
of old black music in Terry Zwigoff's *Ghost World* (2001). Although the film
takes its title and characters from the graphic novel by Daniel Clowes,
Zwigoff has said that he added the character of Seymour to the cinematic
version of the story, knowing from the outset that only Buscemi could play
the part. An extremely versatile actor, Buscemi has made the most of his un-
conventional looks. As Carl in *Fargo,* he is regularly characterized as "funny
lookin'" (see chapter four). He has been cast as a wimpy loser in films such
as *Reservoir Dogs* (1992), *Airheads* (1994), and *The Big Lebowski* (1998). He
has played a romantic gay man in *Parting Glances* (1986) as well as a violent
and overbearing ward heeler from the 1930s in *Kansas City* (1996) and a taciturn contract killer in *Things to Do in Denver When You're Dead* (1995). If any
generalizations can be made about Buscemi as an actor (he has also directed
and written for films and television), they would involve his ability to project
intelligence and a bit of a self-mockery in his roles. Hence his extremely busy
career in the independent film industry.

As in the novel, Enid (Thora Birch) and Rebecca (Scarlett Johansson) are
recent high school graduates with no real plans but with plenty of contempt for
everyone else in their unnamed southern California town. Taking an interest
only in people who are profoundly strange, they direct special scorn at anyone
who is ordinary and/or enthusiastic. The film begins with Enid mimicking the
manic dancing of Lakshmi Chayya in the 1965 Bollywood film *Gumnaam* as
it plays on her television. Later she appears to be listening to heavy metal rock.
Otherwise, she ridicules punk rock, Reggae, and a local band called "Alien

Autopsy." Her attraction to Bollywood music is presented not necessarily as heartfelt but as part of her rebel's devotion to anything exotic or unusual as well as her keen sense of kitsch. Only when she encounters Seymour does Enid drop her adolescent nihilism and, at least temporarily, take music more seriously.

Seymour first appears after Enid and Rebecca see his notice in the personals in a local newspaper. In his message, Seymour suggests that he shared something with a "striking blonde" when he helped her find her contact lens as they were getting off an airplane. Enid calls Seymour to pose as the blonde and then convinces their friend Josh (Brad Renfro) to drive her and Rebecca to the 1950s retro diner where she has told Seymour she will meet him. As the three teenagers watch in perverse fascination, Seymour arrives and waits at the counter, desultorily drinking a vanilla milk shake before he leaves alone. Later, when Enid and Rebecca see him selling records at a garage sale, they approach him in the same spirit of sadistic fun. When Enid asks if he has any Indian music, Seymour humorlessly informs her, "I don't really collect foreign." Seymour does, however, recommend an LP, "Country Blues Classics, Vol. 3," urging her to check out the cut by Memphis Minnie. (*There were in fact four volumes in this series, released on the Blues Classics label in the 1960s. The enterprising producers of the discs made sure that their album covers consisted of little more than severe black type on white paper. The lack of elaborate cover art and liner hype lent authority to the series and gave it much more cachet than more fussily produced LPs might carry. And by numbering the volumes in the series, the producers offered completists still another opportunity to seek plenitude. My friend Lenny has all four volumes.*) Seymour claims to know the person who owns the extremely rare original recording by Memphis Minnie that is on the LP. But when Enid listens to the LP at home, she has an unexpectedly powerful reaction to a different track, Skip James's 1931 recording of "Devil Got My Woman." (*Although there is in fact a Memphis Minnie cut on "Country Blues Classics, Vol. 3," the recording by Skip James does not appear on any of the volumes in the series. Is Terry Zwigoff tormenting the collectors in his audience?*) Although she never articulates exactly what she hears, we see her listening intently to James's eccentric guitar and the haunting, ragged melismas of his falsetto singing. For the first time something has touched her, and she becomes convinced that Seymour is different from the rest. Paying him a back-handed compliment that is nevertheless high praise, she tells Rebecca, "He's the opposite of everything I hate."

Fig. 46. Seymour (Steve Buscemi) is in fact more interested in Enid (Thora Birch) than she is in him in *Ghost World* (2001, United Artists/MGM). Jerry Ohlinger's Movie Material Store, Inc.

But Seymour has no real future with Enid, and not just because he is more than twice her age (fig. 46). He observes how "loser collectors" like himself fill up their lives with useless junk. He even makes the explicit connection between his zeal for collecting and his lack of a girlfriend. Unlike films such as *High Fidelity* and *Zebrahead*, *Ghost World* connects a white man's studious passion for black music to his corresponding failure with what might be appropriate women. Insisting that Seymour should have no trouble finding a female companion and hoping to heal the wound she inflicted by pretending to be the woman he saw on the plane, Enid makes a few feeble attempts at matchmaking. At Seymour's request they go to a noisy club where an elderly black guitarist (J. J. "Bad Boy" Jones) skillfully picks out his tunes while only Seymour pays attention. Meanwhile, Enid has convinced a young red-haired woman with an ample bosom to join Seymour at his table. Although the young woman listens attentively as he speaks, Seymour can only lecture her on the differences between ragtime and authentic blues, richly aware that this kind of knowledge is getting him nowhere. She says that she especially loves the group of young white boys, "Blueshammer," who soon take the stage, declaring that they are about to sing "way down in the

Delta blues." While the group ineptly sings in conventional pop-rock style about "pickin' cotton," the redhead dances provocatively. When another dancer bumps Seymour, he spills beer on his trousers. *(Watching Seymour surrounded by philistines as he tries to listen to the music he loves, and later as he is unable to prevent himself from alienating the redhead with his correct but didactic distinctions among musical genres, I experienced a moment of overwhelming identification with the nerd. My guess is that anyone who does not share the tastes of the masses—even people who love what is oxymoronically known as "alternative rock"—can share Seymour's feelings at this point.)*

Although Seymour makes no progress with the redhead, he still has the attentions of Enid, who at least shares his contempt for the various poseurs in the club. The film is unusual in bringing an actual African American into the film to perform what is constructed as authentic black music and not just as romantic accompaniment for lovable white protagonists. That no one except Seymour listens to the music and that the white audience responds enthusiastically to the white rockers is a deft critique of the racial imbalances that the popular music industry—and the Hollywood cinema—have kept alive. As a proudly independent film, *Ghost World* carefully exposes the practices that Hollywood both exploits and conceals.

The film has even more to say about the racial contradictions submerged in American culture when Seymour shows Enid a separate portion of his collection that does *not* include recordings. Seymour has preserved several advertisements and artifacts that document a history of racist advertising at Cook's Chicken, a chain of restaurants that employs Seymour at its corporate headquarters. One of several advertisements for "Coon Chicken" is a larger-than-life image of a smiling minstrel face. Seymour has arranged the set of old advertisements and menus in chronological order to show how Coon Chicken gradually replaced its grotesquely smiling black faces with antiseptic white faces as it became Cook's Chicken.[3] Of course, Seymour is implicated in this racist past not just because he works for Cook's Chicken but because his polymorphous fascination with blackness has led him to preserve the old documents. Enid is soon given a hard lesson in how these ambivalences are played out when she brings the large minstrel face to her art class. Although the flamboyantly artsy, hyper-sincere teacher (Illeana Douglas) expresses great admiration for the poster as a work of art, several people object when the face is subsequently displayed in an exhibit of student art. When the poster is publicly removed, a photographer is there to document the incident. Enid and her art teacher are not the only people who regret the incident. When the photograph is published in the local newspaper, the executives at Cook's Chicken know that Seymour has brought the item out of his collection into the public eye, and he is fired.

Meanwhile, Enid has taken the reckless step of sleeping with Seymour just as he is beginning to establish a relationship with Dana (Stacey Travis), the blonde woman with whom he had originally hoped to reconnect through the ad in the personals. When Dana finally responds to the ad, explaining that she was still in a relationship when she first read it, Enid is there to convince the once-burned-twice-shy Seymour that this might be the real thing. His relationship with Dana is off to a promising start, in spite of the fact that she listens to the music of Ashford and Simpson and takes an unseemly, gung-ho attitude toward her job at a real estate office. But Seymour is much more taken with Enid and is totally smitten after they have sex. He breaks off with Dana and begins pursuing Enid with constant (unanswered) phone calls, only to find out later that she was the one who staged his humiliation at the restaurant. Having lost two girlfriends and his job, Seymour picks a fight with Josh when he learns that he had driven Enid and Rebecca to the restaurant. A dim-witted martial arts enthusiast (Dave Sheridan)—very much the instinctual, ostentatiously masculine "brute" on the Greimas square above—joins the fight, and Seymour ends up in the hospital.

Feeling guilty for not returning his phone calls prior to the fight, and devastated that Seymour has found out about her prank, Enid pays him a visit in the hospital. When he says that he is not angry with her because he knows that she thinks he is a "dork," Enid responds, "You're not a dork. You're like . . . (*pause*) . . . my hero." She then shows him her book of drawings that are filled with idealized images of Seymour. But there is no happy ending for either the teenager or the record collector. The film ends with Enid leaving town on a bus to nowhere and Seymour sitting in the office of a female psychiatrist (Diane Salinger), who clearly regards him as a lost cause. Seymour is left with nothing but his record collection. (*The biggest disappointment for me is that Enid loses interest in Seymour's music at the same time that she loses interest in Seymour. The last music she listens to is a scratchy old record preserved from her childhood, "A Smile and a Ribbon," by Patience and Prudence. Even worse, David Kitay's score for the film is suffused with standard Hollywood*

*pathos, announcing that the film itself shares little of the irreverence of its char-
acters and inviting us to feel sorry for lost souls like Enid and Seymour. I was hoping the film would find a way to redeem one or both of the principals through a
renewed passion for great black music. Why couldn't the film have ended with
Seymour and Enid listening to some of Duke Ellington's best records from the
1930s? "Delta Serenade," perhaps? Or could it be that the film is punishing Enid
because she abandoned Skip James for Patience and Prudence? Or perhaps the film
is actually becoming more conservative at its ending. Does Enid's abandonment of
her outsider tastes in music therefore represent her social rehabilitation and thus
her decision to leave her old life behind? These are complex questions.)*

Although *Ghost World* was scarcely intended for a large, mainstream audience, it was much more marketable than Terry Zwigoff's previous film, the
1994 documentary *Crumb*.[4] A careful look at the brilliant cartoonist and collector of early blues and jazz, the film begins with a long tracking shot across
the bizarre items in R. Crumb's living room, finally ending with the artist on
the floor crouching in a fetal position next to shelves full of records. He is
swaying gently to the music. The film makes several references to his collection, especially at the end when he is carefully packing his records into boxes
as he moves out of his old house.

Throughout the film, Robert Crumb wears what might generously be
called "vintage clothes," including a series of jaunty hats that no one has
worn since the 1940s. He regularly expresses contempt for American culture,
including its embrace of his own art work. Although he is best known for the
cartoon and slogan "Keep on truckin'," he sternly warns people against saying to him, "Hey R., keep on truckin'." He is also famous for his cover art on
an early LP by Janis Joplin with Big Brother and the Holding Company, but
Crumb says that he hated their music and that he would fall asleep at psy-
chedelic rock concerts. We see him at an outdoor café drawing caricatured
images of "ordinary" people for whom he shares the same contempt as Enid
of *Ghost World*. Under Crumb's gaze, blandly attractive people suddenly
seem as grotesque as his drawings. But in a rare moment, Crumb explains
why the blues, which he seems to collect exclusively on old 78s, almost brings
out in him a love for humanity: "You hear the best part of the common people, their way of expressing their connection to eternity, or whatever you
want to call it. Modern music doesn't have that sense of calamitous loss. . . .
People can't express themselves that way anymore." The camera then catches

him leaning back to listen to a scratchy old recording of "Last Kind Word Blues," performed by Geechie Wiley. Although the concept of authenticity in folk music is especially easy to deconstruct, there is real poignancy in this brief scene when Crumb talks about what he likes and not about what he hates. His deep connection to the music is even apparent in his series of trading cards, "Heroes of the Blues," with their reverential portraits of artists such as Sleepy John Estes, Blind Willie McTell, and Charlie Patton.

When Crumb talks about "calamitous loss," he could be referring to his own happy childhood, a brief period that seems to have been thoroughly destroyed when his parents began having problems. Charles, Robert's older brother, says the trouble began when he was about nine and his mother suffered side effects from the amphetamines she was taking to keep her weight down. He says that his parents fought so violently that his father would put on make-up before he left for the office to cover up the scratches on his face. As for the father, Charles calls him "an overbearing tyrant" and "a sadistic bully" and recalls regular beatings. But in retrospect Charles partially attributes the beatings to his own unconscious need for punishment. Robert says that his father broke his collarbone on Christmas day when he was five years old. Although the father died in 1982, he has left his mark on each of his three sons. (There are also two sisters, but they declined to be interviewed for the film, and we are told nothing about their lives as adults.) Charles became an unemployed recluse, living with his mother and surviving on antidepressants. We are told in a title card at the end of *Crumb* that Charles committed suicide shortly after filming came to an end.

Robert's younger brother Maxon appears to be even more deeply disturbed than Charles. He lives alone in what appears to be a welfare hotel with virtually no furniture in his small room. In conversation with Robert, Maxon talks about his history of epileptic seizures and his habit of sexually molesting women he sees on the street. He laughs about the day he acted on an irresistible urge and pulled down the pants of a woman he suddenly decided to follow into a store. At one point Maxon sits on a bed of nails while swallowing a long piece of cloth that will supposedly cleanse his system as it passes through his intestines over a period of several days. During the scenes in which Robert is filmed with each of his brothers, he laughs heartily and appears to be enjoying himself, although he might also be making light of their appalling lives for the sake of the film crew. Nevertheless, for all his hostilities and obsessions, compared to his two profoundly alien-ated brothers, Robert appears happy and well-adjusted.

Crumb's career as an artist apparently began when he joined Charles in creating comic books that provided fantasy alternatives to their unhappy lives. Although Charles stopped drawing in 1962, Robert says that he still feels his brother looking over his shoulder, judging everything that he draws. While all three of the brothers refused to adopt conventional adult roles, only Robert was able to live a decent life while exploring his childhood anxi-eties and fantasies. Crumb is not ashamed to catalogue the items that ex-cited him sexually when he was growing up. The list includes Bugs Bunny and a pair of boots that his aunt used to wear. He takes perverse pride in his eccentricities, embellishing one of his magazine covers with the phrase, "How glorious it is and also how painful to be an exception."

Of course, much of the material for which Crumb is best known is deeply offensive on multiple levels. Zwigoff presents commentators who criticize his treatment of women and blacks, at one point attributing it to his fears of impotence and powerlessness. His defenders, including his wife, Aline, also a cartoonist, argue that Crumb is not afraid to unleash his id and

Fig. 47. Cartoonist and record collector R. Crumb poses with his son, Jesse (*left*), and his brother Maxon (*center*). Photofest Film Archive.

depict his darker side. Aline even says that it is best that Crumb work through his hostilities in his drawings so that he can live free of them in his personal life. At one point, the camera shows Crumb's "advertisement" for a canned product called "Wildman Sam's Pure Nigger Hearts," complete with racist caricatures of a black woman. Crumb says that the idea came to him in the 1960s when he was taking LSD. Only later did he begin to analyze its origins. He does not make the logical claim that the drawing is satirical in the great tradition of Jonathan Swift. He muses rather that it expresses "some black, deep thing in the American collective mind. . . . It has to do with turning everything over for a buck."

Crumb connects R. Crumb's disastrous childhood both with his passion for old blues recordings and with the contents of his drawings, including the "Nigger Hearts" cartoon. The film hints that Crumb has dealt with his own emotional pain by finding it compellingly recast in the "authentic" folk voices of black blues singers. His dismay at the shallowness of modern life takes many forms, including one tirade about people who become walking adver-tisements by wearing legible clothing embossed with corporate logos. He also denounces the inept 1972 film based on his character Fritz the Cat, calling it "an embarrassment to me for the rest of my life." For Crumb, much of con-temporary entertainment is a bastardization of something real, whether it is Crumb's own creations or the sense of "calamitous loss" he hears in old blues recordings. However offensive the "Nigger Hearts" cartoon may be, Crumb would have us place it in quotations marks, disassociating it from his racial politics and casting it as a critique of how American life degrades and com-modifies the soul as well as the *heart* of African American culture.

Zwigoff has probably based the Seymour of *Ghost World* on R. Crumb. Both have a fascination with African American culture that drives them to pile up old blues records as well as more unsavory representations. Whether they know it or not, both are implicated in the racism of the representations with which they surround themselves. In addition, both have an ironic view of their obsession with old recordings. Although Crumb is filmed telling his teenage son that he will kill him if he breaks one of his records while they are packing them in boxes and then mutters to the camera about workmen who may or may not be taking proper care as they wheel the crates into a moving van, he also talks about the absurdity of living with "all these damn records." In one gentle swipe at Crumb (and himself), Zwigoff put a scene into *Ghost*

World with Enid holding up a record of "R. Crumb and His Cheap Suit Sere-naders," on which Crumb sings some of his favorite old songs and even plays the banjo. Enid holds up the LP for only a moment before Seymour says, "Nah, that one's not so great." (Zwigoff himself plays cello on the LP, and it is entirely possible that he based the Seymour of *Ghost World* on himself as much as on Crumb.) Even if Crumb's surrogate in *Ghost World* is portrayed as a pitiful loser, Zwigoff has maintained a friendship with Crumb as well as with his daughter, Sophie, who supplied the many drawings in *Ghost World* that are attributed to Enid.

As *Crumb* comes to an end, we see Robert and Aline preparing to move to a small village in France. Although he insists that this is purely his wife's idea, Crumb seems content to pack up his records and leave America behind. There is no suggestion that he is henpecked, and we regularly see him ex-pressing physical affection with other women, including former girlfriends. When asked about her husband's habit of "fooling around" with other women, Aline quickly replies that she fools around with other men. Throughout the documentary, Crumb is masculinized in ways that would have been out of the question for Steve Buscemi's Seymour. With his frac-tured sense of style, his Coke bottle glasses, and his lingering attachment to fetishized objects from his childhood, Crumb is, on the one hand, the em-bodiment of nerdism as the subversive challenge to patriarchal masculinity that Straw cannot find in the community of rock music collectors. On the other hand, Crumb is a man of substantial talent who goes about his work with self-knowledge and humility. Although he may have developed a hard shell to adapt to surroundings that proved fatal to at least one of his siblings, the Crumb we meet in Zwigoff's film emerges as a person of wit and sensi-tivity beneath an unkempt exterior. Although he hardly promotes himself as hypermasculine, Crumb's place on the square would probably be much closer to the hipster than to the nerd.

In fact, the postmodern docudrama *American Splendor* (2003), which appeared just as this book was going to press, actually casts the debonair young actor James Urbaniak as R. Crumb. The star of the film, however, is Harvey Pekar, a friend of Crumb's since the 1970s. For many years, Pekar has written the text for comic books and "graphic novels" that Crumb and oth-ers have illustrated. Paul Giamatti plays Pekar throughout most of the film, but the real-life Pekar also makes several appearances. Although Harvey

Pekar has written a great deal of jazz criticism, and although we regularly see swaybacked shelves full of LPs amidst the squalor of his apartment, the film has little to say about the music to which Pekar actually listens. Unlike *Crumb,* in which the cartoonist talks about his love for the blues and its sense of "calamitous loss," and unlike many of the narratives that Pekar himself has included in his comic books, *American Splendor* has no scene in which Pekar articulates what it is about black music that fascinates him.

An important musical feature of *American Splendor,* however, is a score by Mark Suozzo with trumpet solos by Dave Douglas, who intentionally imitates the sound of Miles Davis in the late 1950s. Many scenes in the film are decidedly less unpleasant thanks to the pathos and beauty of what Douglas and the other musicians are playing on the soundtrack. In this sense, *American Splendor* has a bit in common with *The Talented Mr. Ripley, Pleasantville,* and the many other films that use the dark, pure tone of a jazz trumpet to give certain scenes an emotional resonance they would not otherwise possess.

For the purposes of this chapter, however, *American Splendor* is extremely important for presenting R. Crumb as a hip, even glamorous artist with easy access to women, in stark contrast to Pekar, who emerges as deeply dysfunctional and implacably angry at life. If nothing else, *American Splendor* continues the work of *Crumb* by portraying R. Crumb as the ideal to which the white male collector of jazz and blues aspires. Scrupulously ignoring the most prominent codes of proper attire and grooming *(and God knows I have been to concerts where 90 percent of the men would have been thrown out of even a mildly pretentious restaurant),* the collector's appearance asserts that he has risen above such superficial concerns. But he is not entirely oblivious to all codes of bodily display. Unlike the headbanger in a mosh pit or the inert bourgeois at the symphony, the connoisseur of blues and jazz nods insouciantly with a carefully cultivated balance between detachment and involvement. Thus does the collector make use of the highly refined masculine codes he has learned from black musicians. Norman Mailer's white Negro apocalyptics and ultimate orgasms notwithstanding, the nerdish collector strives to become the hipster artist's double off the bandstand. The nerd seeks this transcendence in his soul even if the uninitiated cannot possibly decode its exterior manifestations.

And this is why the dominant codes of representation will never be kind to the collector and why the subversive challenges presented by the nerd are seldom taken seriously. In a culture with a mammoth entertainment industry vigorously promoting spectacular masculinity and jingoistic display, the nerd becomes a marginal figure because, like Crumb, he has refused to accept the most entrenched values of that culture. It would be difficult to imagine a mainstream Hollywood film endorsing the sentiments of someone like Crumb, who did, after all, leave America for France, where people have more respect for black music. The jazz and blues collector may be most hip and subversive when he creates an identity that is unrepresentable in mainstream culture.

(And even if I'm wrong about all of this, I still have my record collection.)

PART FOUR

BLACK MAGIC, INVERTED

CHAPTER EIGHT

Robert Altman's
Jazz History Lesson

Just after the release of *Kansas City* in August 1996, Robert Altman told several interviewers that his jazz-infused film was constructed *like* jazz.[1] Altman has been justly celebrated for his ability to coax memorable performances out of actors by turning them loose without a script. Elliott Gould certainly did his best work riffing with Altman. His extraordinary improvisations in Altman's *The Long Goodbye* (1973) and *California Split* (1974) make most of his performances in other films seem wooden by comparison. In *Kansas City,* as in all of Altman's films, there was much jazz-inspired ad-libbing during the rehearsal process, but the planning behind the film was anything but ad hoc. *Kansas City* was scrupulously researched and meticulously assembled in ways that barely resemble the in-the-moment improvisations of a jazz performance. And like the performances of Marlon Brando (see chapter one), a great deal of what seems like improvisation only looks that way. Like the best jazz artists, Altman, his staff, and his actors know exactly what they are doing as they impart spontaneity to a rigorously rehearsed performance.

As with his earlier film *Short Cuts* (1993), Altman co-wrote the screenplay for *Kansas City* with Frank Barhydt, like Altman a Kansas City native. Altman and Barhydt's film was fiction, but its Kansas City of 1934 was based on facts. The soft-spoken boss Tom Pendergast, the ineffectual governor Guy Park, the respectable criminal John Lazia, and the shootings at a polling place on election day are all presented with as much attention to the history books as can be expected from a Hollywood film.[2] The automobiles, the hair-styles, the telephones, the storefronts on Eighteenth and Vine, and the old Beaux-Arts Union Station all look much as they did in 1934. Carolyn Stilton (Miranda Richardson), the wife of a fictional politician, even gives a little speech about "Goats and Rabbits," although the film never explains that these were nicknames for local political factions.[3]

With similarly understated fidelity to jazz history, *Kansas City* represents the artists who invented a distinct style of music in that wide-open city. Count Basie, Lester Young, Mary Lou Williams, Ben Webster, and Jo Jones, all of whom were in Kansas City in 1934, are played by real-life jazz musicians in the film. According to Geri Allen, who appears as the legendary pianist/arranger Mary Lou Williams, the filmmakers went out of their way to make the musicians feel comfortable in Kansas City, providing them with well-tuned pianos and re-hearsal facilities even in their dressing rooms. Altman then took the unusual step of filming their performances "live," eventually accumulating enough footage for a separate seventy-two-minute video featuring only the musicians.[4]

Altman relied on Hal Willner to assemble the jazz musicians who domi-nate the soundtrack in *Kansas City*. Willner had previously convened the jazz group around Annie Ross for Altman's *Short Cuts,* a film based on several un-related short stories by Raymond Carver. Drawing upon the work of Robert T. Self, I have argued that the jazz singer Tess (played by Annie Ross) and her daughter, Zoe (Lori Singer), provide a key to understanding how the many nar-ratives of *Short Cuts* might fit together (Gabbard, *Jammin'* 283–293). On the one hand, Tess the jazz singer represents those who wear their emotions on their sleeves while Zoe the classical cellist represents those who repress their feelings until they explode. On the other hand, some characters in *Short Cuts* are improvisers like Tess while others seem to need "scripts" such as Zoe reads when she performs. Tess and Zoe then provide a program of sorts for under-standing almost all the characters in the film. Throughout *Short Cuts* the music of Zoe or Tess is often the "glue" that holds together disparate scenes in-volving unrelated characters. Significantly, Tess and her daughter are the only two characters in the film who do not grow directly out of stories by Carver.

For *Kansas City,* Willner brought in an array of mainstream and avant-garde jazz artists, sometimes with stunning results.[5] When pianist Allen ap-pears as Mary Lou Williams with her hair worn up, for example, she bears an

Fig. 48. Jazz pianist, composer, and arranger Mary Lou Williams in the 1930s when she was based in Kansas City. Photofest Film Archive.

uncanny musical *and* physical resemblance to a woman whom Allen herself has admired and studied. In the same spirit in which they wrote the Goats and Rabbits speech, knowing that only a handful of viewers would catch the reference, Altman and Barhydt have unobtrusively introduced many small details from jazz history. They accurately place the real-life Addie Parker (Jeff

Feringa) at a Western Union office and at her home where boarders occupy rooms on the second floor. Most viewers were probably unaware that this woman's son is Charlie Parker, who is also faithfully portrayed as a fourteen-year-old saxophonist in his school's marching band. In another carefully researched moment, Kevin Mahogany sings "I Left My Baby" from behind a bar, a reference to the blues shouter Joe Turner, who originally worked as a singing bartender at the Sunset Club in Kansas City. At no point in the film, however, does anyone in the film mention Turner by name. When the black gangster Seldom Seen (Harry Belafonte) does in fact speak the name of a jazz musician, he refers to "Bill Basie." Basie has said that he did not become *Count* Basie until 1936 while working at the Reno Club (Shapiro and Hentoff 300–301). At its most esoteric, the film has Seldom ask about "that doctor friend of Bennie Moten,"[6] a reference to the successful Kansas City band-leader who employed musicians such as Basie, Webster, and Jimmy Rushing. Moten died in 1935 while having his tonsils removed by the same doctor with whom he had socialized the night before (Barnes 208–209).

Nevertheless, *Kansas City* takes a few liberties with jazz history. Seldom Seen and the musicians are situated at the "Hey Hey Club." There was in fact a "Hey *Hay* Club" in Kansas City, but it was too small to accommodate all the musicians and dancers who appear in the film's spacious Hey Hey Club. The club is clearly a composite of several of the city's better known clubs, especially the Reno. In the film's musical centerpiece, Coleman Hawkins (Craig Handy with his dreadlocks concealed inside a large hat) wages a tenor saxophone battle with Lester Young (Joshua Redman in a modified porkpie). Hawkins did in fact square off against Young in Kansas City, but the legendary encounter took place in December 1933 at the Cherry Blossom Inn while Hawkins was in town with Fletcher Henderson and his orchestra (W. Allen 290). Hawkins left Henderson early in March 1934 and sailed for England a few weeks later at the end of the month, not returning to the States until 1939 (Chilton 96). He could not have been in Kansas City on election day in 1934 when the action of the film takes place. The film might also be criticized for a scene at the end when Ron Carter plays Duke Ellington's "Solitude" as a solo for pizzicato string bass. The most innovative bassists of the period, such as Milt Hinton and Jimmy Blanton, did not begin recording bass solos until 1939; it is unlikely that the bass was regarded as a solo instrument in 1934.[7]

But these are not the kinds of complaints that jazz purists have lodged against the film. Peter Watrous, the principal jazz writer for the *New York Times* when the film was released, spoke for many when he made two basic criticisms. He charged that the film "has turned the music and musicians into servants of the plot and the film's ambiance," and that the music "isn't particularly idiomatic of the time and place . . . as if rock-and-roll predated it, not the other way around" (Watrous 26). This second complaint must be answered with a question as to how jazz musicians today could successfully perform and improvise in a style that is more than sixty years old. According to Michael Bourne, Willner did in fact start out directing the musicians to imitate recordings from the 1930s, but he soon realized that "if we *concentrate* on that, it'll end up dull" (25). There have long been "ghost bands" touring the United States that play note-for-note imitations of old Swing Era recordings by Glenn Miller or the Dorseys. Jazz, however, especially the music of Basie, Ellington, and Henderson that is performed in *Kansas City*, was not meant to be played the same way every night. The handful of repertory jazz orchestras that have recreated this music in

Fig. 49. Harry Belafonte as Seldom Seen in Robert Altman's *Kansas City* (1996, Sandcastle 5 Productions/Fine Line Features). Photofest Film Archive.

recent years often succeed more in embalming the music than in bringing it back to life. Willner and the musicians who came to Kansas City for location shooting eventually agreed to play in their own, more extroverted styles while trying to suggest the "flavor" of their predecessors' playing.

There was probably no solution, however, that would have pleased the more implacable jazz aficionados. I have maintained that the discourses of jazz writing during the last several decades have almost always cast the music as an autonomous art outside history and cultural circumstance (Gabbard, "Introduction"). In chapter seven I argue that jazz enthusiasts manage to by-pass the many problems with their essentializing and fetishizing of black artists by seizing on the myth of jazz autonomy and claiming the moral high ground. The serious jazz enthusiast is not likely to be swayed by arguments about the specific purposes the music has actually served, whether it be ac-companiments for drinking, gender coding among musicians, or back-ground for a Hollywood film. Watrous's first complaint—that the musicians were only "servants" of the plot—is thus related to the second. In both cases he appears unwilling to acknowledge established cinematic practice or the validity of any other attempt to put the music into a different context. Wa-trous also overlooks the many subtle ways in which the musicians are in fact closely related to the action and are frequently essential to the meaning of the film. In fact, *Kansas City* may have succeeded more than almost any other fiction film in folding jazz performance into a cinematic narrative.

GLUING IT TOGETHER

The musicians in *Kansas City* play throughout the day and night at the Hey Hey Club, the domain of Seldom Seen, an articulate but sinister gangster based on a real-life figure from Kansas City history who allegedly carried his money and drugs in a cigar box (Bourne 24).[8] Ostensibly, the actual plot of the film is, like the two films discussed in chapter four, a kidnapping narra-tive. And like *Ransom* and *Fargo*, *Kansas City* is more about race than about a kidnapping. The story is built around the attempts of Blondie (Jennifer Jason Leigh) to retrieve her husband, Johnny O'Hara (Dermot Mulroney), from the Hey Hey Club, where Seldom holds him captive. Earlier Johnny smeared burnt cork on his face and robbed Sheepshan Red (A. C. Smith), a wealthy black gambler on his way to the Hey Hey Club. Seldom quickly figures out the ruse and informs the victimized gambler, "You've been robbed by Amos and Andy."

Johnny is brought in by Seldom's henchmen following the confession of his accomplice, a black cab driver named "Blue" Green (Martin Martin). While Seldom contemplates how he will punish Johnny, Blondie kidnaps Carolyn Stilton in hopes that her highly placed husband can use his influence to set Johnny free. Henry Stilton (Michael Murphy), however, is on a train to Washington, and Blondie and Carolyn spend most of the film together waiting for messages to get through. All of this happens during the last moments of an election campaign, when the politicians who might have been able to intercede with Seldom are distracted, to say the least. And almost all of the action takes place while the Hey Hey Club musicians perform throughout the night and into election day. Although this music is heard in the actual club as well as on the background soundtrack, there is no other music in the film except for a high school band playing at the train station early in the film.

As in *Short Cuts*, the music occasionally "glues" scenes together and provides ingenious moments of continuity, as when Carolyn and Blondie begin to relax with one another at the film's halfway point just before the camera cuts away to reveal Mary Lou Williams playing piano at the Hey Hey Club. The scene at the opening of the film when the two women first meet in Carolyn's bedroom is accompanied only by the occasional rumble of thunder. Although the music of the jazz musicians plays regularly behind most other scenes— even those that are far away from the actual music—Carolyn and Blondie usually interact without musical accompaniment. After Carolyn lights Blondie's cigarette and the two begin to chat for the first time without hostility, music swells up behind them. Eventually the two childless women share their grief over the death of the Lindbergh baby. As Self points out, the scene is especially ironic since the death of the child was responsible for the "Lindbergh Law," a federal statute mandating the death penalty for kidnappers (Self 19). In spite of this moment of shared mourning, Blondie is already sentenced to death, thus strongly differentiating this scene from all those moments in other films when black music invisibly intensifies the romance between white people. The music in *Kansas City* is not invisible and not there solely to make us feel better about white protagonists having a brief moment of intimacy.

Significantly, the music that plays behind Carolyn and Blondie as they discuss the "beautiful baby, beautiful couple" features the lone female musician, Geri Allen, who is performing when the scene changes to the Hey Hey Club. The music from the previous scene continues uninterrupted, a bit of sound-

Fig. 50. With Addie Parker (Jeff Feringa) (the mother of Charlie Parker) in the background, Blondie (Jennifer Jason Leigh, *left*) maintains control over Carolyn (Miranda Richardson, *right*) in *Kansas City* (1996, Sandcastle 5 Productions/Fine Line Features). Photofest Film Archive.

track magic that is typical of the film. In spite of the grim outcome of their relationship, the sympathy that develops between Blondie and Carolyn is one of the most intriguing elements in the film, and Altman has achieved much by allowing Miranda Richardson and Jennifer Jason Leigh to write most of their own speeches. As in *Short Cuts,* the music allows an emotional aspect of one scene to carry over into another that would otherwise seem entirely unrelated. In many ways this is standard Hollywood practice—what Claudia Gorbman has called "narrative cueing" (73)—but Altman's film uses the technique to emphasize the subtleties of women's talk in contrast to the more direct statements of the male characters. Surprising the audience by revealing that Geri Allen/Mary Lou Williams has been playing behind the first moments of bonding between the two female leads is one of the ways in which Altman, Barhydt, and Willner have rethought the conventional practice of cinema sound.

CUTTING IT TOGETHER

Kansas City is especially inspired in its use of music when Seldom's men take Blue Green out to an alley and stab him repeatedly with their knives, finally leaving him to a pack of hungry dogs. This scene is punctuated by the saxophone battle between Young and Hawkins. The two tenorists engage in some fancy cutting of their own (as do Altman and his editors), trading phrases and choruses in a flamboyant show of phallic competitiveness. Altman has expressed admiration for Craig Handy, who *acts* the part of Coleman Hawkins even though he speaks no dialogue. Says Altman, "Handy could be a movie star. Craig does that look when Joshua starts soloing. Craig does that look at him like, 'Who *is* this bird?' And then he takes his coat off. And people get it, even people who don't know what a cutting contest is" (Bourne 22).[9] Yet all of this happens within the inherently collaborative context of a jazz performance. When the combatants finally put down their weapons, they shake hands as a sign of mutual respect. The tenor contest and Blue's journey to death are "cut" together so that the black men in the alley are killing one of their own at the same time that the black men at the Hey Hey Club are engaging in the richest form of cooperation.

In fact, no two people in the film ever connect as exquisitely as do the musicians. Virtually no nonmusical schemes are realized: Johnny's blackface holdup is a failure; Blondie's attempt to rescue Johnny is equally disastrous; phone calls to political cronies never produce results; even Pearl (Ajia Mignon Johnson), the black teenager who has come to Kansas City to give up her baby, does not meet the white women from the Junior League who arrive at the train station too late to find her. Without a trace of didacticism, Altman has held up jazz as a vivid contrast to everything that was wrong with Kansas City in 1934.

Nevertheless, Altman has also subtly implicated the jazz musicians in the city's racial and sexual politics. An early scene features a solo by tenor saxophonist James Carter, who is meant to be the young Ben Webster. After reeling off an especially flamboyant phrase, Carter defiantly thrusts his horn to the side and juts out his chest and lower lip. Although he does not play in a style much like Webster's, Carter may be "sampling" the bravura that often characterized the older musician's playing. Late in his career Webster was a master of the romantic, heavy-breathing ballad. But as Rex Stewart has written, "during his early period, he blew with unrestrained savagery, buzzing and growling through chord changes like a prehistoric monster challenging a foe" (128). Carter/Webster's musical and macho posturing strategically accompanies Johnny O'Hara's arrival at Seldom Seen's inner sanctum at the Hey Hey Club. Johnny's first words are, "I thought we could talk this over like gentleman," but Seldom resists all his overtures. The jockeying for power and masculine superiority among musicians parallels the game played out between Johnny and Seldom. Although Seldom obviously has control over whether Johnny lives or dies, Johnny still has room to assert his masculinity, especially in the scene near the end when he arrogantly explains to Seldom why a black man ought not to kill a white man.

But as Eric Lott has shown, this is not a game for a white man, especially one from the working classes. Although real economic and social power has historically been kept out of the hands of blacks in American culture, African American men have established the rules for masculine performativity at least since the 1840s, when minstrelsy became the dominant form of popular entertainment in American life. In the twentieth century, the comportment of white athletes on the court or playing field has become increasingly based on the body language of black athletes, just as white jazz and popular musicians have engaged in studied imitations of how black men behave as they make music. In *Kansas City,* Johnny O'Hara effectively adopts both aspects of minstrelsy's legacy. He transgresses against law and custom after blacking up, not unlike the minstrel man (and his audiences) for whom the practice authorized antisocial behavior. But Johnny also adopts the swaggering, hypermanly comportment of the working-class white man who unconsciously mimics black masculine display.

Altman has dramatized male anxiety about being male in films such as *McCabe and Mrs. Miller* (1971), *Thieves Like Us* (1974), *Buffalo Bill and the Indians* (1976), *Come Back to the Five and Dime, Jimmy Dean, Jimmy Dean* (1982), and *The Player* (1992), to name just a few. His white *and* his black male characters run the gamut in terms of how they play out their masculinity. Unlike the vast majority of Hollywood directors, Altman neither romanticizes nor pathologizes blacks and their interactions with whites. He seldom employs familiar myths, such as the loyal black retainer we know so well from mainstream films such as *Driving Miss Daisy* (1989) and *Striptease* (1996). And he has certainly never made use of a black angel. Although Altman has often put angry black men on the screen (*M*A*S*H* [1970], *Nashville* [1975], *Streamers* [1983], *Short Cuts* [1993]), he has also depicted the complexity and ironies of even the most casual interactions among people of different races (*A Wedding* [1978], *H.E.A.L.T.H.* [1979], *Short Cuts* [1993]). One of the most remarkable aspects of *Kansas City* is its representation of the wide range of interactions between blacks and whites. Some of these interactions are tense; some are completely matter-of-fact; sometimes blacks have the upper hand; other times whites are in control; and sometimes no one is in control.

Altman took an almost perverse pleasure in bringing black characters into his work as early as 1959, when he directed episodes of the syndicated television program *The Troubleshooters*, a weekly series starring Keenan Wynn and the Olympic decathlon champion Bob Mathias as glorified construction workers. In one episode he had cast a black actor as the owner and bartender of a saloon frequented by the regulars in the series. The program's sponsor objected on the grounds that the actor was not right for the part (Altman, Conversation with the author). When Altman hired a second black actor to replace him, the sponsor again objected, and Altman asked that any objections be put in writing. The producer of the program then told Altman that the sponsors did not want to show a black man as the owner of a saloon, that a white actor must play the part, and that they would never put such statements into a written document. Altman then tried something else: "So I hired an actor and I tattooed him—every bit of his skin, like Queequeg in *Moby Dick*. . . . I put him in tails and a top hat, gave him a German accent and an Indian name. It was so bizarre that it didn't make any sense, but they [the sponsors] just loved it" (Altman, Conversation). Later on, too many episodes provoked clashes, and Altman was asked to leave *The Troubleshooters*, as was often the case in his career as a director for television (McGilligan 274). Altman would later see to it that African Americans played a regular role in his repertory panoramas.

The black and white characters in *Kansas City* have few interactions typical of the Hollywood mainstream. Seldom's imperious reception of the audacious but dim Johnny O'Hara is as unusual as the scene when Blondie takes Carolyn into Addie Parker's house on Olive Street for a few hours of rest as they hide from the police. When Blondie awakens from a nap, she finds the elderly black women in the Parker living room nodding politely while Carolyn, stoned on laudanum, holds forth on race relations. Earlier, in a minor but revealing subplot, the young Charlie Parker (Albert J. Burnes) latches onto the pregnant Pearl. Parker takes her along to the Hey Hey Club, where he adoringly points out Lester Young. They watch in amusement as Seldom's men unceremoniously expel Blondie after she has demanded the return of her boyfriend.

The scene in which Blondie is carried out of the Hey Hey Club shows that Altman is more interested in the complexities of race relations than in an un-critical celebration of Kansas City music and musicians. The black players laugh and make fun of Blondie with their instruments as she passes the band-stand kicking and screaming. The wide-open politics of Kansas City gave blacks some degree of autonomy in their own domain; Altman and Barhydt have suggested that the musicians relished the situation in which they could publicly display their power in the face of a white person. In fact, the film's constant attention to power imbalances involves much more than race and gender relations; it is everywhere in a film that chronicles an election cam-paign fought with bullets and clubs as much as with ballots. Robert Self has pointed out that *Kansas City* is one of several films made during a presidential election year in which Altman tied personal dramas to political activities (Self xix). The connection is explicit in *H.E.A.L.T.H.* (1980), *Secret Honor* (1984), and *Tanner 88* (1988). Although not as overt in its political foregroundings, *Buffalo Bill and the Indians* from 1976 features an appearance by Pat Mc-Cormick as Pres. Grover Cleveland and dramatizes the power struggles be-tween whites and Indians. Altman contributed to the nation's bicentennial celebration—when politics and patriotism became entertainment—with a film that problematizes this same combination. *Kansas City* holds up the city's jazz as the great unintentional monument of the Pendergast era, but the film is more sophisticated than *Buffalo Bill* in finding parallels between poli-tics and a form of entertainment that is especially rich in meaning.

RACING THE AUTOBIOGRAPHY

Although I began this chapter by suggesting that Altman exaggerated when he attributed a jazz-like structure to his film, I would like to return to that statement in this conclusion. Until now I have treated Altman and his col-laborators as scrupulous professionals, fully in control of the meaning of their film. But there is material in the film and in Altman's post–*Kansas City* interviews that justifies a more overtly psychoanalytic reading of the film. In particular, I see Altman unconsciously returning to the scene of an idealized childhood and forging an identification with the young Charlie Parker.

In his interviews, jazz itself seems related to a sense of maternal pleni-tude for Altman. He has spoken of a love for jazz that began when he was nine years old and first heard a 1934 recording of Duke Ellington's "Solitude." In a radio interview, Altman told Leonard Lopate that Glendora Majors, the family's black housekeeper "who raised me," sat him down next to the phonograph and said, "Bobby, now you listen to this. This is the best music there ever was." He then said that "Solitude" is still his favorite song. Altman has also told interviewers that he started going to the jazz clubs in Kansas City when he was fourteen, exactly the same age as the Charlie Parker of *Kansas City.* If there is any character in the film with whom Altman is likely to identify, it is Charlie Parker, and if there is a noncinematic art form to which Altman aspires, it is surely jazz.

Not surprisingly then, *Kansas City* offers an idealized view of Parker, not to mention his mother, whose portrayal in the film may have some relation to Altman's fond memories of Glendora Majors. But as always, representations in cinema are massively overdetermined. The view of Parker in particular and jazz in general may also have been affected by Matthew Seig, listed as one of *Kansas City*'s two co-producers. Seig has directed jazz documentaries on Thelonious Monk, Billie Holiday, Sarah Vaughan, John Coltrane, and Count Basie, most of them shown on PBS. As I suggested in chapter six, Seig's *Thelonious Monk: American Composer* (1991) is almost hagiographic when compared to Charlotte Zwerin's *Thelonious Monk: Straight No Chaser* (1988), a film that emphasizes the pianist/composer's mental illness. Seig also directed *Lady Day: The Many Faces of Billie Holiday* (1991), a similarly idealized look at the legendary singer, especially when compared to Robert O'Meally's thoughtful book on which the video is based. Along with Gary Giddins's videos on Louis Armstrong and Charlie Parker, the work of Seig represents a revision of the dominant modes of jazz biography on film. Clint Eastwood's *Bird* (1988) is much more typical of a well-established tradition of jazz narrative in which a genius musician, usually black, is brought down by drugs, alcohol, and an audience of Philistines. While the Parker of *Bird* is a cipher, Altman's Parker is devoted to the music of his hometown, especially the work of Lester Young. Seig may have played a role in giving us a more charitable view of the young Parker.

Kansas City, however, goes a bit further than simply rejecting the familiar story of Charlie Parker, the self-destructive drug addict. The fourteen-year-old Parker of *Kansas City* even appears to have honorable intentions toward Pearl. He looks after her by taking her to the Hey Hey Club to hear Lester Young, unquestionably the major influence on Parker's early style. The

Fig. 51. Jazz saxophonist and composer Charlie Parker grew up in Kansas City. Photofest Film Archive.

real-life Parker spent a good deal of time in the balcony of the Reno Club, where he could sit undisturbed and listen to Young soloing with the Basie band or at after hours jam sessions. Although he has tended to idealize the young Parker, Altman has chosen a moment in the artist's life when he was merely another listener in the world of Kansas City jazz, not unlike Altman's description of himself as a fourteen-year-old.

    Kansas City is very much about imitation and inspiration. In some ways it is a film about a woman who behaves like a woman in a film. As Blondie, Jennifer Jason Leigh does a sustained impression of her role model Jean Harlow, who appears on screen with Clark Gable in a climactic scene from *Hold Your Man* (1933) while Blondie and Carolyn wait in a movie theater for Henry Stilton to call. At the end, when Blondie has returned to her peroxide Harlow look and is finally reunited with Johnny, the lovers play out a desultory version of the Gable/Harlow scene before they both end up on the floor dead. Imitation is also at the heart of Johnny's misadventures in blackface. When he wipes the burnt cork off his face, Johnny looks at himself in the mirror and says, "So long, Amos." Accordingly, Seldom Seen repeatedly mentions Amos and Andy as he taunts Johnny.[10] Seldom also says, "You come swinging in here like, like Tarzan. Right in the middle of a sea of niggers. Just like in the picture show. You like picture show?" When Johnny replies, "I can take it or leave it," Seldom says, "I recommend you leave it." This is advice that both Johnny and Blondie should have observed. It also touches on a major theme in the works of Altman—the discrepancies between the images presented by the entertainment industry and the realities behind them. Although Altman has not exactly imitated what he sees in the picture shows, he has on some levels been inspired by Charlie Parker.

Kansas City is unique for marking the first time in a long career that Altman has clearly turned to his own experience as a consumer of entertainment. His affinity for Charlie Parker goes well beyond their common experience as young men listening to jazz. Like Parker, Altman is an artist who assimilated a body of material that few regarded as art and then went on to create his own brilliant but eccentric brand of that art. Altman further resembles the jazz artist in his regular reliance on improvisation throughout his career. Just as Parker was a drug addict for most of his adult life, Altman has battled various forms of addiction for most of his life (McGilligan).

If Lott is right that black men have long provided models of manliness for white American males, it is also true that the male jazz musician expresses his masculinity in more subtle ways than does the athlete, the rock star, or the white suburban teenager with baggy shorts, a turned-around baseball cap, and a loping walk. The jazz musician expresses much more than just manliness. In fact, as I have suggested elsewhere, black jazz musicians have even developed codes for problematizing received notions of masculinity (Gabbard, *Jammin'* 138–159). Improvising black musicians have inspired many of America's most important white artists, including Marlon Brando (see chapter one). Among directors, we could list a diverse group consisting of Martin Scorsese, John Cassavetes, Henry Jaglom, Stan Brakhage, Dennis Hopper, and Christopher Guest. Like Altman, they all practice a "jazz aesthetic." Like the others, and like jazz musicians such as Parker, Altman has also learned much from the great artists who preceded him. But by identifying with a black jazz musician, Altman has gone even further than the others. Perhaps unconsciously, perhaps not, Altman has sought "the cool, virility, humility, abandon, or *gaité de coeur* that were the prime components of white ideologies of black manhood" (Lott 52). He has not, however, put these qualities at the service of lovable white people, nor has he made a fetish of African American gender display.

At Addie Parker's, Pearl tells Blondie that she dreamed about her the night after she witnessed her expulsion from the Hey Hey Club. Pearl says that in her dream Blondie was dancing and Charlie Parker was playing the piano. Blondie is nonplussed by this confession but has other things on her mind. She does not pursue the issue. One wonders if the dream ends as disastrously for Blondie as does her brief adventure with Carolyn. At the end of *Kansas City,* Blondie and Johnny are dead. Carolyn has pointed a gun at Blondie in her negligee just as Blondie had held a gun on the negligee-clad Carolyn at the beginning of the film. Carolyn and Henry then return to a marriage that is more empty than ever. Seldom Seen, the one character who has had anything at all to say about the music, counts the money he has made from his gambling tables. An alto saxophone hanging from his neck, Charlie Parker is back at the Hey Hey Club, having drifted off to sleep in the balcony, perhaps like the historical Charlie Parker after a long night at the Reno Club. As the credits role, a small jazz ensemble performs Altman's favorite song, "Solitude." The film does not reveal what Parker is dreaming about as he dozes at the Hey Hey Club, but it is likely that his dreams, like Altman's, resemble those of few other artists.

CHAPTER NINE

Spike Lee Meets Aaron Copland

A t the beginning of *He Got Game* (1998), written and directed by Spike Lee, the credit sequence contains an unusual juxtaposition. In consecutive title cards the American composer Aaron Copland (1900–1990) is credited with "Music" and the rap group Public Enemy is listed for "Songs." These credits link a composer widely associated, perhaps inaccurately, with the American heartland to an urban, highly political rap group. A correspondingly diverse set of images appears behind the credits sequence. Usually in balletic slow motion, young Americans play basketball in a variety of locations, including pastoral landscapes in the Midwest and concrete playgrounds in the inner city. Behind the title card with Copland's name a young black man dribbles a ball along the Brooklyn Bridge, perhaps an acknowledgment that both Copland and Spike Lee grew up in Brooklyn and that they may have more in common than audiences expect. Throughout the credits sequence the audience hears the steel-driving clangor of Copland's *John Henry*. Although this composition is among Copland's more dissonant works, it has an appropriately portentous quality, not unlike the beginnings of many big-budget American films. Copland in fact specialized in the auspicious, often opening his compositions with grand gestures, even fanfares. He was also familiar with the conventions of film music. He wrote the soundtrack score for *Of Mice and Men* (1939), *Our Town* (1940), and *The Red Pony* (1949), as well as a few short films, and his score for *The Heiress* (1949) won an Academy Award. Portions of the soundtrack music for *Our Town* can even be heard in *He Got Game*.[1]

Fig. 52. Director, writer, and actor Spike Lee on the set. Photofest Film Archive.

He Got Game takes place during the few days when Jesus Shuttlesworth (Ray Allen) must decide where he will attend college. The most sought-after high school basketball player in the nation, Jesus is recruited by a large group of college coaches, many of whom appear as themselves in the film. Even his girlfriend, Lala (Rosario Dawson), is involved with an agent who wants to profit from Jesus's decision. Jesus's father, Jake Shuttlesworth (Denzel Washington), is in a state penitentiary serving a long prison sentence for killing his wife in an incident of domestic violence when Jesus and his sister, Mary (Zelda Harris), were children. The warden (Ned Beatty) tells Jake that the governor, who is a graduate of "Big State," wants Jesus to play basketball at his alma mater and that Jake may have his sentence reduced if he can convince Jesus to attend Big State. Carefully watched over by prison guards in civilian clothes, Jake is taken to a sleazy motel on Coney Island where he must overcome the enduring bitterness of a son who still blames him for the death of a beloved mother. At the motel Jake becomes involved with Dakota (Milla Jovovich), a prostitute who returns to her home in the Midwest after she makes love to Jake. At the climax of the film, Jake challenges Jesus to a game of one-on-one basketball, telling Jesus that he will permanently stay out of Jesus's life if he loses. If Jake wins, the son must sign the letter of intent for Big State that Jake carries with him. Jake loses the game and is taken back to prison, but the next day Jesus announces at a press conference that he will attend Big State. The warden, however, tells Jake that since he did not actually get Jesus's signature on the letter of intent, the governor may not honor his promise to reduce Jake's sentence.

With its multicultural cast of basketball players, including young white women as well as African American men, the opening sequence of *He Got Game* does not actually racialize the music of Copland, in spite of the fact that the legendary John Henry was black. But about ten minutes into the film, after the principal characters have been introduced, Spike Lee is more didactic in mixing Copland's music with images on the screen. When a group of black youths arrive on a court at night and begin a vigorous game of full-court basketball, the soundtrack music is "Hoe-Down," the final movement of Copland's 1942 ballet *Rodeo*. Spike Lee has made a powerful statement by combining images of young black men playing basketball with music written by the one composer in the classical tradition considered by many to be "the most American." Writing in the *New York Times* in anticipation of the centennial of Copland's birth, Anthony Tommasini referred to the composer as "Mr. Musical Americana" (Tommasini 2:1). Copland's music, especially a composition as robust as "Hoe-Down," can signify the American spirit at its most positive. Wit, energy, spontaneity, romance, bravado, optimism, and grace all seem to emanate from the music, as if Copland's dancing cowboys transparently express the soul of the American people. These kinds of associations have more to do with the reception of Copland's music than with anything intrinsic to it, but Spike Lee has made the most of commonly accepted associations by linking "Hoe-Down" with exuberant young black men on a basketball court. In a move that would have pleased Ralph Ellison, Lee may be asserting that these African Americans youths are as uniquely and thoroughly American as anything that Copland's ballet music might signify. For Ellison, African Americans are most themselves when they improvise and play changes on the bricolage of American culture. And Lee has said, "When I listen to Aaron Copland's music, I hear America, and basketball is America" (Sterritt 15). But just as Lee has made the obvious statement—all African Americans are American—he is also stating the inverse—all Americans are African American. Like Ellison before him, who said that being truly American means being somehow black, Lee has made his assertion knowing that many white Americans cannot accept it. So long as this remains the case, even flawed films such as *He Got Game* deserve our attention.

THE INVISIBLE SIGNIFIER

In his choice of Aaron Copland, Spike Lee may also have sought to reverse the familiar Hollywood practice of using the invisible and "inaudible" sounds of black music to accompany the actions of white people (Gorbman 73). As composers of film music frequently point out, if audiences listen too closely to the background score, something has gone wrong. The most successful composers find subtle ways to supplement the action on the screen, often playing to cultural assumptions of which audiences are scarcely aware, cer-

Fig. 53. Singer, pianist, and bandleader Ray Charles invisibly adds romance to *Groundhog Day*. Jerry Ohlinger's Movie Material Store, Inc.

Fig. 54. Singer, pianist, and composer Nat King Cole, an invisible but crucial presence in *Groundhog Day*. Jerry Ohlinger's Movie Material Store, Inc.

tainly not while the film narrative is in full gear. This convention is at its most benign when an unseen African American singer provides a romantic atmosphere for white lovers. As I suggested in chapter two, Clint Eastwood has made broad use of this practice in *Play Misty for Me* (1971) and *The Bridges of Madison County* (1995). So have the people who made *Next Stop Wonderland* (1998) (see introduction), *The Talented Mr. Ripley* (1999) (see chapter three), and *The Green Mile* (1999) (see chapter five). To cite one more example among many, in *Groundhog Day* (1997), Bill Murray romances Andie MacDowell in a small-town location that includes virtually no black people even though at the most romantic moments the soundtrack includes Ray Charles singing "You Don't Know Me" and Nat King Cole crooning "Almost Like Being in Love."

In a more sinister use of the voices of blacks to signify something other than black subjects, a film will make a menacing group of youths seem even more menacing by playing rap music on the soundtrack even if all the youths are white. Andrew Ross has pointed out that in *Batman* (1989) the

Joker is played in whiteface by the white, middle-aged Jack Nicholson but that the character arouses white anxieties about black youths by speaking in rappish rhymes and spray-painting graffiti on famous paintings in a museum while prancing to the funk of Prince (Ross 31). In all of these films, music says what the filmmakers are unwilling or afraid to say with images. While Eastwood and the makers of films such as *Groundhog Day* engage in "permissible racism" by benignly associating African American artists with intensified romance and sexuality, the singers are acknowledged only in the end credits, their black bodies kept off screen in order to maintain the centrality of white characters. In *Batman,* director Tim Burton and his collaborators have avoided charges of overt racism by *not* showing black hooligans on the screen, but they have made the Joker more threatening by linking him to African American musical performances that scare the hell out of many white Americans.

In *He Got Game,* Spike Lee has turned these conventions upside down. Instead of using black music as a supplement for white characters on the screen, Lee allows the music of a white composer to enhance the playfulness, grace, and masculinity of black youths on the basketball court. Lee may even have supposed that the early scene with "Hoe-Down" would be widely excerpted outside of its original context. Even for those who do not know the plot of the film or the identity of the ballplayers, the meaning of the scene is clear. When I presented a shorter, spoken version of this chapter, I made the case for Lee's reversal of standard Hollywood practice most forcefully by showing that scene. There are surely any number of academic presentations on Lee, Copland, and/or film music that have made or will make use of the same scene. By simply bleeping out the one use of the word "shit" on the soundtrack, the clip could even be a useful teaching tool in a grade-school music appreciation class. This would bring the music of Copland home to a generation of American students more in touch with black urban culture than ever before. But even this scene must be understood in the larger context of *He Got Game,* of Spike Lee's other films, and of Aaron Copland's career. By combining the music of Copland with images that do not immediately appear apposite, Lee has made viewers think about new sets of associations. By tracing out an even larger group of associations, this chapter is in effect continuing the work of the film. Ultimately, I have little interest in what Spike Lee actually knows about Aaron Copland. I care more

about how racial, sexual, political, and musical discourses play off one another in and around *He Got Game.*

CONSTRUCTING AMERICA

As the theorists of postmodernism have argued, sounds and images do not
adhere to grand narratives but circulate freely among systems of meaning
that escape the conventional boundaries of academic disciplines. And as the
new musicology has taught us, musical meaning has as much to do with listening communities as it does with well-established attempts to "anchor" it
in reassuring discourses.[2] Spike Lee has made several attempts to anchor the
compositions of Copland to specific meanings at crucial moments in *He Got
Game,* often lifting music out of a more familiar context so that it can signify
in new ways. In the "Hoe-Down" sequence, however, Lee follows traditional
practice and casts Copland as an "American" composer in the most positive
and unproblematic sense. But Copland's identity as Mr. Musical Americana
becomes highly problematic if we examine his own story.

Copland did in fact seek new ways of creating a music that was recognizably
American, even in his earliest works. Rejecting many of the Eurocentric elements in American classical music, Copland paid special attention to American
folk melodies and quoted them in his compositions without irony or patronizing gestures.[3] He also found tonalities that gave his music a spacious, uplifting
quality that is today considered "American" even if the same chords that seem
to symbolize the wide-open plains of the American countryside can have different meanings in other contexts.[4] Copland's Jewish roots have also been connected to passages in his music, as when Howard Pollack suggests that a central
motive in the *Piano Concerto* of 1926 hint at "the calls of the shofar" (522).

But if Copland intended his music to represent the essence of America,
he did so in a spirit that was by no means blandly jingoistic. Especially in the
1930s his politics were well left of center, leading him at one point to write
what he called "my communist song," a setting for a Marxist lyric by Alfred
Hayes (Pollack 276). Although he never joined the Communist Party, his 1934
song, "Into the Streets May 1st," won the prize in a competition sponsored by
the *New Masses,* a prominent magazine for "the proletarian avant-garde"
(Denning 140). In writing this music, Copland succeeded by combining a
musical style that might be called "revolutionary" with an appeal to mass
taste (Pollack 276). Copland later disavowed the song, but its composition

Fig. 55. Composer Aaron Copland. Photofest Film Archive.

foreshadowed certain stylistic aspects of *Fanfare for the Common Man* (1942).
Although *Fanfare* was written to bolster the morale of Americans in the early
stages of World War II, and although by the end of the millennium the piece
was being used in television commercials for the U.S. Marine Corps, the
music must also be regarded as a powerful statement of the composer's leftist sentiments. Pollack suggests that even Copland's invocations of Abraham
Lincoln, Billy the Kid, and John Henry can be understood alongside Communist Party leader Earl Browder's efforts to bring ultranationalist sentiments into the party's rhetoric (Pollack 279).[5]

Nor should Copland's homosexuality be overlooked in the consideration of a music that has been characterized as "manly" as well as American.
Keep in mind that the sounds of Rodeo and Billy the Kid that wash over the
robustly masculine bodies in He Got Game were written for the ballet. Compared to the black athletes in Lee's film, the actual dancers who have performed these ballets look like gay men in cowboy drag, which in many cases
they are. Indeed, as Susan McClary instructed Robert K. Schwartz when he
wrote his article about the sexuality of male composers, "The straight boys
claimed the moral high ground of modernism and fled to the universities,
and the queers literally took center stage in concert halls and opera houses
and ballet, all of which are musics that people are more likely to respond to."
As a gay man, Copland was surely fascinated by men who performed their
masculinity in the dance, the cinema, and the opera, and he wrote memorable music for all of these genres. Pollack even suspects that there are homosexual subtexts to much of Copland's work:

> This would include the macabre eroticism of Grohg, the portrait of a rebel in
> Billy the Kid, the acceptance of difference in The Second Hurricane, and the
> male bonding in Of Mice and Men and The Tender Land. Moreover, Rodeo, The
> Heiress, The Tender Land, and Something Wild, all of which concern a young
> woman's sexual and emotional self-discovery, could be seen as "coming
> out" tales of one kind or another. (Pollack 526)

Of course, it is also possible to hear much of this same music as a "beard" to
help Copland survive in a culture where Jews and homosexuals often have to
pass for heterosexual gentiles. Regardless, in finding musical codes to express
masculinity and heterosexual romance, Copland was demonstrating that he,
like innumerable other gay composers, filmmakers, and performers, was
highly sensitive to the performative nature of sexuality and gender.

Not every critic was comfortable associating a gay Jewish leftist from
Brooklyn with the most basic sounds of America. A variety of writers have
denounced Copland's attempts to create a uniquely American classical
music. Many of these attacks were unself-consciously anti-Semitic, such as
the statement by E. B. Hill that in his Music for the Theatre (1925) Copland
was guilty of "the usual clever Hebraic assimilation of the worst features of
polytonalité" (Oja 335). Perhaps the most vicious assault on Copland came

from the Jewish writer/composer Lazare Saminsky, who wrote in 1949 that Copland possessed "a small, cool creative gift, but an ego of much frenetic drive, a devious personality with a feline *savoir faire,* with his fine commercial acumen and acute sense of the direction of today's wind" (Pollack 520).

Half a century after these attacks, the music of Copland has won the admiration of a sufficient number of critics to overcome the old slurs on his politics, ethnicity, and sexuality. More significantly, he influenced a large contingent of younger composers who understood his ability to capture what could pass for the authentic American vernacular. If Copland is considered today to be the most American of American composers, it is primarily because so many other writers of music felt his influence in this way. In fact, even the less positive aspects of Copland's compositions have been conceptualized as *echt* Americana. Wilfrid Mellers has said that Copland's "fragmentary, cubistlike forms and the static, nonmodulatory harmonies" represent "uprootedness and disintegration, reflective of American alienation" (Pollack 529). It may have been these aspects of Copland's music that inspired Spike Lee to use the opening, conflicted section of *Billy the Kid,* the ominous *Orchestral Variations,* and the less celebratory portions of *Lincoln Portrait* for a story about the tensions between a father serving a long prison sentence and a son in constant danger of being used up and tossed aside by a culture that values him only as a commodity.

CORPORATE POPULISM OR REVOLUTIONARY ART?

Spike Lee's choice of Copland's music for a film about black basketball players might seem surprising in the light of perceptions about the director's politics. Lee is known as the director of *Malcolm X* (1992), a biopic of the black Muslim leader, and *Get on the Bus* (1996), a film about black men journeying to hear Louis Farrakhan at the Million Man March of 1995. Lee ends all his films with Malcolm X's phrase, "By any means necessary." *Do the Right Thing* (1989), which inspired some white commentators to charge Lee with inciting racial violence, is surely the most controversial film that Lee has made to date. That film paid close attention to the only surviving photograph of Malcolm X with Martin Luther King Jr. In most discussions of identity politics, King is associated with the hope that black Americans can survive comfortably within the American mainstream, while Malcolm X represents the nationalist view that African Americans must survive on their own apart from white America. At the end of *Do the Right Thing,* Lee ran two quotations, one from King and one from Malcolm X. King's eloquent endorsement of nonviolence is *followed* by Malcolm's powerful defense of violence in self-defense, suggesting to some that Lee was endorsing Malcolm's statement. The fact that Lee ends his films with a quotation from Malcolm and that he made a film about Malcolm and not about King also suggests that Lee is more comfortable with the nationalist sentiments of Malcolm.

But many critics found Lee's *Malcolm X* to be a conventionally bland Hollywood biography. Amiri Baraka denounced Lee as the "quintessential buppie" who brought his own "petit bourgeois values" into the film (Baraka, "Spike Lee at the Movies" 146). And it is surely significant that Smiley, the character in *Do the Right Thing* who constantly holds up the photograph of the two black leaders, can barely speak because of a severe stutter. The film's regular association of Smiley with the photograph may represent the inability of Lee or anyone else to articulate a satisfying synthesis of what the two extraordinary black men had to say.

The release of *Do the Right Thing* also inspired Jerome Christensen to charge that Spike Lee was a "corporate populist," more interested in selling the Nike Corporation's Air Jordan sneakers than in making politically responsible films. The same charge could be aimed at *He Got Game,* especially when Jake Shuttlesworth expresses great delight as he purchases a pair of "the new Jordans" shortly after his temporary release from prison. Throughout the 1990s, Spike Lee and Michael Jordan were the two public figures most associated with Nike sports shoes. Lee directed television commercials for Nike that featured Jordan, and Jordan himself appears in *He Got Game.* In fact, Jordan can be seen in the film twice, once in a brief clip when he utters the three-word title of the film and again as the subject of a heroic statue in front of the United Center in Chicago that appears in the opening credits sequence. In the statue, Jordan strikes the same pose that appears as an icon on Nike products.

Even the use of Copland's music in *He Got Game* can be interpreted as a corporate maneuver, since Copland is a great deal more accessible than any number of composers who could have been arrogated by Lee to signify American values. Although George Gershwin might have been even more accessible, Lee probably did not choose him because Gershwin was too implicated in the old game of "love and theft" with which whites have approached black culture. Furthermore, Woody Allen had already made extravagant use of

Gershwin's music in *Manhattan* (1979). Lee certainly could have made a more daring choice than Copland if he had used the music of, say, Charles Ives. Once Copland's music was chosen, however, many of his recordings heard in the film were issued on the CBS/Sony label and made available for purchase on the CD *He Got Game: Spike Lee Presents the Music of Aaron Copland* (Sony Classical SK 60593). *Elvira Madigan* (1967) sold a Mozart piano concerto, *Ordinary People* (1980) sold Pachelbel's *Canon,* and *Platoon* (1986) sold Samuel Barber's *Adagio for Strings.* Why should *He Got Game* not sell *Rodeo* and *John Henry?* Lee surely knew that CDs with music from a film could be as financially remunerative as the film itself, even if Lee's Copland CD would probably enrich music publisher Boosey & Hawkes and the Copland estate more than it would the filmmaker.

But the charge that Lee is merely a shill for corporations such as Nike and Sony must be considered alongside the film industry's commitment to corporate advertising that virtually began with the birth of the American cinema (Hansen 51–71). For an artist to survive today in *any* marketplace without some connection to corporate interests is scarcely possible. Todd Boyd compares Lee to Charles Barkley, who appeared in *He Got Game* prior to his retirement from professional basketball in 1999. Aggressive and voluble both on the court and off, Barkley was fond of making statements such as "I'm a '90s nigga . . . I told you white boys you've never heard of a '90s nigga. We do what we want to" (Boyd 132). Writing about Spike Lee, Boyd says, "Lee's presence is quite like that of Barkley, a compromised image of Blackness for mass consumption in return for the financial power to challenge the racial status quo elsewhere" (138). W.J.T. Mitchell has even suggested that *Do the Right Thing* can be read as a *critique* of corporate populism, in which "no utopian public image or monument is available to symbolize collective aspirations" and in which purchasing a pair of sneakers is, sadly, among the few ways for dispossessed individuals to find a sense of personal identity (Mitchell 124).

In *He Got Game,* Jesus has no mother, does not trust his father, and is beset by predatory individuals who have little concern for him as a person. He can rely on no stable institution or, in Mitchell's words, "a monument" to make sense of his predicament. Instead he must contend with a cast of self-interested characters that includes his girlfriend, his uncle, his high school coach, a sleazy agent, college coaches, the media, and promiscuous white coeds, not to mention the governor of New York. Even his little sister tells Jesus that she hopes his money will buy them a home on Long Island so that she can leave the projects of Coney Island. Other than his cousin, the only character who does not seek a profit from Jesus and seems genuinely concerned about his welfare is "Big Time Willie," a local godfather who drives a red Mercedes and claims to have put the word out on the street that Jesus must be left alone. Willie warns Jesus about drugs, alcohol, and the HIV-infected women who lie in wait for him and cautions the young man about the ballplayers who thought they could "make it out of Coney Island" but "didn't amount to shit." Jesus smiles when he corrects Willie by naming Stephon Marbury, even though he is the only athlete he can identify who provides a valid role model.

The mention of Marbury, the high-scoring NBA point guard who, like the fictional Jesus Shuttlesworth, played for the Lincoln High School Rail-Splitters on Coney Island, is one entry in a virtual encyclopedia of basketball lore that runs through the film. The familiar faces of Dean Smith, Lute Olson, John Chaney, John Thompson, Nolan Richardson, Rick Pitino, Reggie Miller, Charles Barkley, Bill Walton, Shaquille O'Neal, and of course Michael Jordan all appear in *He Got Game*. Lee even stops the progress of his plot to let high school play-

Fig. 56. The winning basketball team from Coney Island in *He Got Game* (1998, 40 Acres and a Mule Filmworks/Touchstone Pictures/Buena Vista Pictures). Photofest Film Archive.

ers speak directly to the camera about what the game means to them (fig. 56). There is a sense of pride and possibility in this early sequence when the five young men on the championship high school team talk about the game. Jesus, for example, says that for him "basketball is like poetry in motion." We later learn that Jesus Shuttlesworth was not named for the biblical character but for Earl Monroe, whose nickname was "Jesus" when he played in Philadelphia prior to becoming a star with the New York Knicks. When Jake tells Jesus about the origins of his name, he points out that the press referred to Monroe as "Black Jesus," but that the people in Philadelphia simply called him "Jesus." The discourses of big-time athletics can be meaningful to marginalized groups and, as Boyd powerfully argues, they can provide sites of resistance to dominant culture. Stanley Crouch has even suggested that "the game of basketball is Negro history itself, a thing of inspiration and horror, magic and disillusionment, compassion and sadism. . . . Discipline, wariness, compassion, and good judgment are of absolute importance" (Crouch, *Always in Pursuit* 257).

It is significant that Big Time Willie, who speaks so compellingly of the dangers that Jesus faces, is played by Roger Guenveur Smith, the same actor who played the stuttering Smiley in *Do the Right Thing* and who has appeared in most of Lee's films. A character who is basically incoherent in one film can be uniquely articulate in another. Hollywood films rarely dramatize the conflicts faced by a young black man, especially one like Jesus Shuttlesworth who is portrayed as largely instinctual and unreflective. In many ways, he recalls Ellison's Invisible Man, who learns little as he tries to find his way in a culture of predators until wisdom comes as "I began to accept my past" (496). Jesus cannot speak with the eloquence of the Invisible Man, but he, too, finally learns to accept his past and reconciles with his father.

If we look for a political statement in a film such as *He Got Game,* we must find it within the complex web of achievement and co-optation that surrounds Lee's characters. Victoria A. Johnson has written:

Lee's "politicized" voice is most conflicted . . . as his films grant expression to the voices that are typically marginalized in relation to the mainstream, only for those oppositions to be subsumed by larger commodification practices that recoup them for popular sale as black history and politics. Perhaps in spite of themselves, however, Lee's films may represent a provocative, positive fusion of a prolific, chameleon-like visual-aural aesthetic—a fusion that incorporates diverse youth concerns (in terms of response rather than generational affiliation) and plays with spectator activity and popular knowledge in an unprecedented fashion. (70)

He Got Game exposes the predicament of Jesus Shuttlesworth, who would seem to be among the most successful members of black youth culture. The film regularly contrasts Jesus's anxieties with the popular media's upbeat view of college athletics, embodied most memorably in the manic figure of Dick Vitale, the sportscaster and former college coach who is even more over the top than usual in his brief appearance in *He Got Game*. A fictional character standing in apposition to Vitale is John Turturro's Billy Sunday, the coach at "Tech U" who tries to recruit Jesus with rhetoric more reminiscent of his namesake than of a basketball coach. Chick (Rick Fox), the college player who is escorting Jesus on his campus tour, smirks at Jesus during Sunday's speech. Like Smiley, Radio Raheem, and many other characters in Lee's films, the black athletes must find alternative means to speak their minds.

Nevertheless, for all its celebration of the game and its flamboyant personalities, *He Got Game* does not hold out much hope for Jesus Shuttlesworth. As Big Time Willie persuasively argues, and as the film continually demonstrates, Jesus is entering a cutthroat world of agents, coaches, and hangers-on. Any number of mishaps can quickly end his career, even before he arrives in the National Basketball Association. As many have pointed out, an African American male has a better chance of becoming a successful doctor or lawyer than of playing in the NBA. The film is much more about the oedipal reconciliation between father and son than about a young man's rise to success in professional athletics.

INTERTEXTS, OEDIPAL AND OTHERWISE

Even if Spike Lee is not entirely devoted to reaping the corporate benefits of his interventions, he cannot be expected to survive in the American film industry without making some accommodations with global capital. Nevertheless, he has consistently taken chances in his films, and he is not afraid to experiment at the edges of the Hollywood style. The visual feel of *He Got Game* is in many ways as experimental as its soundtrack. Lee takes chances with different types of film stock and with flashes of light throughout the film, and he presents the opening moments of his film in staggered sequence, jumping back and forth between Jake's first conversation with the warden and the events leading to his arrival at the motel on Coney Island. But there are other aspects to *He Got Game* that cannot be ignored once we acknowledge that the presence of Copland's music opens up a number of intertexts. I have already mentioned the montage of white and black ballplayers that the credit sequence links to Copland's *John Henry*. Although the lyrics for the tune reproduced in Copland's music tell the story of a black man, Lee associates the legendary steel-driver with both black and white athletes.

Later, in the scene in which Jesus hears the appeal of Coach Billy Sunday at Tech U, the young athlete is exposed to an elaborate video played over the gymnasium's huge monitors and public address system. Although it features Copland's much-honored *Fanfare for the Common Man,* the video primarily reflects the histrionic religiosity of Coach Sunday. Playing with the connotations of the name Jesus, the video includes bits of footage from George Stevens's kitsch epic *The Greatest Story Ever Told* (1965). In the fast montage of images, we even see a mock cover of *Sports Illustrated* in which Jesus poses on a cross wearing his basketball uniform and a crown of thorns. Lee has made Copland's music part of a postmodern pastiche, deflating the auspicious sounds associated nowadays with individuals and institutions more well-heeled than the average "common man." *Fanfare for the Common Man* has been recruited, after all, for bombastic purposes by the Rolling Stones, Woody Herman's New Thundering Herd, Emerson, Lake, and Palmer, Elvis Presley, and Grand Funk Railroad, not to mention the producers of numerous television news programs. The popular media's transformations of *Fanfare* constitute a set of intertexts that Lee happily acknowledges at the same time that he treats the rest of Copland's music without irony.

But Lee may not have intended to unleash all the intertextual possibilities in a film with so much of Copland's music. For example, by using "Hoe-Down" to ennoble a spirited game of playground basketball, Lee and his collaborators inevitably suggest comparison with Agnes de Mille's scenario for *Rodeo*. The "Hoe-Down" section of the ballet was basically a dance of sexual aggression in which the cross-dressing, adventuresome Cowgirl reveals her femininity, only to be subdued in a vigorous dance by the overbearing Buck. In *He Got Game* Copland's music for *Rodeo* has been joined to an action that has nothing to do with women but everything to do with phallic aggressivity and male display. That Copland was writing as a gay man intrigued by staged masculinity undermines the black athletes' seemingly natural display of gender. At the same time the music looks forward to the subordination of women that is an all-too-significant element in *He Got Game*.

The film's final music before the end credits is from *Billy the Kid*, the ballet that Copland wrote in 1938 to a scenario by Eugene Loring. Like Jesus Shuttlesworth, the Billy of Loring's scenario witnesses the accidental death of his mother when he is still a child. In a rage, the twelve-year-old Billy publicly kills the man who shot his mother as she passed by during a gunfight. Billy is protected from the crowd by Pat Garrett, who functions in the early stages of the ballet as a surrogate father for the boy. Garrett rides with Billy for a period, but then becomes disillusioned, takes a job as a lawman, and ultimately fires the shot that kills Billy. This narrative begins and ends with a solemn procession of people headed westward, some of whom fall by the wayside or succumb to madness. The music of this processional plays prominently throughout the final scene of *He Got Game* after Jesus seems to have definitively rejected his father. We first hear it on the soundtrack as the camera shows Jake, back in prison for we know not how long, writing a letter to his son. When we see Jesus reading the letter, he is clearly moved by his father's words. The music continues as Jake risks being shot by a guard when he walks into the off-limits area of the prison basketball court and hurls a ball over the wall. The basketball magically arrives at the gymnasium at Big State where Jesus practices alone. He picks up the ball, examines it, and smiles. He may even be crying, but it is difficult to identify tears among the streams of perspiration on his face. The events of the film end here along with Copland's music.

In its original incarnation as music for a ballet, the processional from *Billy the Kid* depicted the epic movement of settlers across the American continent. Copland surely wrote it in the spirit of the radical populism of the 1930s, dramatizing the struggles of ordinary men and women who built America before capital turned their descendants into exploited members of the working class. Some who made the westward journey were slaves and freedmen who helped settle the West and who formed a large contingent of the men called cowboys (Durham and Jones). Some of the black men who journeyed west surely ended up like Jake in *He Got Game* and fell by the wayside. The *Billy the Kid* ballet is usually staged so that dancers, following the westward direction of the early settlers, move right to left, from the audience's point of view, during the processional. On the one hand, it is significant that Jake throws the ball toward

Fig. 57. Jake Shuttlesworth (Denzel Washington) with his son, Jesus (Ray Allen), in *He Got Game* (1998, 40 Acres and a Mule Filmworks/Touchstone Pictures/Buena Vista Pictures). Photofest Film Archive.

the left of the frame and that it lands to the right in the gymnasium where Jesus is practicing; the processional from *Billy the Kid* complements the frustrated westward aspirations of a black man in prison. On the other hand, it is ironic that music associated with oedipal aggressivity is recruited to add emotional depth to the reconciliation between father and son at the end of *He Got Game*. I have no idea if Spike Lee or Alex Steyermark, who is listed as the film's music supervisor, were aware of the oedipal struggle between Billy the Kid and Pat Garrett that is central to the ballet's narrative. For that matter, I do not know if Copland's politics, sexuality, or ethnicity were under consideration as Lee and Steyermark picked out the music for *He Got Game*. Nevertheless, by combining Copland's music with the incidents in the film, Lee and his collaborators have activated subtexts involving racial politics and gender construction, as well as oedipal conflict.

THE FILMMAKER AND HIS FATHER

With its powerful oedipal elements, *He Got Game* might be regarded as the third in a series of partially autobiographical films by Spike Lee. The director has long regarded his own father with a great deal of ambivalence. Bill Lee, who has been an important bass player in the New York jazz community for several decades, refused to play electric bass or accommodate himself to more popular musics in the 1960s (Lee with Jones 163). As a result, the Lee family could not live on his income, and Spike Lee's mother Jacquelyn went to work as a schoolteacher to support Spike and his siblings. Spike Lee has said that his mother was "the heavy" in the household in contrast to his father's passivity (43). She died of cancer when Spike Lee was nineteen, and a few years later Bill Lee began living with a Jewish woman, much to the chagrin of his son, who resented what he perceived as an insult to his mother's memory as much as he resented the color of his father's new companion. (I cannot help wondering if the white prostitute with whom the father has sex in *He Got Game* may—in the thoughts of Spike Lee—bear some relationship to Bill Lee's white companion.) Even a largely hagiographic biography observes that Spike Lee and his father could barely speak without arguing, even during the years when Bill Lee was writing memorable music for his son's early films (Haskins 35).

I have argued that *Mo' Better Blues* (1990) is a wish-fulfillment fantasy in which Spike Lee rewrites his own story (Gabbard, *Jammin'* 155–156). Bleek Gilliam (Denzel Washington), the jazz musician protagonist of the film, grows up in a house in which the father and the son are dominated by the mother, played with great authority by the vocalist/composer/actress Abbey Lincoln. Unlike Spike Lee's father, however, Bleek Gilliam abandons jazz and grows up to become a strong father who gently gives orders to his wife in a final scene that precisely reproduces all but the matriarchal dominance depicted in the film's opening. In *Crooklyn,* an even more overtly autobiographical film from 1994 written by Spike Lee's sister Joie Lee, the father is a jazz pianist who greatly disappoints his oldest son by insisting that the family sit through the father's sparsely attended recital on a night when the son would much rather be watching the New York Knicks play in the NBA finals. Spike Lee was in fact the oldest son of Bill and Jacquelyn Lee, and his lifelong devotion to the Knicks is well known.

Alfre Woodard plays the mother in *Crooklyn* as a loving but overwhelmed and often angry woman who struggles mightily to keep a large family afloat. Although Woodard's character is not entirely sympathetic at first, her death is played for great pathos toward the end. Significantly, the father in *Crooklyn* is played by Delroy Lindo, the talented but sinister-looking actor who would later play a murderous drug-dealer in Lee's *Clockers* (1995) as well as the FBI agent who is the major obstacle to the white hero in *Ransom* (see chapter four). If *Crooklyn* can be read as incidents from Spike Lee's childhood, *He Got Game* might be regarded as a narrative of Spike Lee in young adulthood. The later film dramatizes the crises of a talented young black man from Brooklyn who must cope with all those who would profit from his fame. The protagonist's mother in *He Got Game* is even more idealized than the mothers in Lee's previous films. Seen briefly in flashbacks, Martha Shuttlesworth sends her son loving letters while he is away at camp. In the film she is played by Lonette McKee, who appeared in Lee's *Jungle Fever* (1991) as a successful career woman with a white father and a black mother who explodes when her husband (Wesley Snipes) takes up with a white woman (Annabella Sciorra). In *He Got Game*, McKee looks much younger than the Abbey Lincoln of *Mo' Better Blues* and is perhaps more strikingly beautiful than the Alfre Woodard of *Crooklyn*.

Although the father in *He Got Game* has actually killed the mother, the film is told primarily from his point of view. And as played by Denzel Washington, the character is among the most complex figures in any of Lee's films. Crouch was abundant in his praise for Washington's performance as Jake Shuttlesworth: "Pathetic, arrogant, insecure, stoic, brutish, tender, suspicious, disciplined, sadistic, fatherly, and choking with desire for his son to forgive him, this character has classic American dimensions, wide like the country but intensified by the laser precision of an ethnic authority so fundamentally human that it bores through all walls of class and social division" (Crouch, *Always in Pursuit* 258). In the flashback that precedes the mother's death, Copland's grim *Orchestral Variations* plays on the soundtrack as Jake drives Jesus mercilessly on the basketball court, calling him "a little bitch" and at one point hurling a ball directly into his face. But we also see that the end result is mostly positive; Jesus is the nation's most sought-after high school player. The audience's sympathy is drawn immediately to Jake if only because he is played by Washington, who certainly possesses more charisma than Ray Allen, the real-life NBA basketball player who plays Jesus. The intense dislike that Jesus expresses for his father alongside the extremely sympathetic treatment given to Jake by the film suggest that Spike Lee is as ambivalent as ever about his own father.

Perhaps as a result of the powerful oedipal content in *He Got Game*, the women of the film do not fare well. Like Freud's male child, Jesus must renounce the oceanic feeling associated with the mother—and her surrogates—

and embrace the values of his father in order to achieve manhood. Jesus is given many reasons to move beyond the stage of dependence upon a woman. During the scene in which Big Time Willie lectures Jesus about the dangers of women, he asks, "How you spell pussy? H.I.V." Jesus's girlfriend, Lala, openly cavorts in a swimming pool with D'Andre (Leonard Roberts), whom she identifies as her brother, while Jesus looks on. Presumably looking after the best interests of his son, Jake later breaks D'Andre's nose and then reminds Jesus of the story of Samson and Delilah. Jesus subsequently understands the extent to which Lala cares only for herself and sends her away with the phrase "Good riddance." In addition to sexual experiences with the duplicitous Lala, Jesus has sex with two large-breasted coeds at Tech U who are obviously interested primarily in recruiting him to their college. Jake has sex with the prostitute Dakota, who professes her love for a vicious pimp with a pockmarked face. These sexually degraded women stand in stark contrast to the idealized Martha, whose photograph Jesus kisses shortly after he has seen Lala in the pool with D'Andre.[6] When Jake visits Martha's grave and embraces the headstone, we hear "Grover's Corners" from Copland's score for *Our Town*, perhaps the most lyrical music in the film. But Martha is dead, the victim of the film's brutal oedipal struggles. She is the only positive female character in the film perhaps because she is safely out of the picture during the film's crucial scenes. *He Got Game* suffers most from its unapologetic embrace of misogyny and unreconstructed masculinity.

ANNOTATING WHITE MUSIC

A well-trained deconstructionist could follow many other chains of signifiers at each of the links between Spike Lee and Aaron Copland. I conclude this exercise by identifying another set of associations that follows from the work of this essay but that may be more consistent with the intentions of the filmmakers. Although they do not take up as much time on the soundtrack as do the compositions of Copland, the songs of Public Enemy drive home many of the film's ideas. As with much of rap music, the songs are highly didactic. Consider Chuck D's lyric:

> *People use, even murder's excused*
> *White men in suits don't have to jump*
> *Still a thousand and one ways to lose with the shoes*

Indeed, the world painted by Public Enemy holds almost as little promise for Jesus Shuttlesworth as it does for his imprisoned father. But within the film, the songs provide a microcosm of the interracial connections that grow out of the juxtaposition of Copland and black basketball. Public Enemy comments on white music, especially a tradition of popular music in the white mainstream that tends to hide its debt to African American traditions. This commentary provides a relevant and perhaps even oppositional comment on the use of Copland.

Public Enemy is surely Spike Lee's favorite rap group. Their version of "Fight the Power" was the anthem for *Do the Right Thing* even if that film was dominated musically by the symphonic jazz of Bill Lee, which strongly suggested the influence of Aaron Copland.[7] The musicians who make up Public Enemy have taken their role seriously as spokesmen for marginalized and exploited people, often denouncing record companies that prevent artists from interacting more directly with their audiences. At the end of the 1990s, the group was fighting with Def Jam Records, which refused to release some of the group's music. Group member Chuck D received some public attention when he took the music to the Internet and made it avail-

Fig. 58. The rap group Public Enemy: Chuck D (*left*), Terminator X (*center*), and Flava Flav (*right*). Photofest Film Archive.

able in high quality audio format to anyone with a computer, a sound card, and a modem. Def Jam subsequently released the withheld music.

For *He Got Game*, Public Enemy composed a number of songs in which they articulate values of revolutionary youth and present themselves as candid commentators on urban life. Their song "He Got Game" is especially significant for its title as well as for its prominence in the end credits. In fact, the song kicks in immediately after the last strains of Copland's *Billy the Kid* and the image of Jesus holding the basketball magically delivered to him by his father fade away. Public Enemy's "He Got Game" is the last music audiences hear as they leave the theater. The opening sounds of the song are a sampling of the 1967 recording of "For What It's Worth" by the folk rock group Buffalo Springfield. Actually, Public Enemy does more than just sample the recording. The entirety of "He Got Game" is layered over the earlier record. The chime-like whole notes alternating between E and B in portions of "For What It's Worth" can be heard throughout all of Public Enemy's record. Chuck D actually convinced Stephen Stills to join the group in the studio so that he could re-record his thirty-one-year-old lyrics to "For What It's Worth" (Brunner 61). Even so, Public Enemy's Flava Flav plays the trickster, engaging in call and response with Stills. When the aging rocker sings, "There's a man with a gun over there," Flava responds with a knowing "Yeah, that's right. Hah hah."

The rapper's intrusions into the mild protest rock of the 1960s become especially plangent when the female voices of the Shabach Community Choir of Long Island are heard late in the recording. Although they sing the same lyrics as Stephen Stills, the choir was added to the mix by Public Enemy. The female singers embody the African American gospel traditions that have found their way into white popular music, usually as a means of validating the "authenticity" of the white singer. Innumerable white vocalists have performed in front of a group that consists primarily or exclusively of black singers and dancers, including the Rolling Stones, Laura Nyro, Carole King, Talking Heads, Madonna, and more recently Vonda Shepherd, who was a regular presence on the weekly television program *Ally McBeal*.

By essentially holding up Buffalo Springfield's music to the scrutiny of black artists, the appropriation of African American voices by white artists becomes especially obvious, not at all like the invisibility of black singers in Hollywood's *The Bridges of Madison County, Groundhog Day,* and so many other films. Similarly, Public Enemy's annotations of "For What It's Worth" allude to the role of the civil rights movement in the rhetoric of the student protest movements of the 1960s. When Stephen Stills sang about the ominous presence of men with guns, he was referring to the Sunset Strip Riots of 1966, in which police harassed young people, many of them in hippie mufti, who were attracted to the region's nightlife. Later, the song became associated with the attacks by police and National Guardsmen on Vietnam-era protestors. Regardless, Stills was poaching on the much greater fears that African Americans felt as they faced down police in the civil rights struggles of the 1950s and 1960s. The knowing responses of Flava Flav to the lyrics of "For What It's Worth" register the gap between the anxieties of white hippies like Stills and the daily exposure to racism experienced by black Americans.

But then Public Enemy has also done its share of poaching by appropriating the white musicians of Buffalo Springfield for their performance. By employing Public Enemy, Spike Lee has again called attention to the common but invisible practice of mixing black music into performances by white artists. Lee and Public Enemy reveal the inseparability of "white" popular music and African American traditions, a synthesis so profound that to separate the two would be, in the words of Ellison, an attempt at "a delicate brain surgery with a switch-blade" (*Collected Essays* 283). I am quoting Ellison's review of *Blues People,* the book by Amiri Baraka (then LeRoi Jones) that first made a powerful case for the centrality of the black experience in jazz and blues. Ellison was charging Baraka with overlooking the extent to which African American culture has become an inseparable part of the American mainstream. Aaron Copland did after all look to jazz in his early years to find an American vernacular. He later looked to folk traditions that had effectively absorbed Negro influences long before Copland got to them. By the time he was writing his great ballets and film music, it had become impossible to identify which elements in Copland's music were indisputably "white" and which were the undiluted products of black culture. Because Ralph Ellison was writing as a high modernist in his critique of Baraka, he was less interested in the identity politics and institutional boundaries that Baraka was then developing, ultimately with great success. But I am convinced that Ellison, as a modernist and an integrationist, would have been very pleased with Spike Lee's appropriation of Aaron Copland.

Conclusion

I n recruiting the music of the white composer Aaron Copland to enhance a story about black people, *He Got Game* elegantly and precisely reverses what has become standard musical practice in Hollywood. Many other films have, of course, undertaken comparable if less specific projects. Robert Townsend's micro-budgeted *Hollywood Shuffle* (1987) aggressively exposes the film industry's perpetuation of inner-city stereotypes. *Suture* (1993), a more subtle, more ironic outsider film, upends racial clichés by casting Dennis Haysbert, who is black, as the brother of Michael Harris, who is white. Or at least that's the way it seems to anyone watching the film. To the people *in* the film, the two are indistinguishable, presumably because they are so alike in spirit or perhaps because the film is suggesting that conventional notions of identity are more unstable than most of us would like to admit.

More mainstream films have also confronted the common but under-acknowledged anomalies of race in American culture. *Bring It On,* directed by Peyton Reed in 2000, directly addresses white "love and theft" of black culture. Ostensibly a celebration of well-drilled high school cheerleading teams grafted onto a coming-of-age teenpic, *Bring It On* traces the fortunes of a squad of white cheerleaders that wins national championships by copying the routines of a team of black cheerleaders that lacks the financial means to attend the competitions. The film lets its white heroine, Torrance (Kirsten Dunst), off the hook early by revealing that her predecessor as head cheerleader during the previous year had driven to an inner-city school to

videotape the movements of the black team. Dunst's squad ultimately fin-
ishes second to the African American team after they discover the theft and
purposefully raise the money to mount a challenge at the next national competition. Although Dunst remains the film's central, highly sympathetic
character, the film does make an attempt to humanize the black characters.
At film's end, Dunst congratulates the leader of the black team (Gabrielle
Union), and the two express mutual respect.

The New Guy (2002), like Bring It On a relatively unambitious coming-
of-age story, also works at dissecting America's racial ironies. DJ Qualls plays
Dizzy, a wimpy high school boy terrorized by local bullies. Misdiagnosed by a
psychologist (Illeana Douglas) as suffering from Tourette syndrome and
stoned on the tranquilizers she prescribes, Dizzy is arrested and convicted for
disturbing the peace. He is locked up with Luther (Eddie Griffin), a young
black man who has perfected the art of in-your-face menace. Taking pity on
his utterly helpless cellmate, Luther instructs him on the finer points of acting tough in order to gain control of crucial situations, such as imminent
abuse from schoolyard roughnecks. Although the racial interactions are
played for laughs, and although the film is still another tale about a black
character providing salvation for a white character, The New Guy clearly
demonstrates the extent to which white male toughness is primarily a matter of whites imitating blacks. The film is also refreshing for casting the
short, small-framed Eddie Griffin as Luther, whose highly effective manifestations of masculinity, as well as their appropriation by Dizzy, are revealed as
a performance and little else.

Bring It On and The New Guy suggest that I am not the only person who
has noticed some trends in how American films deal with race. It is even possible that a few filmmakers have decided to bring to the fore certain racial issues that are often essential but unacknowledged in mainstream cinema. But
as I hope I have demonstrated throughout this book, all too many Hollywood
films indicate that, even at the start of a new millennium, white Americans
are still as oblivious to their large debt to black culture as they are unwilling
to grant African Americans the full weight of their humanity. I also hope
that my arguments are not read as the simple demand that white filmmakers
stop casting black actors in parts that have begun to seem too familiar. If
nothing else, the actors need the work. And the surviving family members of
those invisible musicians can use the royalty payments. People who know

Johnny Hartman's widow, Tedi, have told me, for example, that she is a lovely person who thoroughly deserves the windfall she received after the extensive use of her husband's voice in *The Bridges of Madison County*.

I would also insist that many of the films discussed in this book have moments of truth that should not be overlooked. Those love scenes in *The Bridges of Madison County* may put Hartman's voice at the service of white lovers while concealing his identity, but I am surely not alone in finding the scenes extremely moving. In fact, they truthfully represent the degree to which white romance *is* frequently accompanied by black music. My point has been that the film follows a well-entrenched cinematic pattern that ultimately furthers the marginalization of blacks in American society. If there is a degree of racism in the pattern that runs through *The Bridges of Madison County, Next Stop Wonderland, Pleasantville, Groundhog Day*, and the rest, there is also high tribute to the achievements of black artists.

An instructive example of how a film can register this kind of tribute without simultaneously ignoring the identity of a black musician is a scene toward the end of *Stardust Memories* (1980), written and directed by Woody Allen. When Allen, as filmmaker/protagonist Sandy Bates, searches for a moment that has given some meaning to his life, he recalls a Sunday morning in spring with Dorrie (Charlotte Rampling), an Englishwoman with whom he was completely in love at the time. Relaxing in his New York apartment after a walk in Central Park, Sandy puts on a recording of Hoagy Carmichael's "Star Dust," performed by Louis Armstrong at a historic 1931 recording session. When Armstrong begins his dazzling re-creation of the lyrics, Dorrie looks up from the newspaper she has been reading while reclining on the floor and sees that Sandy is staring at her. The camera concentrates on her face as she smiles back at him, obviously seeing the love in his eyes. Allen lets Armstrong perform his entire vocal chorus without interruption while the audience watches the beatific face of Dorrie/Rampling. It's magic. And to his credit, Allen identifies Armstrong by name and even finds the title for his film in the lyrics that Armstrong so elegantly interprets ("My star dust melody, the memory of love's refrain . . .").

But this moment is hardly typical of turn-of-the-century American cinema. If nothing else, we are seldom allowed to hear so much great music without people talking over it. And even when a filmmaker takes the extra step of putting the image of a black musician into a film, the familiar project of forcing the music to serve a white protagonist can continue unabated. I conclude this book with one final example from the Hollywood cinema, one that pushes beyond the convention of black music as invisible lubricant for white romance but that ingeniously preserves the old hierarchies at the same time. In Cameron Crowe's *Vanilla Sky* (2001), David (Tom Cruise) throws a birthday party for himself in his opulent New York apartment just as he is beginning to fall in love with Sofia (Penélope Cruz). To amuse the exclusively white guests, one of David's employees has installed an active, life-size, holographic representation of John Coltrane playing his soprano saxophone in the middle of the apartment. The black-and-white image is performing one of the many recordings of Rodgers and Hammerstein's "My Favorite Things" that Coltrane transformed into roiling tours de force. The hologram, however, is treated strictly as a curio, albeit an extremely sophisticated one. Sofia, one of the only people paying attention, playfully slices Coltrane's image with her hand and pokes it with her finger, producing flashes of light before the hologram reassembles. Coltrane's image is on the screen for less than twenty seconds. More importantly, Sofia's experiments with the hologram are quickly followed by a reaction shot of David looking at her with smiling fascination. Coltrane and his music are almost lost within the assemblage of party guests and their voices, and the hologram and the saxophone solo are of no importance to the film except as an occasion for a white hero to admire the child-like innocence of a new love object. As is more often the case than not, the film pays no debt to black culture beyond a royalty check to the Coltrane estate.

The purpose of this book has been to assess how American culture, as represented by a huge industry that I have called white Hollywood, has been running up a substantial debt to African American culture at the end of the twentieth century and the beginning of the twenty-first. As of this writing, the debt is growing fast and the payments are small change.

Notes

1. The ancestors of Africans who were brought to South America as slaves are also "African Americans," and people of African descent played an important role in the genesis of vernacular music in Brazil. But because racial mixing has produced much less anxiety in Brazil and other Latin American nations, I use the phrase "African American" exclusively for people with some degree of African heritage who grew up in the United States.

2. Seshadri-Crooks writes, "There is the ethnographically oriented school that regards Whiteness as pertaining to white people or Caucasians where the attempt is to induce self-consciousness or awareness of one's racial privilege and racial embodiment. See for instance Ruth Frankenberg, the *Critical Race Theory* volumes edited by Richard Delgado, Vron Ware, Wray and Newitz, etc. There is also the more materialist analysis of Whiteness as an ideological construct, such as Alexander Saxton's, and David Roediger's. The journal *Race Traitor* invokes both these types of analyses" (161).

3. The most important studies include Lott's *Love and Theft*, Rogin's *Blackface*, Bernardi's *Birth*, and Lipsitz's *Possessive Investment*.

4. For Shohat and Stam, syncretism takes an anti-essentialist attitude toward the mix of geographically displaced people in a single nation and "refuses to police identity along purist lines" (41). The concept comes primarily from post-colonial theory, but Shohat and Stam find that it provides a useful framework for thinking about race and ethnicity in the United States.

5. I have also tried not to be an essentialist. Just as the term African American can be problematized by raising the subject of African slaves brought to Latin America, we must also keep in mind the many drops of white blood and white cultural influence that run through the lives of black Americans. The term white should

also be problematized. As Ralph Ellison argued and as Spike Lee has demonstrated, to be white in America means to be a little bit black.

CHAPTER ONE—MARLON BRANDO'S JAZZ ACTING
AND THE OBSOLESCENCE OF BLACKFACE

1. Following Harold Bloom, I use the term "misreading" nonjudgmentally. According to Bloom, all artists misread predecessor artists in order to create their own works of art. Among several books in which Bloom developed this idea, see *The Anxiety of Influence* and *A Map of Misreading*.

2. In *The Political Unconscious*, Fredric Jameson applies the term to literary works. Film scholars have found a wide variety of approaches to applying the psychoanalytically inflected ideological criticism of literary theorists, such as Jameson, to the American cinema. See, for example, the collections edited by Grant, James and Berg, and Collins, Radner, and Collins, and the books by Linda Williams and Michael Rogin, as well as my own *Jammin' at the Margins*.

3. For thorough explorations of the racial logics driving *Birth of a Nation* and much of early American cinema, see Williams, *Playing the Race Card* 96–135, and Rogin, *Blackface, White Noise* 73–156.

4. And in the year 2000, as a centerpiece at the New York Film Festival, a freshly struck print of *Body and Soul* (1925), directed by Micheaux and starring Paul Robeson, was screened in Avery Fisher Hall with a new musical score performed by the Lincoln Center Jazz Orchestra under the direction of Wynton Marsalis.

5. A few years later, filmmakers such as Robert Altman and John Cassavetes would acknowledge the influence of jazz and encourage their actors to improvise. For Altman, see chapter eight. For Cassavetes, see Carney.

6. North was an extremely successful and versatile writer of music for American films. Although he successfully integrated a certain jazz feel into the soundtrack for *Streetcar*, he made little use of jazz during the rest of his career, always writing in a style that was appropriate to his projects. His best known films include *Viva Zapata!* (1952), *The Rose Tattoo* (1955), *The Rainmaker* (1956), *Spartacus* (1960), *Cleopatra* (1963), *Who's Afraid of Virginia Woolf?* (1966), *Bite the Bullet* (1975), *Under the Volcano* (1984), *Prizzi's Honor* (1985), and *The Dead* (1987).

7. Also see the essays by Margolis and Esman.

8. Surprisingly, Brando has said that his work on *Last Tango* was "a violation of my innermost self" (Naremore 196).

9. Beiderbecke's parents never approved of their son's profession. After several years of traveling and sending each of his records home to his parents, Beiderbecke returned to discover all his packages on the top shelf of a closet, still unopened (Sudhalter 245).

10. For the best account of the discourses among jazz writers of the 1940s, see Gendron 121–157. For a broader account of the fascination with "the primitive," see Torgovnick.

11. Still another Davis/Brando connection involves their understanding of record-

ing technology. Davis used electronic hardware to create new effects, playing softly but tightly into a microphone, and later in his career, making use of a "wah-wah" pedal. Brando was often accused of mumbling, but he was also relying on the technological amplification of his voice in order to avoid stale old declamatory styles of stage speech.

12. Although eventually rejected, a cigar was often in the mouth of Brando's Kowalksi during rehearsals of the original stage version of *Streetcar*. In describing Stanley's sexuality, Elia Kazan wrote, "he sucks on a cigar all day because he can't suck on a teat" (Kolin 28). The choice of words is revealing. By writing "teat" rather than "tit," Kazan evokes the infantile qualities of Stanley rather than the oral pleasures of a sexually mature adult.

13. I have used the terms "phallic" and "postphallic" to describe the styles of jazz trumpeters in *Jammin' at the Margins* (138–159).

14. The model of jazz improvisation that informs this chapter should be distinguished from the perilous improvisatory adventures at the outer reaches of free jazz admirably analyzed by John Corbett in "Ephemera Underscored."

15. For an excellent account of Davis's "mistakes" in performance, see Walser.

CHAPTER TWO—BORROWING BLACK MASCULINITY:
DIRTY HARRY FINDS HIS GENTLE SIDE

1. See Rogin, "'Make My Day!'" When Eastwood uttered the words as Harry Callahan in *Sudden Impact,* he was daring an armed black man to murder a white woman so that he could shoot him.

2. Although a film such as *Tightrope* (1984) matches Eastwood with an aggressively feminist leading lady (Genevieve Bujold), centers his fear of involvement, and repeatedly suggests equivalences between the "normal" masculinity of the hero and the pathological behavior of a killer, the film ends with a return to conventional notions of gender as Eastwood rescues Bujold and then pursues the villain to his death (Smith, *Clint Eastwood,* and Mayne). Much the same can be said of *Unforgiven* (1992), which begins as a thoughtful critique of the Western genre but ends with Eastwood recovering his masculinity and gunning down a highly unsympathetic group of antagonists.

3. Thanks to the bulging clipping files in the Cinema Study Center at the Museum of Modern Art, I was able to read reviews of *Bridges* in over thirty daily newspapers and in more than a dozen mass-market magazines.

4. I am indebted to Tania Modleski for the concept that Hollywood films "arouse and contain" the various anxieties of their audiences. See Modleski, *Feminism without Women,* 77.

5. As the trajectory from *Bonnie and Clyde* to *Body Heat* to *Basic Instinct* indicates, the film industry has portrayed sexually desirable women as progressively more threatening over the years. See Gabbard and Gabbard, "Phallic Women."

6. In "The Dialectic of Female Power," Knee discusses the inability of Eastwood's character to express himself in *Play Misty for Me,* in spite of his job talking on

the radio. Bingham points out the unusually prolix character of Eastwood's McBurney in *The Beguiled* and of his John Wilson in *White Hunter, Black Heart*. In general, however, Eastwood's characters tend to be laconic or simply inarticulate.

7. Also hear the performance of John Martyn over the end credits to *The Talented Mr. Ripley*. See chapter three.

8. See Michael Rogin's important essays on the white appropriation of African American culture in movies, all of them collected in *Blackface, White Noise*.

9. As one reader of this chapter has suggested, however, Callahan could just as easily be saying that he is doing it for the one and only person whose approval he requires—himself.

10. Recorded in New York on August 11, 1980, *Once in Every Life* was released on the now defunct Bee Hive label. The personnel includes well-established jazz musicians Joe Wilder (trumpet), Frank Wess (tenor sax, flute), Billy Taylor (piano), Al Gafa (guitar), Victor Gaskin (bass), and Keith Copeland (drums).

11. Eastwood may have attempted to acquire the rights to the Coltrane/Hartman LP, but he could have been frustrated by Alice Coltrane, who administers her late husband's estate with notoriously strong requirements for anyone wishing to make use of the music. For example, when Spike Lee asked if he could pay tribute to John Coltrane by using the title of his 1964 LP, *A Love Supreme*, for the film that eventually became *Mo' Better Blues*, Alice Coltrane said he could use the title only if he agreed to take all foul language out of the film.

12. In taking Hartman's songs off the original Bee Hive LP for the film and soundtrack CDs of *The Bridges of Madison County*, Eastwood and his staff made the rash decision to slow down the recordings to the point that Hartman's voice sounds artificially low and the tempi become dirge-like. When they featured the original recordings of Charlie Parker in *Bird*, Eastwood's people digitally lifted the sound of Parker's saxophone out of its original context and then brought in working musicians to play along with the old solos. In *Jammin' at the Margins*, I argue that this process was probably intended to make Parker more accessible to movie audiences (88). Eastwood probably chose to slow down Hartman's 1980 recordings to deepen their romanticism, but at least for me the effect produces more distortion than romance.

13. The program is in the jazz on video collection at the Library of Congress. Like just about everyone who has ever used that extraordinary collection, I thank Larry Appelbaum for bringing the tape to my attention.

14. Writing about Sinatra as a movie actor, Keir Keightley has said that "Sinatra's persona is continuously being masculinized in order to be re-feminized, and feminized in order to be re-masculinized." Much the same can be said of Sinatra's singing career.

15. The 1966 version of "Girl Talk" is available on the compact disc *Johnny Hartman, Unforgettable* (Impulse! IMPD-152). The song was originally issued on a pop album by ABC/Paramount, a company in the same family of labels as the more jazz-oriented Impulse!

16. I have also argued that the recent and largely unprecedented appearance of jazz in television commercials, often as the signifier of affluence and sophistication,

is strong evidence that jazz has acquired real cultural currency. See the introduction to my anthology, *Jazz among the Discourses* 1-2.

17. Dietz and Schwartz wrote "I See Your Face Before Me" in 1937 for the show *Between the Devil*. Frank Sinatra recorded the song on his classic LP *In the Wee Small Hours* (1955). Johnny Hartman recorded the song twice, first on his Bethlehem LP *Songs from the Heart* (1955), and subsequently on the 1980 Bee Hive album that Eastwood used for *Bridges*.

18. *The Bridges of Madison County* is primarily a series of flashbacks. In a strange scene that follows shots of the daughter, Caroline (Annie Corley), reading about her mother's trip to the roadhouse with her lover, she and her brother, Michael (Victor Slezak), seem to be setting off sexual charges in one another as they discuss the revelations in their mother's diary. When I first saw the film, I momentarily expected a scene of brother/sister incest, as if the erotics of the film were spilling over into the lives of all the characters.

19. The choice of the song may actually have been dictated by the dialogue. Kincaid's one-liner in the movie is taken from a more prolix passage in the novel: "I have one thing to say, one thing only, I'll never say it another time, to anyone, and I ask you to remember it: In a universe of ambiguity, this kind of certainty comes only once, and never again, no matter how many lifetimes you live" (Waller 117).

20. Eastwood chose to cast Morgan Freeman in the role of Ned in *Unforgiven* even though the part had not been written for a black actor. When asked why he did not then have the script rewritten to acknowledge Freeman/Ned's color, Eastwood said, "It's just hipper not to mention it" (Bingham 241). One wonders if Eastwood also understands how much the film is in fact changed by showing Ned's crucifixion/lynching at the hands of Little Bill (Gene Hackman) and his lackeys, thus justifying their eventual slaughter. With the hip white hero avenging racist violence at the end, the horror of his killing spree—and the film's revelation that a storied gunfighter of the Old West is in fact a sociopath—is substantially undermined.

CHAPTER THREE—PASSING TONES:
THE TALENTED MR. RIPLEY AND PLEASANTVILLE

1. "You Don't Know What Love Is" was written by the white team of Don Raye and Gene DePaul for the 1941 film *Keep 'em Flying*, one of several starring vehicles for Bud Abbott and Lou Costello. Although the song has been recorded by a long list of white musicians, the best known versions are by black jazz singers, such as Billie Holiday and Dinah Washington. Other black singers who have made memorable recordings of the song include Billy Eckstine, Etta James, and Cassandra Wilson. In addition, "You Don't Know What Love Is" has been expertly recorded by many of the most important black saxophonists, including John Coltrane, Sonny Rollins, Eric Dolphy, and Booker Ervin.

2. Working through the forest of books and essays on "The Postmodern," I would distinguish theorists who see postmodernism as a set of stylistic practices (Hutcheon, Krauss, McHale) from theorists, such as Jameson (*Postmodernism, or, the Logic of Late Capitalism*), who see it much more in terms of the commodification of every

sector of American life and the attendant interpenetration of economy, politics, and culture. I thank Jeff Smith for sharing his thoughts with me on this complex subject and its huge bibliography.

3. In fairness, I should acknowledge that there are mainstream American films that attack affirmative action more aggressively than does *Pleasantville*. Consider, for example, *Ricochet* (1991), a film about a law enforcement professional named Styles (Denzel Washington). As Elizabeth Alexander cogently argues, the film shows that Styles has risen through the ranks because of his sense of personal style (hence his name) rather than for ability or hard work.

4. James Baldwin's *Giovanni's Room* (1956), written at roughly the same time as Highsmith's first Ripley novel, is typical of American narratives with self-hating homosexual protagonists. For the cinema, see Vito Russo's *The Celluloid Closet*, with its long and exhaustive appendix, "Necrology," listing the many gay characters who are killed off in Hollywood films. The fact that *The Talented Mr. Ripley* concludes with a gay hero facing disaster places it much more in the mainstream of Hollywood film than in the traditions of independent film or the European art cinema.

5. Gavin's biography of Chet Baker is thorough and unflinching. Also see de Valk's shorter book on the trumpeter as well as Baker's own memoir, *As Though I Had Wings*. To see Baker in action, watch Bruce Weber's 1988 film, *Let's Get Lost*, which regularly contrasts the photographic image of Baker the youthful Adonis with the ravaged jailbird at the end of his life.

6. As I suggested in note 4 above, *The Talented Mr. Ripley* is best understood within American traditions of filmmaking. The film was, of course, made by an English director and released first in the United Kingdom. Nevertheless, the film employs several American stars and character actors and is taken from a novel written by an American. Most importantly, *The Talented Mr. Ripley* was Anthony Minghella's first film after his *The English Patient* (1996) won several Academy Awards in the United States. If nothing else, the film was received as a Hollywood movie by its American audience.

7. As Gloria Monti has observed, within the hothouse of racial discourses it is not entirely fair to refer to someone unproblematically as "white." Susan Kohner, for example, was the daughter of a Mexican mother and Hungarian Jewish father. Just as Keanu Reeves is unequivocally marked as white in *The Matrix* (see chapter five), Kohner is a mixed-race actor marked as black in *Imitation of Life* (1959).

8. See my discussion of Davis and the jazz trumpet's role in establishing masculinity in *Jammin' at the Margins*, 141–146.

9. The brief moment from *Eugene Onegin* in *The Talented Mr. Ripley* is distinguished by extraordinary stagecraft. Appropriately for Tom, the scene is the duel when Onegin kills his best friend, Lenski. At first, when the camera goes in tight to show a pair of authentic-looking pistols in an elegant box, the opera seems staged primarily for viewers of the film. The camera also carefully picks up the stage snow catching the light behind the singer playing Onegin. But when Lenski falls to the floor, bright red silk spreads out from under him in a stunning, stylized representation of the wounded man's blood. The fragment of *Eugene Onegin* was staged by Anthony Minghella's wife, Carolyn Choa, who used the red silk to bring a Kabuki-like effect to the scene.

10. The music supervisor for *Pleasantville* was Bonnie Greenberg, one of many people in the film industry discussed by Jeff Smith in what may be the only scholarly discussion of the profession, "Taking Music Supervisors Seriously." Greenberg has been very busy as a music supervisor, contributing to more than thirty-five films since 1988. Like all members of her profession, she must deal with clearances and copyrights, and she must also construct playlists to complement the ownership structures among the megacorporations that make movies and sell recordings of a film's soundtrack. CDs of songs from a film often prove as lucrative as the films themselves. But music supervisors also have the ability to transform a film though careful selection of old and new recordings at strategic moments.

11. As I point out in *Jammin' at the Margins,* the triumph of jazz in the 1950s as a music for the learned and the affluent is presented in an entirely noncelebratory fashion in the Elvis Presley vehicle *Jailhouse Rock* (1957). When the Presley character meets his girlfriend's parents and their jazz aficionado friends at a party, he brusquely storms out, denouncing them for their insider commentary about a jazz record by "Stubby Ritemeyer." See *Jammin'* 124–126.

12. In spite of my claims that *The Talented Mr. Ripley* might be conceptualized as an American film, there is no question that albums such as *Kind of Blue* and *Time Out* were in fact considered by a large group of English people to be works of art. Please keep this in mind in any comparison of *The Talented Mr. Ripley* with a much more conventional Hollywood film like *Pleasantville.*

13. Etta James recorded "At Last" in 1960, one of several anachronisms in the film's musical chronology. The filmmakers surely knew that only music geeks and film music scholars would care. I plead guilty, but see chapter seven.

CHAPTER FOUR—THE RACIAL DISPLACEMENTS OF *RANSOM* AND *FARGO*

1. Although the vertical measurements of male stars are zealously guarded secrets, Mel Gibson appears to be about 5' 7" tall. In Hollywood, at least for male stars, faces clearly matter more than bodies. The industry has thoroughly mastered the art of disguising the diminutive physical stature of leading men such as Gibson, Alan Ladd, Paul Newman, Kirk Douglas, Al Pacino, and Tom Cruise. In the case of Mel Gibson, however, height may have something to do with his strident attempts to present himself as manly. Gibson spent much of the 1990s making films that insist on male perseverance, often, as William Luhr has pointed out, to the point of extreme masochism. In *The Man without a Face* (1993) and *Braveheart* (1995), two films that Gibson himself directed, the hero attempts to live up to what Luhr accurately characterizes as an idealized if not impossible notion of masculinity.

2. For a revealing account of how specific paintings were chosen to make the Mullens' apartment look opulent but viewer-friendly, see Berman.

3. Among the many commentators on the myth of the American hero, see Fiedler, Slotkin, Chase, and Ray.

4. The emasculating and feminizing pressures of family life that bear down on Tom Mullen in *Ransom* have even drawn the attention of critics in the popular press.

Here is an excerpt from Aaron Gill's review from *Time Out New York:* "Like so many Hollywood thrillers, *Ransom* is built on a reactionary psychological subtext. If Tom (Mel Gibson) is the archetypal father, rendered impotent by his feminine love for his son (just indulge me for one minute), only by denying that love and reasserting his masculine impulse can he again find his rightful place in the universe (i.e., on top). Hey, it worked for Agamemnon, right?" (Gill 59). Agamemnon killed his daughter, not his son, but the reviewer has correctly identified the film's ambivalence about family.

5. *Ransom!* was directed in 1956 by Alex Segal with a screenplay by Cyril Hume and Richard Maibaum, who get credit for "story" in the 1996 version. There is of course no black FBI agent in the original film.

6. When *The Time Machine* was remade in 2002 by Simon Wells, a descendant of H. G. Wells, the class issues central to the original novel were even more obscured. Late capitalism is not the reason why Morlocks live below and Eloi live above the earth's surface in the future. The 2002 film blames the colonization of space for knocking pieces of the moon into the earth and disrupting civilization. This time the Morlocks are animated creatures resembling apes and dogs more than cavemen. The leader of the underground forces is played by Jeremy Irons, who speaks with his usual aristocratic English accent. He is also the whitest character in the film, resembling an albino with long white hair. To further confuse the racial and class distinctions, several of the more important Eloi in the film are played by African American actors.

7. According to an only partially facetious book by Paul Fussell, clothing inscribed with written letters marks the wearer as belonging to the prole classes, those who seek to gain prestige by associating themselves with the name of a university or a successful product printed on their T-shirts and baseball caps.

8. I have relied on Sharon Willis's *High Contrast* for this citation as well as for much of the argument in this section of the chapter.

9. Leslie Fiedler is the critic most associated with this tradition in American literature. For cinema and television, also see Pfeil (1–36), Willis (27–59), Wiegman (149–202), and Penley (135–138).

10. I use the term "anatomy" in the tradition of Robert Burton's *The Anatomy of Melancholy* and its subsequent appropriation by Northrop Frye.

11. According to Neal Karlen, the actual statue of Paul Bunyan outside Brainerd wears a much more benevolent smile. The Coens deliberately substituted a statue with a grin that Karlen has called "ghoulish" (19).

12. John Turturro's blocked writer in a spooky hotel in *Barton Fink* recalls Jack Nicholson in *The Shining*. The letters "P.O.E." are scrawled on a bathroom wall in *Raising Arizona*, thus recalling Sterling Hayden's abbreviations for "Purity of Essence" on his scratchpad in *Dr. Strangelove*; the same letters are seen backwards in a mirror, recalling the murder/redrum image in *The Shining*, etc.

13. See Gabbard, "Redeemed by Ludwig Van," my account of how music functions in the films of Stanley Kubrick.

14. See "FAQs": http://www.josefeliciano.zoovy.com/category/jose.faqs.

15. See Lehman and Luhr's account of *Dragon: The Bruce Lee Story* (1, 2).

16. Inferring someone's country of origin by last name is not always reliable, but to my ear "Yanagita" suggests Japan and "Park" suggests Korea. If in fact Steve Park, an actor of Korean descent, is playing a man of Japanese descent, the Coens have once again shown a lack of concern about the identity of people of non-European descent.

CHAPTER FIVE—BLACK ANGELS IN AMERICA:
MILLENNIAL SOLUTIONS TO THE "RACE PROBLEM"

1. In King's novel, the connections between Christ and John Coffey are much more obvious, and the scars on John Coffey's back are mentioned more frequently. As Audrey Colombe has observed, Coffey's initials are even J. C.

2. George Lucas does not seem to be bothered by the constant charges that most of his computer-generated characters are built on racist stereotypes. The Jamaican-accented, minstrelesque Jar Jar Binks is most often mentioned, but Lucas has also relied upon familiar notions of Otherness in basing his *Star Wars* characters on racist myths about Asians, Africans, and diasporic Jews and Arabs.

3. A case can be made that Keanu Reeves should not simply be identified as "white." His father, whose ancestors came from China and Hawaii, met and married his English mother in Lebanon. On the one hand, many who function as "white" in American culture have a similar mix of "non-white" people in their backgrounds. On the other hand, there is no question that Reeves is designated white and middle-class (and thus even more white) in *The Matrix*. Much the same can be said of Cameron Diaz, whose Latina heritage is irrelevant to the character she plays in *A Life Less Ordinary* and most of her other films.

4. In King's novel of *The Green Mile*, there is at least one passage in which Paul Edgecomb marvels at how John Coffey managed to escape lynching.

5. As in *The Matrix*, the music of Duke Ellington plays a small part at a crucial moment in *The Legend of Bagger Vance*. If Neo in *The Matrix* is "Beginning to See the Light" thanks to the interventions of the Oracle, Adele invites Junuh to join her in a "Mood Indigo." In both films, as in so many Hollywood films, white people become more sensitive (and thus, in some situations, more sexual) in the presence of black music.

CHAPTER SIX—EVIDENCE: THELONIOUS MONK'S
CHALLENGE TO JAZZ HISTORY

1. The problems raised by documentary cinema's inevitable claim to truth dominate much writing on the subject. Among many useful volumes, see Rosenthal, Renov, and Barnouw. The best single work on biographies, autobiographies, and documentaries about jazz musicians is by Harlos. Also see the chapter on the "jazz biopic" in my *Jammin' at the Margins*.

2. Dickerson was cinematographer on all of Spike Lee's films from *She's Gotta Have It* (1986) through *Malcolm X* (1992). He has also directed several films for

television and the cinema, including *Juice* (1992), *Surviving the Game* (1994), and *Bulletproof* (1996).

3. Paul Smith compares the lighting of Eastwood's body in many of his films to the lighting afforded Whitaker in *Bird:* the way that Parker/Whitaker signifies "decadence and dissolution" bears a significant relationship to "the ways in which Eastwood's own body both represents and signifies whiteness" (241).

4. This situation began to change with a conference on Monk held at the University of North Carolina in 1998. The papers at this conference became the kernel of an issue of *Black Music Research Journal* (Tucker, Special Issue) that included an early draft of this chapter. In addition, Robin D. G. Kelley's theoretically sophisticated book-length study of Monk's life and work is forthcoming.

5. The intention was probably to make Monk's music less threatening and obscure by associating him with the revered and popular Basie, who also played piano in a spare, percussive style. Nevertheless, the placement of Basie did not please Monk. He later complained to his personal manager, Harry Colomby, that Basie was "looking at" him while he was playing. According to Colomby, Monk eventually vowed that "the next time he plays somewhere I'm going to look at him." (Not surprisingly, this information is not in Seig's film but in Zwerin's.)

6. I have borrowed the term "authenticating voices" from William Kenney, who applies it both to whites who edited and wrote introductions to slave narratives in premodern eras as well as to Rudy Vallee, who wrote a preface to Louis Armstrong's first autobiography.

7. Orrin Keepnews, who produced the many recordings Monk made for the Riverside label in the 1950s and 1960s, is also a talking head in Seig's film, but he is called upon more to address the specifics of Monk's life than to speak to the larger significance of the man and his music.

8. The recording session in fact took place in December 1967 after Monk's tour of European cities in October and November of 1967.

9. The scene at the recording session is difficult to follow. The editing does not make clear how much time has elapsed between the various segments of the footage, and Monk's speech is indistinct. Teo Macero seems to be mocking Monk at the same time that he goes out of his way to be enthusiastic about his presence in the studio. Commenting on an earlier draft of this chapter, Mark Tucker suggested that the presence of the camera in the studio transforms the two into something of a comedy team—the sly Monk with his sardonic grin and the broadly slapstick Macero with his desperate attempts at being hip and funny. Ultimately, the sequence seems designed to reveal the power struggle between the musician and the producer as well as the demands that the recording industry awkwardly imposes on an artist who was both a serious musician and an eccentric personality.

10. Russell's *Bird Lives* is an excellent example of the romantic narrative of the self-destructive black genius suffering from exploitation and the ignorance of audiences. In cinema, a similar course is taken by director Sidney J. Furie in *Lady Sings the Blues* (1972) and by Bertrand Tavernier in *Round Midnight* (1986). In his book, Laurent de Wilde appropriates the same discourse to explain Monk's refusal to play during the last years of his life.

11. After a period in the late 1950s and early 1960s when the American cinema presented highly sympathetic portrayals of psychiatrists and other mental health professionals in at least twenty-five feature films, the industry dramatically changed its practices and began portraying psychiatrists as unprofessional, incompetent, and/or vindictive. See Gabbard and Gabbard, *Psychiatry and the Cinema*.

12. For an excellent study of Wiseman's work, see Grant, *Voyages of Discovery*.

13. I thank Christopher Harlos for getting me started on this list.

CHAPTER SEVEN—REVENGE OF THE NERDS:
REPRESENTING THE WHITE MALE COLLECTOR OF BLACK MUSIC

1. The scene is so memorable that it is included on *Nothing to Fear: A Rough Mix*, a kaleidoscopic CD of sampled music and talk produced by the turntable king Steinski. I thank Michael Jarrett for calling this artifact to my attention and for being an especially reliable native informant about musical worlds I never even knew existed.

2. At one point in *Bamboozled*, Wayans begins hallucinating that the minstrel-head toy bank on his desk has come to life. This piece of racist memorabilia, its hand reaching out for a penny to stuff into its smiling red mouth, is an exact replica of the one that the unnamed hero of *Invisible Man* accidentally breaks in his room at Mary's boarding house. Because the bank does not belong to him, the Invisible Man is too ashamed to confess what he has done, but neither can he find the right time or place to rid himself of the fragments of the detested object. It ends up becoming a permanent fixture in the briefcase that was given to him by the white city fathers who had tormented him back home. Both the briefcase and the broken toy bank are charged with racist associations, but the Invisible Man cannot shed them until the final pages of the novel. Spike Lee was almost surely recreating this complex encounter with racist culture at the climax of *Bamboozled*. For this and many other insights, I thank David Yaffe.

3. There actually was a chain of Coon Chicken Inns in the western United States in the early years of the twentieth century that actually became Cook's Chicken. See http://members.aol.com/mlgcci/mlgcci.htm.

4. According to the Internet Movie Database (www.imdb.com), *Ghost World* earned more than $10 million at the box office. *Crumb* earned about $3 million, not bad for a documentary and definitely more than the filmmakers anticipated.

CHAPTER EIGHT—ROBERT ALTMAN'S JAZZ HISTORY LESSON

1. Altman explains this comparison in some detail in the interview with Leonard Lopate and in the article by Bourne.

2. Altman says that he himself recalls most of what happened in Kansas City in the 1930s and has not mentioned if he or anyone else looked at history books.

In researching the music and politics of Kansas City in the 1930s, I have con-
sulted Barnes, Dance, Dorsett, Giddins, Shapiro and Hentoff, Murray, Pearson,
Porter, Reddig, and Russell.

3. The speech is even accurate in terms of how a character such as Carolyn might
   represent her situation as the wife of a man who emerged from local politics to
   become an advisor to FDR in Washington. Disoriented from a large dose of laudanum and speaking for no particular reason to the bewildered cleaning woman
   Addie Parker, the aristocratic Carolyn carefully distances herself and her husband from the corrupt Goats and Rabbits while hinting at their sympathy with
   the more powerful faction.

4. Since the 1930s, the vast majority of Hollywood movies have filmed actors and
   even real-life musicians miming performances to pre-recorded music. A rare exception was the French/American co-production *Round Midnight* (1986), but
   unlike the musicians in *Kansas City,* the players in *Round Midnight* often appeared uncomfortable playing on camera, and their performances suffered as a
   result.

5. Willner brought the following musicians to Kansas City: James Carter, Craig
   Handy, David Murray, Joshua Redman (tenor saxophones); Jessie Davis, David
   "Fathead" Newman Jr. (alto saxophones); Don Byron (clarinet); Olu Dara,
   Nicholas Payton, James Zollar (trumpets); Curtis Fowlkes, Clark Gayton (trom-
   bones); Victor Lewis (drums); Geri Allen, Cyrus Chestnut (piano); Ron Carter,
   Tyrone Clark, Christian McBride (bass); Russell Malone, Mark Whitfield (gui-
   tar); and Kevin Mahogany (vocal).

6. The doctor in question is not identified by his real name in the film, probably to
   avoid legal complications. After Johnny O'Hara offers "his guts" to Seldom Seen,
   the doctor is presumably the one who surgically removes them before sending
   Johnny home to die.

7. Various other complaints might be made about the film's representation of
   Kansas City jazz. The musicians at the Hey Hey Club play carefully arranged compositions for large jazz orchestra, such as Fletcher Henderson's "Queer Notions,"
   although they also seem to be engaging in a jam session. Dan Morgenstern has
   pointed out that a poster that appears early in the film

   The Hey Hey Club Battle of JAZZ
   All Day • All Nite MONDAY
   Lester YOUNG vs. Coleman HAWKINS
   Plus! Noteable Appearances by Mary Lou WILLIAMS
   Ben WEBSTER and OTHERS
   WHO is the KING of the RIGHTEOUS RIFF?

   was completely inconsistent with KC practice, where cutting contests were almost always spur-of-the-moment events. If nothing else, there could have been
   no guarantee that Hawkins would show up at an after-hours place while on tour
   with the Henderson Orchestra (Morgenstern, Conversation with the author).

8. According to von Ziegesar, the "real" Seldom Seen was a Kansas City gangster
   named Ivory Johnson (12).

9. These aspects of the cutting contest between Hawkins and Young are somewhat consistent with the widely quoted account of the event that Mary Lou Williams gave to the jazz periodical *Melody Maker* in 1954. "The word went around that Hawkins was in the Cherry Blossom and within half an hour there were Lester Young, Ben Webster, Herschel Evans and one or two unknown tenor players piling into the club to blow. Bean [Hawkins's nickname] didn't know the Kansas City tenormen were so terrific and he couldn't get himself together though he played all morning . . . when we got there Hawkins was in his vest taking turns with the KC men. It seems he had run into something he didn't expect" (quoted in Chilton 91).

10. The original "Amos 'n' Andy" radio show became hugely successful during its second year on NBC in 1929. The eponymous characters were played by the white actors Freeman F. Gosden and Charles J. Correll, who would later play their roles in blackface in the 1930 film *Check and Double Check*. In his interview with Lopate, Altman said that he and Harry Belafonte were working on a new film based on "Amos 'n' Andy." Apparently nothing ever came of the idea.

CHAPTER NINE—SPIKE LEE MEETS AARON COPLAND

1. It would be difficult to overstate the influence of Copland's music on the history of music for American films. To choose just one example, in the same year as the release of *He Got Game*, John Williams's score for Steven Spielberg's *Saving Private Ryan* (1998) was extremely Coplandesque.

2. In "Rhetoric of the Image," Roland Barthes argues that the polysemy of a photograph in a magazine can be stripped of a wide range of possible meanings and anchored to a specific few by means of the caption below the picture. Claudia Gorbman has employed this concept of *ancrage* by arguing that soundtrack music can anchor the profusion of images in a film to selected sets of meanings. See Gorbman 32.

3. Compare Copland's quotations with those of jazz musicians who relish the opportunity to insert fragments of inapposite melodies into their compositions. Perhaps the best example is Charlie Parker's frequent references to Percy Grainger's "Country Gardens," as if to conjure up a bourgeois drawing room while playing in a smoky nightclub full of bohemians. See my "The Quoter and His Culture."

4. Tommasini has argued that chordal structures that suggest the American heartland in Copland's work can also be found in music that Palestrina wrote in sixteenth-century Italy (36).

5. But in *The Cultural Front*, Denning argues that invocations of Lincoln were more typical of "the official Americanisms of the Depression" (131). Members of the Popular Front and other radical groups were more likely to associate themselves with the abolitionist John Brown.

6. The sexual politics of the film are further complicated by the racial dynamics at Tech U, where Jesus is surrounded by white coeds who are, in the words of Chick, "freaks." When Chick and Jesus walk across the campus with two white girls, they encounter a group of black coeds, one of whom says, "That's not right,

Chick." While Jesus speaks with one of the white girls, Chick attempts to mollify the black girls by saying that he will see them at church on Sunday. Later, Chick explains in detail why he prefers white girls, who will wash his "dirty drawers," as opposed to black girls, who "make you work too hard."

7. Writing at least a year before the release of *He Got Game,* Victoria Johnson referred to Bill Lee's score for *Do the Right Thing* as "Coplandesque" (55).

Works Cited

Adams, Doug. "Composition Theory: Carter Burwell Interviewed." *Film Score Monthly* Oct./Nov. 1998: 29–33.

Alexander, Elizabeth. "'We're Gonna Deconstruct Your Life!': The Making and Un-Making of a Black Bourgeois Patriarch in *Ricochet.*" *Representing Black Men.* Ed. Marcellus Blount and George P. Cunningham. New York: Routledge, 1996. 157–171.

Allen, Geri. Conversation with the author. 12 Oct. 1996.

Allen, Walter C. *Hendersonia: The Music of Fletcher Henderson and His Musicians.* Jazz Monographs 4. Highland Park, Ill.: Walter C. Allen, 1973.

Altman, Robert. Conversation with the author. 2 Dec. 1982.

——. Interview with Leonard Lopate. New York Public Radio. WNYC, New York. 16 Aug. 1996.

Attali, Jacques. *Noise: The Political Economy of Music.* Trans. Brian Massumi. Theory and History of Literature 16. Minneapolis: U of Minnesota P, 1985.

Baker, Chet. *As Though I Had Wings: The Lost Memoir.* New York: St. Martin's, 1997.

Baker, Dorothy. *Young Man with a Horn.* Boston: Houghton Mifflin, 1938.

Baldwin, James. *Giovanni's Room.* New York: Doubleday, 1956.

——. "Sonny's Blues" (1965). *Hot and Cool: Jazz Short Stories.* Ed. Marcela Breton. London: Bloomsbury, 1991. 112–129.

Baraka, Amiri (as LeRoi Jones). *Blues People: Negro Music in White America.* New York: Morrow, 1963.

Baraka, Amiri. "Spike Lee at the Movies." *Black American Cinema.* Ed. Manthia Diawara. New York: Routledge, 1993.

Barnes, Harper. *Blue Monday.* St. Louis: Patrice Press, 1991.

Barnouw, Erik. *Documentary: A History of the Non-Fiction Film.* New York: Oxford UP, 1993.

Barthes, Roland. "Rhetoric of the Image." *Image—Music—Text.* Trans. Stephen Heath. New York: Hill and Wang, 1977.

Baudrillard, Jean. *Le Système des objets.* Paris: Gallimard, 1968.

Berman, Avis. "In the Script, the Art Says, 'They're Rich.'" *New York Times* 3 Nov. 1996. 2:43.

Bernardi, Daniel, ed. *The Birth of Whiteness: Race and the Emergence of U.S. Cinema.* New Brunswick: Rutgers UP, 1996.

———. ed. *Classic Hollywood, Classic Whiteness.* Minneapolis: U of Minnesota P, 2001.

Berrett, Joshua. "Louis Armstrong and Opera." *Musical Quarterly* 76.2 (1992): 216–241.

Bingham, Dennis. *Acting Male: Masculinities in the Films of James Stewart, Jack Nicholson, and Clint Eastwood.* New Brunswick, N.J.: Rutgers UP, 1994.

Bloom, Harold. *The Anxiety of Influence: A Theory of Poetry.* New York: Oxford UP, 1973.

———. *A Map of Misreading.* New York: Oxford UP, 1975.

Blumenthal, Bob. "Clint Eastwood: Bridging Jazz and Film." *Jazz Times* Sept. 1990: 30.

Bogle, Donald. *Toms, Coons, Mulattoes, Mammies, and Bucks.* New ed. New York: Ungar, 1992.

Bosworth, Patricia. *Marlon Brando.* Penguin Lives Series. New York: Viking, 2001.

Bourne, Michael. "Goin' to Kansas City and Robert Altman Takes You There!" *Down Beat* Mar. 1996: 22–27.

Boyd, Todd. "The Day the Niggaz Took Over: Basketball, Commodity Culture, and Black Masculinity." *Out of Bounds: Sports, Media, and the Politics of Identity.* Ed. Aaron Baker and Todd Boyd. Bloomington: Indiana UP, 1997. 123–142.

Brady, John. *Bad Boy: The Life and Politics of Lee Atwater.* New York: Addison-Wesley, 1997.

The Bridges of Madison County soundtrack CD. Advertisement. *The Nation* 26 June 1995: 917.

Brunner, Rob. "Game Boys." *Entertainment Weekly* 1 May 1998: 61.

Burnham, John. "The Influence of Psychoanalysis upon American Culture." *American Psychoanalysis: Origins and Development.* Ed. J. Quen and E. Carlson. New York: Brunner/Mazel, 1978. 52–72.

Burton, Robert. *The Anatomy of Melancholy.* New York: New York Review of Books, 2001.

Carbine, Mary. "'The Finest Outside the Loop': Motion Picture Exhibition in Chicago's Black Metropolis, 1905–1928." *Camera Obscura* 23 (1990): 8–41.

Card, Wallace. "Is This Trap Necessary: Ann-Margret and Treat Williams Hop aboard a TV Remake of *Streetcar.*" *People Weekly* 15 Aug. 1983: 98.

Carney, Raymond. *The Films of John Cassavetes: Pragmatism, Modernism, and the Movies.* Cambridge Film Classics. Cambridge: Cambridge UP, 1994.

Carr, Jay. "Spike Lee Spotlights Race Relations." *Spike Lee's "Do the Right Thing."* Ed. Mark A. Reid. Cambridge Film Handbooks. Cambridge: Cambridge UP, 1997. 134–137.

"Carter Burwell in Conversation: Music for the Films of Joel and Ethan Coen." *The World of Sound in Film.* Ed. Philip Brophy. Sydney, Australia: Australian Film and Television School, 1999. 15–39.

Chase, Richard Volney. *The American Novel and Its Traditions.* Baltimore: Johns Hopkins UP, 1980.

Chilton, John. *The Song of the Hawk: The Life and Recordings of Coleman Hawkins.* Ann Arbor: U of Michigan P, 1990.

Ching, Barbara. "The Possum, the Hag, and the Rhinestone Cowboy: Hard Country Music and the Burlesque Abjection of the White Man." *Whiteness: A Critical Reader.* Ed. Mike Hill. New York: New York UP, 1997. 117–133.

Christensen, Jerome. "Spike Lee: Corporate Populist." *Critical Inquiry* 17.3 (Spring 1991): 582–595.

Cleage, Pearl. "Mad at Miles." *The Miles Davis Companion.* Ed. Gary Carner. London: Omnibus Press, 1996. 210–216.

Cohan, Steven. *Masked Men: Masculinity in the Movies of the Fifties.* Bloomington: Indiana UP, 1997.

Colombe, Audrey. "White Hollywood's New Black Boogeyman." *Jump Cut* 45 (Fall 2002). http://www.ejumpcut.org/archive/jc45.2002/colombe/index.html. Aug. 4, 2003.

Collins, Jim, Hilary Radner, and Ava Preacher Collins, eds. *Film Theory Goes to the Movies.* AFI Film Readers. New York: Routledge, 1993.

Corbett, John. "Ephemera Underscored: Writing around Free Improvisation." *Jazz among the Discourses.* Ed. Krin Gabbard. Durham: Duke UP, 1995. 217–240.

Crouch, Stanley. *Always in Pursuit: Fresh American Perspectives.* New York: Vintage, 1999.

——. "Bird Land." *The New Republic* 27 Feb. 1989: 25–31.

——. Conversation with the author. 29 Jan. 1997.

——. "Jazz Criticism and Its Effect on the Art Form." *New Perspectives on Jazz: Report on a National Conference Held at Wingspread, Racine, Wisconsin.* Ed. David N. Baker. Washington: Smithsonian Institution, 1990. 71–87.

Crowdus, Gary, and Dan Georgakas. "Thinking about the Power of Images: An Interview with Spike Lee." *Cineaste* 26.2 (Mar. 2001): 4–9

Cuscuna, Michael. Conversation with the author. 12 Dec. 1995.

Dance, Stanley. *The World of Count Basie.* New York: Scribner's, 1980.

Davis, Miles, with Quincy Troupe. *Miles: The Autobiography.* New York: Simon and Schuster, 1989.

Delgado, Richard, ed. *Critical Race Theory: The Cutting Edge.* Philadelphia: Temple UP, 1995.

Delgado, Richard, and Jean Stefanic, eds. *Critical White Studies: Looking behind the Mirror.* Philadelphia: Temple UP, 1997.

Denning, Michael. *The Cultural Front: The Laboring of American Culture in the Twentieth Century.* London and New York: Verso, 1997.

de Valk, J. *Chet Baker: His Life and Music.* Berkeley, Calif.: Berkeley Hill, 2000.

DeVeaux, Scott. *The Birth of Bebop: A Social and Musical History*. Berkeley and Los Angeles: U of California P, 1997.

——. "Constructing the Jazz Tradition: Jazz Historiography." *Black American Literature Forum* 25.3 (1991): 525–560.

de Wilde, Laurent. *Monk*. Trans. Jonathan Dickinson. New York: Marlowe, 1997.

Dobson, Frank E. "Poise, Authority, and Privilege: Race in Eastwood's *White Hunter, Black Heart*." Society for Cinema Studies conference, Holiday Inn Crowne Plaza, New York, March 1995.

Doherty, Thomas. *Pre-Code Hollywood*. Film and Culture Series. New York: Columbia UP, 1999.

——. *Teenagers and Teenpics: The Juvenilization of American Movies in the 1950s*. Boston: Unwin Hyman, 1988.

Dorsett, Lyle W. *The Pendergast Machine*. New York: Oxford UP, 1968.

Douglas, Ann. "50th Anniversary for Actors Studio and Its 'Streetcar' Ride to Renown." *New York Times* 3 Oct. 1997: E1, 24.

Durham, Philip, and Everett L. Jones. *The Negro Cowboys*. Lincoln: U of Nebraska P, 1965.

Dyer, Richard. *White*. New York: Routledge, 1997.

Erenberg, Lewis A. *Steppin' Out: New York Nightlife and the Transformation of American Culture, 1890–1930*. Chicago: U of Chicago P, 1984.

Eliot, T. S. *What Is a Classic? An Address Delivered before the Vergil Society on the 16th of October 1944*. London: Faber and Faber, 1944.

Ellison, Ralph. *The Collected Essays of Ralph Ellison*. New York: Modern Library, 1995.

——. *Invisible Man*. 1952. New York: Random, 1972.

Esman, A. "Jazz—A Study in Cultural Conflict." *American Imago* 8 (1951): 219–226.

Farmer, Art. Conversation with the author. 12 Nov. 1996.

Fauset, Jessie Redmon. *Plum Bun*. 1928. Boston: Beacon, 1990.

Fiedler, Leslie. *Love and Death in the American Novel*. New York: Stein and Day, 1960.

Fitterling, Thomas. *Thelonious Monk: His Life and Music*. Trans. Robert Dobbin. Berkeley, Calif.: Berkeley Hills, 1997.

Frankenberg, Ruth. *Displacing Whiteness: Essays in Social and Cultural Criticism*. Durham: Duke UP, 1997.

Freud, Sigmund. "A Special Type of Object Choice Made by Men" (1910). *The Standard Edition of the Complete Psychological Works of Sigmund Freud*. Trans and ed. James Strachey. London: Hogarth Press, 1974. 11:164–169.

Friedwald, Will. *Sinatra: The Song Is You*. New York: Simon and Schuster, 1995.

Frye, Northrop. *Anatomy of Criticism: Four Essays*. Princeton: Princeton UP, 1957.

Fussell, Paul. *Class: A Guide through the American Status System*. New York: Summit, 1983.

Gabbard, Krin. "Introduction: The Jazz Canon and Its Consequences." *Jazz among the Discourses*. Ed. Krin Gabbard. Durham: Duke UP, 1995. 1–28.

———. *Jammin' at the Margins: Jazz and the American Cinema.* Chicago: U of Chicago P, 1996.

———. "The Quoter and His Culture." *Jazz in Mind: Essays on the History and Meanings of Jazz.* Ed. Reginald T. Buckner and Steven Weiland. Detroit: Wayne State UP, 1991. 92–111.

———. "Redeemed by Ludwig Van: Kubrick's Musical Strategy in *A Clockwork Orange.*" *Cinesonic: Experiencing the Soundtrack.* Ed. Philip Brophy. North Ryde, Australia: Australian Film Television and Radio School, 2001. 149–167.

Gabbard, Krin, and Glen O. Gabbard. "Phallic Women in Contemporary Cinema." *American Imago* 50.4 (1993): 421–439.

———. *Psychiatry and the Cinema.* Chicago: U of Chicago P, 1987.

Gary, Romain. *White Dog.* New York: New American Library, 1970.

Gates, Henry Louis, Jr. *The Signifying Monkey: A Theory of Afro-American Literary Criticism.* New York: Oxford UP, 1988.

Gavin, James. *Deep in a Dream: The Long Night of Chet Baker.* New York: Knopf, 2002.

Gendron, Bernard. *Between Montmartre and the Mudd Club: Popular Music and the Avant-Garde.* Chicago: U of Chicago P, 2002.

Gennari, John. Conversation with the author. 8 March 2003.

———. "Race-ing the Bird: Ross Russell's Obsessive Pursuit of Charlie Parker." *Canonizing Jazz: An American Art and Its Critics.* Chicago: U of Chicago P, forthcoming.

Giddins, Gary. "Birdman of Hollywood." *Faces in the Crowd.* New York: Oxford UP, 1992. 39–51.

———. *Celebrating Bird: The Triumph of Charlie Parker.* New York: Morrow, 1987.

Gill, Aaron. Rev. of *Ransom,* dir. Ron Howard. *Time Out New York* 1–14 Nov. 1996: 59.

Gioia, Ted. *The Imperfect Art: Reflections on Jazz and Modern Culture.* New York: Oxford UP, 1988.

Goldberg, Jonathan. "Recalling Totalities: The Mirrored Stages of Arnold Schwarzenegger." *Differences* 4.1 (1992): 172–204.

Goldman, Herbert G. *Jolson: The Legend Comes to Life.* New York: Oxford UP, 1988.

Gorbman, Claudia. *Unheard Melodies: Narrative Film Music.* Bloomington: Indiana UP, 1987.

Gourse, Leslie. *Straight, No Chaser: The Life and Genius of Thelonious Monk.* New York: Schirmer, 1997.

———. *Unforgettable: The Life and Mystique of Nat King Cole.* New York: St. Martin's, 1991.

Grant, Barry Keith, ed. *The Dread of Difference: Gender and the Horror Film.* Austin: U of Texas P, 1996.

———. *Voyages of Discovery: The Cinema of Frederick Wiseman.* Urbana: U of Illinois P, 1991.

Griffin, Farah Jasmine. "When Malindy Sings: A Meditation on Black-American Women's Singing." *The New Jazz Studies.* Ed. Robert G. O'Meally, Brent Hayes Edwards, and Farah Jasmine Griffin. New York: Columbia UP, 2003. Forthcoming.

Groch, John. "Afterbirth of a Nation: The Angry White Male's Ride to the Rescue in Contemporary American Cinema." Society for Cinema Studies conference. University of North Texas, Dallas, Texas, March 1996.

Grossberg, Lawrence. "Another Boring Day in Paradise: Rock and Roll and the Empowerment of Everyday Life." *Dancing in Spite of Myself: Essays on Popular Culture*. Durham: Duke UP, 1997. 29–63.

Gubar, Susan. *Racechanges: White Skin, Black Face in American Culture*. New York and Oxford: Oxford UP, 1997.

Hajdu, David. Conversation with the author. 2 June 2003.

Hansen, Miriam. "Adventures of Goldilocks: Spectatorship, Consumerism, and Public Life." *Camera Obscura* 22 (1990): 51–71.

Harlos, Christopher. "The Jazz Life-Text: Autobiography and Biography in Jazz Art." Diss. Duke University, 1998.

Haskell, Molly. *From Reverence to Rape: The Treatment of Women in the Movies*. 2nd ed. Chicago: U of Chicago P, 1987.

Haskins, Jim. *Spike Lee: By Any Means Necessary*. New York: Walker, 1997.

Hernton, Calvin. *Sexism and Racism in America*. New York: Grove, 1988.

Herodotus. *The Histories*. Trans. Robin A. Waterfield. Oxford: Oxford UP, 1999.

Highsmith, Patricia. *The Talented Mr. Ripley*. New York: Coward-McCann, 1955.

Hirsch, Foster. *A Method to Their Madness: The History of the Actors Studio*. New York: Norton, 1984.

Holmlund, Chris. "Aging Clint." Society for Cinema Studies conference, University of North Texas, Dallas, Texas, March 1996.

———. "Sexuality and Power in Male Doppelganger Cinema: The Case of Clint Eastwood's *Tightrope*." *Cinema Journal* 26.1 (Fall 1986): 31–42.

Hornby, Nick. *High Fidelity*. New York: Riverhead Books, 1995.

Hutcheon, Linda. *A Poetics of Postmodernism: History, Theory, and Fiction*. New York: Routledge, 1988.

———. *The Politics of Postmodernism*. New York: Routledge, 1989.

Ignatiev, Noel. *How the Irish Became White*. New York: Routledge, 1995.

James, David E., and Rick Berg, eds. *The Hidden Foundation: Cinema and the Question of Class*. Minneapolis: U of Minnesota P, 1996.

Jameson, Fredric. *The Political Unconscious: Narrative as a Socially Symbolic Act*. Ithaca: Cornell UP, 1981.

———. *Postmodernism, or, the Cultural Logic of Late Capitalism*. Durham: Duke UP, 1991.

Jarrett, Michael. Conversation with the author. 22 Nov. 2002.

Johnson, James Weldon. *The Autobiography of an Ex-Colored Man*. 1912. New York: Penguin, 1990.

Johnson, Victoria A. "Polyphony and Cultural Expression: Interpreting Musical Traditions in *Do the Right Thing*." *Spike Lee's "Do the Right Thing"*. Ed. Mark A. Reid. Cambridge Film Handbooks. Cambridge: Cambridge UP, 1997. 50–72.

Karlen, Neal. "If the Shoe (Snowshoe?) Fits, Well. . . ." *New York Times* 5 May 1996, Sunday Arts and Leisure Section: 19.

Keightley, Keir. "Singing, Suffering, Sinatra: Articulations of Masculinity and Femininity in the Career of Frank Sinatra, 1953–1962." Society for Cinema Studies, Syracuse University, Syracuse, N.Y., March 1994.

Kelley, Robin D. G. "Miles Davis: A Jazz Genius in the Guise of a Hustler." *New York Times* 13 May 2001, Arts and Leisure: 1, 7.

Kenney, William Howland. "Negotiating the Color Line: Louis Armstrong's Autobiographies." *Jazz in Mind: Essays on the History and Meanings of Jazz.* Ed. Reginald T. Buckner and Steven Weiland. Detroit: Wayne State UP, 1991. 38–59.

Kenny, Tom. "Carter Burwell: An Ironic Twist on Film Scoring." *The Mix* Oct. 1997: 269–276.

Kernfeld, Barry, ed. *The New Grove Dictionary of Jazz.* 2 vols. London: Macmillan, 1988.

——. "Two Coltranes." *Annual Review of Jazz Studies* 2 (1983): 7–61.

King, Stephen. *The Green Mile.* New York: Simon and Schuster, 1996.

Knee, Adam. "The Dialectic of Female Power and Male Hysteria in *Play Misty for Me.*" *Screening the Male: Exploring Masculinities in the Hollywood Cinema.* Ed. Steven Cohan and Ina Rae Hark. New York: Routledge, 1993. 87–102.

Koestenbaum, Wayne. *The Queen's Throat: Opera, Homosexuality, and the Mystery of Desire.* New York: Poseidon, 1993.

Kolin, Philip C. *Williams: A Streetcar Named Desire.* Plays in Production. Cambridge: Cambridge UP, 2000.

Kornbluh, Anna. "Romancing the Capital: Choice, Love, and Contradiction in *The Family Man* and *Memento.*" *Lacan and Contemporary Film.* Ed. Todd McGowan and Sheila Kunkle. New York: Otherpress, 2004 (forthcoming).

Krauss, Rosalind. *The Originality of the Avant-Garde and Other Modernist Myths.* Cambridge: MIT P, 1985.

Krutnik, Frank. *In a Lonely Street: Film Noir, Genre, Masculinity.* New York: Routledge, 1991.

Larkin, Philip. *All What Jazz: A Record Diary.* New York: Farrar Straus, 1985.

Larsen, Nella. *Passing.* 1929. New York: Penguin, 1997.

Lee, Spike, with Lisa Jones. *Mo' Better Blues: The Companion Volume to the Universal Pictures Film.* New York: Fireside, 1990.

Lees, Gene. *Oscar Peterson: The Will to Swing.* Toronto: Lester and Orpen Dennys, 1988.

Lehman, Peter, and William Luhr. *Thinking about Movies: Watching, Questioning, Enjoying.* Fort Worth and New York: Harcourt Brace, 1999.

Lipsitz, George. *The Possessive Investment in Whiteness: How White People Profit from Identity Politics.* Philadelphia: Temple UP, 1998.

Lord, Albert Bates. *The Singer of Tales.* Cambridge: Harvard UP, 1960.

Lott, Eric. "All the King's Men: Elvis Impersonators and White Working-Class Masculinity." *Race and the Subject of Masculinities.* Ed. Harry Stecopoulos and Michael Uebel. Durham: Duke UP, 1997. 192–227.

——. *Love and Theft: Blackface Minstrelsy and the American Working Class.* New York: Oxford UP, 1993.

——. "Racial Cross-Dressing and the Construction of American Whiteness." *Cultural Studies Reader.* Ed. Simon During. 2d ed. New York: Routledge, 1999. 241–255.

Luhr, William. "Mutilating Mel: Martyrdom and Masculinity in *Braveheart.*" *Mythologies of Violence in Postmodern Media.* Ed. Christopher Sharrett. Detroit: Wayne State UP, 1999. 227–246.

Mailer, Norman. "The White Negro." *Advertisements for Myself.* New York: G. P. Putnam's, 1959. 311–331.

Malamud, Bernard. "Angel Levine." *The Stories of Bernard Malamud.* New York: Farrar Straus Giroux, 1983. 277–289.

Manso, Peter. *Brando: The Biography.* New York: Hyperion, 1994.

Margolis, N. "A Theory of the Psychology of Jazz." *American Imago* 11 (1954): 263–290.

Margulies, Martin. "Studies in Madness: The Role of Cognitive Style in the Effects of Mental Illness on the Creative Genius of Jazz Pianists Thelonious Monk and Bud Powell." The Thelonious Website: http://www.achilles.net/~howardm/psych1.html. Sept. 10, 2002.

Martin, Henry. *Charlie Parker and Thematic Improvisation.* Studies in Jazz, No. 24. Lanham, Md.: Scarecrow Press, 1996.

Maslin, Janet. "Deadly Plot by a Milquetoast Villain." *New York Times* 8 Mar. 1996: C1.

Mayne, Judith. "Walking the *Tightrope* of Feminism and Male Desire." *Men in Feminism.* Ed. Alice Jardine and Paul Smith. New York: Methuen, 1988. 62–70.

McClary, Susan. *Feminine Endings: Music, Gender, and Sexuality.* Minneapolis: U of Minnesota P, 1991.

McGilligan, Patrick. *Robert Altman: Jumping off the Cliff.* New York: St. Martin's, 1989.

McHale, Brian. *Postmodernist Fiction.* New York, Methuen, 1987.

Meltzer, David, ed. *Reading Jazz.* San Francisco: Mercury House, 1993.

Miklitsch, Robert. "Queer (Audio) Surplus-Value: *The Talented Mr. Ripley.*" Society for Cinema Studies conference, Marriott at Metro Center, Washington, D.C., March 2001.

Miller, Miles D. "Jazz and Aggression." *Psychiatric Communications* (1958): 7–10. Rpt. in *Keeping Time: Readings in Jazz History.* Ed. Robert Walser. New York: Oxford UP, 1999. 234–239.

Mingus, Charles. *Beneath the Underdog.* Ed. Nel King. New York: Knopf, 1971.

Mitchell, W.J.T. "The Violence of Public Art." *Spike Lee's "Do the Right Thing."* Ed. Mark A. Reid. Cambridge Film Handbooks. Cambridge: Cambridge UP, 1997. 107–128.

Modleski, Tania. *Feminism without Women: Culture and Criticism in a "Postfeminist" Age.* New York: Routledge, 1991.

Monti, Gloria. Conversation with the author. 27 Aug. 2001.

Moody, Bill. *Bird Lives!* New York: Walker, 1999.

Morgenstern, Dan. Conversation with the author. 14 Aug. 1997.

Morrison, Toni. *Playing in the Dark: Whiteness and the Literary Imagination.* Cambridge: Harvard UP, 1992.

Mullen, Jim. "Hot Sheet." *Entertainment Weekly* 29 Dec. 1995/5 Jan. 1996: 148.

Murray, Albert. *Stomping the Blues.* New York: McGraw-Hill, 1976.

Murray, Albert, and John F. Callahan, eds. *Trading Twelves: The Selected Letters of Ralph Ellison and Albert Murray.* New York: Modern Library, 2000.

Naremore, James. *Acting in the Cinema.* Berkeley: U of California P, 1988.

Nolan, Frederick. *Lorenz Hart: A Poet on Broadway.* New York: Oxford UP, 1994.

Oja, Carol J. "Virgil Thomson's Harvard Years." *A Celebration of American Music: Words and Music in Honor of H. Wiley Hitchcock.* Ed. Richard Crawford, R. Allen Lott, and Carol J. Oja. Ann Arbor: U of Michigan P, 1990. 331–346.

Okrent, Daniel. "The Greatest Record Ever Made." *Esquire* June 1990: 46.

O'Meally, Robert. *Lady Day: The Many Faces of Billie Holiday.* Boston: Little, Brown, 1991.

Otis, Johnny. *Listen to the Lambs.* New York: Norton, 1968.

——. *Upside Your Head! Rhythm and Blues on Central Avenue.* Hanover, N.H.: UP of New England, 1993.

Parry, Milman. *The Making of Homeric Verse: The Collected Papers of Milman Parry.* Ed. Adam Parry. Oxford: Clarendon, 1971.

Pearson, Nathan W., Jr. *Goin' to Kansas City.* Urbana and Chicago: U of Illinois P, 1987.

Pellegrinelli, Lara. "Dig Boy Dig: Jazz at Lincoln Center Breaks New Ground, but Where Are the Women?" *Village Voice* 8–14 Nov. 2000: http://www.villagevoice.com/issues/0045/pellegrinelli.php. Aug. 4, 2003.

Penley, Constance. *NASA/Trek: Popular Science and Sex in America.* New York: Verso, 1997.

Peretti, Burton W. "Oral Histories of Jazz Musicians: The NEA Transcripts as Texts in Context." *Jazz among the Discourses.* Ed. Krin Gabbard. Durham: Duke UP, 1995. 117–133.

Pfeil, Fred. "Rock Incorporated: Plugging in to Axl and Bruce." *White Guys: Studies in Postmodern Domination and Difference.* New York: Verso, 1995. 71–104.

Pollack, Howard. *Aaron Copland: The Life and Work of an Uncommon Man.* New York: Henry Holt, 1999.

Porter, Lewis. *Lester Young.* Boston: Twayne, 1985.

—, ed. *A Lester Young Reader.* Washington: Smithsonian Institution P, 1991.

Powers, Richard. *The Time of Our Singing.* New York: Farrar Straus Giroux, 2003.

Rabinowitz, Paula. *They Must Be Represented: The Politics of Documentary.* London and New York: Verso, 1994.

Ray, Robert B. *A Certain Tendency of the Hollywood Cinema, 1930–1980.* Princeton: Princeton UP, 1985.

Reddig, William M. *Tom's Town: Kansas City and the Pendergast Legend.* Philadelphia and New York: Lippincott, 1947.

Reed, Ishmael. *Japanese by Spring*. 1993. New York: Penguin, 1996.

Reid, Mark A., ed. *Spike Lee's "Do the Right Thing."* Cambridge Film Handbooks. Cambridge: Cambridge UP, 1997.

Renov, Michael, ed. *Theorizing Documentary*. New York: Routledge, 1993.

Ricker, Bruce. Conversation with the author. 30 July 1995.

Roediger, David. *Towards the Abolition of Whiteness*. London: Verso, 1994.

Rogin, Michael. *Blackface, White Noise: Jewish Immigrants in the Hollywood Melting Pot*. Berkeley: U of California P, 1996.

———. "'Make My Day!': Spectacle as Amnesia in Imperial Politics." *Representations* 29 (Winter 1990): 99–123.

———. "Making America Home: Racial Masquerade and Ethnic Assimilation in the Transition to Talking Pictures." *Journal of American History* 79 (1992): 1050–1077.

Rosenthal, Alan, ed. *New Challenges to Documentary*. Berkeley and Los Angeles: U of California P, 1988.

Ross, Andrew. "Bullets, Ballots, or Batmen: Can Cultural Studies Do the Right Thing?" *Screen* 31.1 (1990): 31.

Russell, Ross. *Bird Lives: The High Life and Hard Times of Charlie (Yardbird) Parker*. New York: Charterhouse, 1973.

———. *Jazz Style in Kansas City and the Southwest*. Berkeley: U of California P, 1971.

———. *The Sound*. New York: Dutton, 1961.

Russo, Vito. *The Celluloid Closet: Homosexuality in the Movies*, rev. ed. New York: Harper and Row, 1987.

Saxton, Alexander. *The Indispensable Enemy: Labor and the Anti-Chinese Movement in California*. Berkeley: U of California P, 1995.

———. *The Rise and Fall of the White Republic: Class Politics and Mass Culture in Nineteenth-Century America*. New York: Verso, 2003.

Schickel, Richard. *Brando: A Life in Our Times*. New York: Atheneum, 1991.

Schuller, Gunther. *Early Jazz: Its Roots and Musical Development*. New York: Oxford UP, 1968.

Schwartz, Robert K. "Composers' Closets Open for All to See." *New York Times* 19 June 1994: 2:1.

Sedgwick, Eve Kosofsky. *The Epistemology of the Closet*. Berkeley: U of California P, 1992.

Self, Robert T. *Robert Altman's Subliminal Reality*. Minneapolis: U of Minnesota P, 2002.

Seshadri-Crooks, Kalpana. *Desiring Whiteness: A Lacanian Analysis of Race*. London and New York: Routledge, 2000.

Shapiro, Nat, and Nat Hentoff. *Hear Me Talkin' to Ya: The Story of Jazz as Told by the Men Who Made It*. New York: Holt, Rinehart and Winston, 1955.

Sharrett, Christopher. "End of Story: The Collapse of Myth in Postmodern Narrative Film." *The End of Cinema as We Know It: American Film in the Nineties*. Ed. Jon Lewis. New York: New York UP, 2001. 319–331.

Shohat, Ella. "Ethnicities-in-Relation: Toward a Multicultural Reading of American Cinema." *Unspeakable Images: Ethnicity and the American Cinema.* Ed. Lester Friedman. Urbana: U of Illinois P, 1991. 215–250.

Shohat, Ella, and Robert Stam. *Unthinking Eurocentrism: Multiculturalism and the Media.* London and New York: Routledge, 1994.

Slotkin, Richard. *Regeneration through Violence: The Mythology of the American Frontier, 1600–1860.* Middletown, Conn.: Wesleyan UP, 1973.

Smith, Jeff. Conversation with the author. 23 Nov. 2002.

———. "Taking Music Supervisors Seriously." *Cinesonic: Experiencing the Soundtrack.* Ed. Philip Brophy. North Ryde, Australia: Australian Film Television and Radio School, 2001. 125–146.

Smith, Paul. *Clint Eastwood: A Cultural Production.* Minneapolis: U of Minnesota P, 1993.

Smith, W. O. *Sideman: The Long Gig of W. O. Smith.* Nashville, Tenn.: Rutledge Hill, 1991.

Stein Crease, Stephanie. *Gil Evans out of the Cool: His Life and Music.* Chicago: A Cappella, 2002.

Sterritt, David. "Spike Lee Chooses Copland Classics for Soundtrack." *Christian Science Monitor* 8 May 1998: 15.

Stewart, Rex. *Jazz Masters of the 30s.* New York: Macmillan, 1972.

Stewart, Susan. *On Longing: Narratives of the Miniature, the Gigantic, the Souvenir, the Collection.* Durham: Duke UP, 1993.

Straw, Will. "Sizing up Record Collections: Gender and Connoisseurship in Rock Music Culture." *Sexing the Groove: Popular Music and Gender.* Ed. Sheila Whiteley. New York: Routledge, 1997. 3–16.

"The Struggles of Johnny Hartman." *Our World.* Oct. 1950: 20.

Sudhalter, Richard M., Philip R. Evans, and William Dean Myatt. *Bix: Man and Legend.* New York: Schirmer, 1974.

Szwed, John. Conversation with the author. 8 Aug. 2000.

———. "Race and the Embodiment of Culture." *Ethnicity* 2.1 (1975): 19–33.

———. *So What: The Life of Miles Davis.* New York: Simon and Schuster, 2002.

Tommasini, Anthony. "Aaron Copland, Champion of the American Sound." *New York Times* 21 Nov. 1999, Arts and Leisure: 2:1, 36.

Torgovnick, Marianna. *Gone Primitive: Savage Intellects, Modern Lives.* Chicago: U of Chicago P, 1991.

Tucker, Mark. *Ellington: The Early Years.* Urbana: U of Illinois P, 1991.

———, ed. Special Issue: "New Perspectives on Thelonious Monk." *Black Music Research Journal* 19.2 (1999).

Tucker, Sherrie. Conversation with the author. 26 Dec. 2002.

———. *Swing Shift: "All-Girl" Bands of the 1940s.* Durham: Duke UP, 2000.

———. "When Subjects Don't Come Out." *Queer Episodes in Music and Modern Identity.* Ed. Sophie Fuller and Lloyd Whitesell. Urbana: U of Illinois P, 2002. 293–310.

von Ziegesar, Peter. "Robert Altman's Journey Home." *New York Times* 27 Aug. 1995, late ed., sec. 2: 9+.

Waller, Robert James. *The Bridges of Madison County*. New York: Warner, 1992.

Walser, Robert. "'Out of Notes': Signification, Interpretation, and the Problem of Miles Davis." *Jazz among the Discourses*. Ed. Krin Gabbard. Durham: Duke UP, 1995. 165–188.

Ware, Vron. *Beyond the Pale: White Women, Racism and History*. New York: Verso, 1992.

Watrous, Peter. "The Movies Miss Another. . . ." *New York Times* 11 Aug. 1996, sec. 2: 26.

White, Armond. "Eastwood's Jazz Substitutes for *Madison* Drama." *The City Sun* [New York] 2–8 Aug. 1995: 23.

Weinraub, Bernard. "The Dark Underbelly of Ron Howard." *New York Times* 12 Nov. 1996: C11.

Wiegman, Robyn. *American Anatomies: Theorizing Race and Gender*. Durham: Duke UP, 1995.

Williams, Linda. *Playing the Race Card: Melodramas of Black and White from Uncle Tom to O. J. Simpson*. Princeton: Princeton UP, 2001.

Williams, Martin. *The Jazz Tradition*. Oxford: Oxford UP, 1970.

Willis, Sharon. *High Contrast: Race and Gender in Contemporary Hollywood Film*. Durham: Duke UP, 1997.

Wilson, John S. "Hartman Singing in 'Voice of Jazz.'" *New York Times* 21 May 1982: 36.

Winston, Brian. *Claiming the Real: The Griersonian Documentary and Its Legitimations*. London: British Film Institute, 1995.

Wood, Robin. *Hollywood from Vietnam to Reagan*. New York: Columbia UP, 1986.

Wray, Matt, and A. Newitz, eds. *White Trash: Race and Class in America*. New York: Routledge, 1996.

Yaffe, David. Conversation with the author. 2 Dec. 2000.

Zabor, Rafi. *The Bear Comes Home*. New York: Norton, 1997.

Index

About the Author

K RIN G ABBARD is professor of comparative literature and English at the State University of New York at Stony Brook. He is the author of *Jammin' at the Margins: Jazz and the American Cinema* (1996) and the editor of *Jazz among the Discourses* and *Representing Jazz* (both 1995). With Glen O. Gabbard, he has written *Psychiatry and the Cinema*, now in a second edition (1999).

About the Type

This book was set in ITC Mendoza, a typeface named for
its designer, the prolific French graphic artist José Mendoza y Almeida.
Mendoza is a neohumanist text face, related in style and structure to the
roman and italic types created in sixteenth-century Paris. It was released
by the International Typeface Corporation in 1991.

Designed and composed by Kevin Hanek

Printed and bound by Sheridan Books, Inc.,
Ann Arbor, Michigan